No Peace Without Freedom

No Peace Without Freedom

Race and the Women's International League for
Peace and Freedom, 1915–1975

Joyce Blackwell

Southern Illinois University Press - Carbondale

Excerpts from Linda Schott, *Reconstructing Women's Thoughts: The Women's International League for Peace and Freedom Before World War II* (copyright © 1997 by the Board of Trustees of the Leland Stanford Jr. University), used with the permission of Stanford University Press, www.sup.org.

Excerpts from Carrie A. Foster, *The Women and the Warriors: The U.S. Section of the Women's International League for Peace and Freedom, 1915–1946* (Syracuse, NY: Syracuse University Press, 1995), and from Harriet Hyman Alonso, *Peace as a Women's Issue: A History of the U.S. Movement for World Peace and Women's Rights* (Syracuse, NY: Syracuse University Press, 1993), used with the permission of Syracuse University Press.

Library of Congress Cataloging-in-Publication Data
Blackwell, Joyce, 1954–
No peace without freedom : race and the Women's International League for Peace and Freedom, 1915–1975 / Joyce Blackwell.
    p. cm.
Includes bibliographical references and index.
1. Women and peace—United States—History. 2. African American pacifists—History. 3. African American women political activists—History. 4. Women's International League for Peace and Freedom. 5. Women pacifists—United States—History. I. Title.
JZ5578.B57 2004
303.6'6—dc22   2004000940
ISBN 0-8093-2564-0 (cloth : alk. paper)

Dedicated with love to
Oriana, Calvin Jr., and Mom
and
In memory of my father, Joseph Blackwell

Contents

Part Two. 1945–1975

Illustrations

Preface

As I prepared dinner one evening in June 1998, I listened to a 1970s song that seemed rather appropriate at the time. While making wildly animated gestures, I lip-synched as the artist bellowed out, "War, oh yeah, what is it good for? Absolutely nothing!" The children laughed, insisting that their mother had been in the kitchen a little too long. I laughed, too, but not for the same reason.

Although the lyrics seemed meaningless for most of 1990s peacetime America, they were extremely significant to me then and seem even more so in 2004. For nine years, I had been researching and writing about the role of African American women in the peace movement. They, too, had repeatedly questioned the purpose of war, often concluding that it was pointless. I never thought before listening to that song that the group of middle-class, elitist women that I had come to know would have something in common with a controversial, left-wing, 1970s young artist named Edwin Starr. Perhaps this feeling about war is all that the black peace activists and Starr had in common. Just as that thought occurred to me, the telephone rang. It was my travel agent informing me that the airline ticket I requested would be available the next morning. For many reasons, I was looking forward to another journey to Swarthmore to examine more boxes of unprocessed data.

I began my study of African American activists in the Women's International League for Peace and Freedom (WILPF) almost a decade ago. As I traveled back and forth to Swarthmore College to peruse dozens of documents, mostly unprocessed, my heart raced with excitement and joy.

I knew that I had stumbled upon a significant topic in the fields of peace history, African American history, and women's history. As time passed, my self-assurance often waned as I questioned how much information was actually available in the many documents that I had carefully examined. I felt that I needed to know considerably more to reconstruct adequately the lives and experiences of the women activists mentioned therein. However, my curiosity about black women and peace compelled me to continue. I wanted to know more about these women, who were willing to sacrifice so much for peace and freedom.

Upon closer examination of the available sources, I realized that they indeed contained a considerable amount of information about black women's peace activism. Nevertheless, to unravel the tightly concealed story, I had to center African American women in the narrative. In doing so, I understood, among other things, that black women's definition of peace and freedom differed somewhat from that of their white peace activist colleagues. For black women, peace and freedom were inseparable. They believed that no one could truly have peace until everyone was free, and only when people were free would everyone enjoy true peace. This pattern of thought shaped their peace activism.

This study explores African American women's participation in the Woman's Peace Party (WPP, which later became known as the Women's International League for Peace and Freedom) between 1915 and 1975. The WPP, which was officially formed in January 1915, opened its membership to African American women later that year. The WPP, in some ways, entered a new era when it accepted African American women. Just as women changed the agenda and direction of the peace movement when they became increasingly involved in what had been an all-male club, so too did African American women alter the path of a cause that had previously lacked racial diversity. It is the peace activism of African American women that made their white colleagues realize that they could not speak about peace without speaking about racial justice. Therefore, African American women activists rooted peace soundly in race and, in doing so, often made WILPF truly live up to the joint purpose in its title— peace and freedom. This activism is most evident in the group's peace experiences from World War I to the end of the Vietnam War.

African American women who either held leadership positions or were active participants in WILPF are the specific focus of this study. These women were intentional in their record keeping, and their correspondence, journals, and other written records shed valuable light on the

African American female experience in WILPF and peace activism between 1915 and 1975.

Whenever possible, I have allowed the available sources to speak for African American peace activists. I have relied heavily on the interviews with three Southwestern black peace activists conducted by Judith Adams, an eminent peace historian at Stanford University, as well as on the unprocessed manuscript collections of Erna Harris and Bertha McNeill, both located at Swarthmore College. The manuscript collection of Mary Church Terrell, located at Howard University, has been equally important to this study. I found these collections to be the richest, indeed the only, sources dealing almost exclusively with black women's peace activism. Other sources proved valuable in that they mentioned black peace activists who directly interacted with their white colleagues in WILPF. Papers include those of Mildred Scott Olmsted, Emily Greene Balch, WILPF (United States section, the national executive board meetings, the Interracial Committee, the Committee on Minorities and Race Relations), and the various WILPF branches.

This approach obviously presents problems. How can a few people speak for African American women activists generally? I concluded that this focus on a small group of key figures was justified not only by the source problem but also by the fact that these women had an influence on WILPF that was out of proportion to their numbers. In the course of writing this book, I came to see my study as part of a continuing process, as offering a few important voices in dialogue among a larger group of people.

Using these most powerful voices, I have tried to weave together material from the available sources in a way that would stimulate and provoke. Though I tried to show the dilemmas that arise for black peace activists in wartime, I have not given space to those who chose to support war. I have tried to include the most powerful and important voices, although I am certain that many remain hidden or lost. In addition to examining the activities, views, and arguments advanced by black peace activists, I explore how these women, though a minority, influenced the movement.

Therefore, in writing *No Peace Without Freedom,* I do not claim to have written a comprehensive history of all African American peace activists in WILPF through all of these years. At best, this book represents a discovery of the past that has been heretofore neglected. I offer it as an historical account of exemplary lives within WILPF and the peace movement.

This work is divided into two parts. Part One concerns African American participants in WILPF between 1915 and 1945, just before the United Nation's founding conference in San Francisco. Chapter 1 briefly examines why white women felt a need to organize their own peace groups at the start of World War I. After a discussion of WILPF's initial goals, this chapter focuses on several bold steps taken by the peace group in its first ten years.

Chapter 2 examines the continuous search by white peace activists for the perfect black woman. In the process of identifying African American peace activists, the chapter addresses when and why African American women joined the organization and why WILPF interested so few black women. The small number of black women who did join the League shared certain experiences and attributes with white pacifists. This chapter also examines the problems with race of WILPF's white members.

Chapter 3 shows how WILPF, frustrated at its inability to successfully appeal to the "perfect" African American woman, established the controversial Interracial Committee. It discusses WILPF's dilemma of building its membership with black women while retaining all of its members committed to peace work.

Chapter 4 analyzes the effect of African American members on the organization. I address several of the links that black dissidents established with the African American community.

Chapter 5 traces the black activists' peace reform activity on an international level before the end of World War II. It also examines the links that black peace activists made between people of the black diaspora and peace and freedom issues.

Part Two examines the role played by African American activists in WILPF during much of the Cold War. Chapter 6 maintains that the efforts of those black peace activists to end racial injustice both at home and abroad did not end after World War II. They continued to link peace and race even in the immediate aftermath of the Second World War. However, the African American woman's fight for peace that began on the home front and spread to the black diaspora continued in a different venue after World War II. I also suggest that World War II was a significant historical watershed in black female peace activism. This chapter also shows that a new group of women appeared on the scene after World War II and explores how these women differed from their predecessors. I briefly examine some of their backgrounds, their organizational affiliations, and their views on race and race relations.

Chapter 7 discusses the international consciousness of post–World War II black dissidents, pointing to similarities and differences between them and their foremothers in the movement. It focuses on the different views expressed by black peace activists about the Vietnam War, while paying special attention to how these activists linked peace and freedom issues with race.

The conclusion returns to the general thematic questions to summarize findings, provide analysis, and draw some broad conclusions. Finally, it reemphasizes the major thesis of this study.

Acknowledgments

In many respects, this study is a collaborative effort. It received detailed and penetrating criticism from scholars of American history. Their many comments improved not only the substance of this book but its style and grammar. Hence my debt to Jacquelyn Dowd Hall, Peter Filene, Suzanne Lebsock, Gerald Horne, and Joel Williamson is overwhelming, and it is more than perfunctory to remark that the errors that remain are literally my own.

I extend my appreciation to others who directly aided in the completion of this study. Frances Early, Larry Wittner, Kathleen Kennedy, Genna Rae McNeill, Linda Schott, Harriet Alonso, and Anne Marie Pois all inspired and assisted me in some of the crucial stages of this study. They provided critical analyses that were helpful. Though she did not read a word of the manuscript, Lolita Brockington closely followed its development to its completion and would not hear of me not finishing it.

I thank the University of North Carolina at Charlotte Faculty Development Committee, the National Endowment for the Humanities, and the University of North Carolina Board of Governors Foundation for grants that enabled me to have the time and resources necessary for the research and writing of this work.

I am greatly obliged to the following institutions and their librarians or archivists for giving me access to their archives and permission to use their manuscript collections: Swarthmore College Peace Collection, Swarthmore, Pennsylvania; Women's International League for Peace and Freedom Archival Department, Philadelphia, Pennsylvania; Library of Congress, Washington, D.C.; the Moorland-Spingarn Collection, Howard

University, Washington, D.C.; Archival Department, Tuskegee University, Tuskegee, Alabama; and New York Public Library, New York, New York. I am especially grateful to Wendy Chmielewski and her staff at Swarthmore College.

I must express appreciation to the Reverend Dominic Owens, whose support meant more to me than he could possibly have known. Moreover, he took time from his busy schedule to correct parts of the manuscript that may not have adhered to the publisher's guidelines.

This work owes much to my editors at Southern Illinois University Press who cared for it and, therefore, made our work enjoyable.

Peggy Ellis typed the manuscript with extraordinary skill, intelligence, and patience. She also acted as perceptive first-line critic and copy editor. I will always be grateful for her services.

Most of all, I thank my children, Oriana and Calvin Jr., for their patience and understanding. They lived though my involvement with this study for nine years without complaining. I also thank my sisters and brothers for their support. Moreover, my friends Linda Torian and Betty Johnson provided assistance at a time when I really needed it. I learned the true meaning of sisterhood.

Finally, I thank all of my friends and colleagues who understood this major undertaking and gave me the space and time I needed to complete the project.

Abbreviations

MFDP	Mississippi Freedom Democratic Party
NAACP	National Association for the Advancement of Colored People
NACW	National Association of Colored Women
NATO	North Atlantic Treaty Organization
WIL, WILPF	Women's International League for Peace and Freedom
WPP	Woman's Peace Party

No Peace Without Freedom

Introduction

In November 1937, white peace activist Caroline Singer made yet another urgent plea to her peace colleagues, asking that the Women's International League for Peace and Freedom (WILPF) open its doors to African American women. She wrote, "I wish to emphasize that, according to its Constitution, the W.I.L. is obliged to extend its membership to women, regardless of race or, properly speaking, ethnic groups." In the same report, she noted, "New York State contained large numbers of Negro women, many of them university graduates." Therefore, it was Singer's sincere hope that "in the near future, a genuine effort [would] be made to secure Negro women as members." Singer finally ended her entreaty on a less optimistic note when she expressed her unhappiness with WILPF's "feeble efforts in this direction."[1]

Singer's concerns about WILPF's lack of racial diversity were not new to her peace colleagues. The organization had long suffered from the lack of a visible African American presence. Although WILPF's national executive board had made a concerted effort to aggressively seek black women for peace work from the time of its inception, twenty-two years later, the organization could still only boast of a small membership. For black women who joined WILPF, certain questions loom large. What conditions triggered the black woman's reaction? What peace issues tended to be significant to them? Why? Did they separate peace issues from race issues? If so, how? If not, why? Are there, and were there, certain classes of black women who contributed to this kind of political and social activism?

In addressing these fundamental questions, limited help is available from published academic studies. Thus this study is part of a recent shift in historical scholarship on African American women, one that emphasizes the women's perspectives and analyzes their actions in light of the social movements of which they were a part, seeing these women in their historical context as activists rather than passive victims.

There were many differences and similarities among these African American WILPFers. The majority was middle- or upper-class. Furthermore, virtually all of them were well educated and several had graduate degrees. Only one, Fannie Lou Hamer, never attended college. Most used their education professionally, in a wide range of occupations. The majority of them were married. Some who were married, like Sadie Sawyer Hughley and Coretta Scott King, shared their commitment to peace work with their husbands, partners, or family members. Most black peace activists worked on a wide range of projects—organizing antiwar activities, speaking, writing, petitioning, participating in race work in their own neighborhoods, and cooperating with whites as much as possible.

There are several striking qualities about African American female peace activists. One is the small number of participants; another is their willingness to challenge formidable political and social structures as African Americans in a racist society. Their motivation to take action, however, did not come from meticulously thought-out political philosophy. When unfavorable social conditions for African Americans became extreme, black peace activists, like many other African American activists, responded as with one mind.

The most extensive manifestation of this phenomenon was during the Vietnam War, when African American peace activists throughout America fiercely engaged in the struggle to end inequality and injustice for all blacks. On one hand, they helped organize marches, protests, conferences, and mass meetings, either through local WILPF branches or predominant black civil rights organizations. On the other, they clearly articulated their opposition to the war and the reasons for their position.

Understanding the full implications of African American women's peace activism is enormous. In this study, the movement spans six decades and manifested itself in a wide variety of activities and organizations. The recurring nature of the events is a mixed blessing. While it offers the possibility of comparisons, it also presents a chronologic problem in that it is difficult to move forward in time when one approaches the topic thematically.

Another problem is that the activities of black peace activists cannot be viewed simply on a political level. The intensity of their activism renders it a social phenomenon whose roots penetrate deeply into the fabric of American society. The factor that empowered the struggle of black female activists came directly from the social context and was intimately related to their own definitions of themselves and their rightful place in society. The challenge, therefore, is to reconstruct both the social and political aspects of the history of activism by African American proponents of peace.

There is first a need to assemble the data about black female activists into a thematic chronology of events, a task never before attempted for the period. Second, there is a need to account for the differences in their activism before and after World War II, when the goals and ideology shifted from a local to a more national scope. A third challenge is to probe into that quality of African American women's activism that is uniquely theirs.

The period from 1915 to 1975 is broad but represents a distinctive time in African American history, an era when the definition of blacks' status in America was actively contested. This study reflects the shifting scale of the problem. In the first half of the period under consideration, 1915 to 1945, blacks responded to their status by advancing a program of self-help and race improvement, as well as launching an antilynching campaign. After World War II, however, African Americans' attitudes changed. Having been employed in well-paying jobs for the first time during the war or witnessing firsthand equal treatment by Europeans while fighting in World War II, African Americans no longer so readily accepted prewar conditions. A growing number began to challenge previous policies and demanded clearer definition of African Americans' civil status. The conflict over that status was eventually dealt with on a national stage in a struggle of major proportions. This study has been divided into two parts, each addressing different phases in the evolution of the process. The picture that emerges shows an interesting and revealing look at a unique group of African American peace activists, whose activism was shaped by multidimensional pressures and whose attitudes and interests evolved in distinctive ways between 1915 and 1975.

Were black WILPFers peace activists or pacifists? There were significant differences between the two types of conscientious objectors. According to Peter Brock and Nigel Young, in *Pacifism in the Twentieth Century,* a pacifist during World War I was an individual who "believe[d] *all* war to be wrong and that *all* methods involving the use of violence to attain a desired end . . . futile in the long run."[2] Using their definition to characterize black women involved in peace work, I maintain that they were not pacifists. Instead, they were peace activists who believed that peace and freedom were inseparable. This definition of peace sometimes placed them in a position to accept war as the only way to insure these two goals. For example, during World War I, pacifists would not have supported war work under any conditions because they saw it as a way of indirectly supporting the war and its inevitable violence. On the other hand, peace activists very well could have supported war work because they would have regarded it as a way of assisting soldiers who needed their help as they fought for a greater cause: protection of one's liberties.

Americans engaged in peace efforts as early as 1815, but the movement remained virtually unknown until 1905 when they became increasingly involved both economically and politically in international affairs. Peace historian Harriet Alonso asserts that the Spanish-American War of 1898 was the international activity that forced America onto the global stage. After the war, America held colonial possessions in the Caribbean and the Pacific that, Alonso maintains, ensured America's involvement in Latin America. America's increasing involvement in Latin America, in turn, confronted peace activist women with a variety of issues, namely Cuba's independence from Spain and imperialism. But, the women were divided on the Cuban issue. While some opposed United States involvement in Cuba's affairs, others believed that it was the right thing to do. Alonso concludes, and I concur, that female pacifists and anti-imperialists saw America's acquisition of Puerto Rico, the Philippines, and Guam as an expression of the linkage among commercialism, colonialism, and militarism.[3]

Once America occupied the Philippines in 1898, women peace activists became increasingly opposed to America's newfound imperialist power. Consequently, this action by the United States compelled women peace critics to protest more aggressively within nonpeace organizations because they saw America's behavior as a "clear-cut case of imposing one nation's will upon another." Women in the National Council of Women, the Woman's Christian Temperance Union, and the National American

Woman Suffrage Association regarded the subjugation of Filipinos as another tactic used by Americans to trounce on other subjects.[4]

At the end of the Spanish-American War, the peace movement grew tremendously, with forty-five new peace organizations appearing between 1901 and 1914. Men led and controlled most of these groups, which forced women members to leave and form organizations that would give them some sense of independence and power. As all-female peace organizations sprung up, mainly in the northeast, a subtle shift in white women's peace rhetoric occurred. They argued that men were more concerned about "their own achievements than in caring for human life."[5] Once these women were enfranchised, they saw it as their "duty to effect legislation and cause changes in government policy" that would ultimately improve the economic and social conditions of men, women and children.[6] Operating on this premise, many female peace activists actively waged a war for peace and freedom in exclusively female organizations.

One of the largest and most significant American peace groups was the Woman's Peace Party (WPP), founded on January 10–11, 1915, in Washington, D.C., a year after World War I began. Some three thousand white women from all across the country assembled in the nation's capital to demand that America's leadership unequivocally oppose the war. Their platform consisted of eleven planks, which ranged from war issues to international relations issues.[7]

Because it was difficult for the women to agree on the planks, the WPP eventually adopted a position of "nonresistance" as its pacifist commitment. The term meant that the WPP would not commit or condone violence, even in self-defense. Although not all of its members supported this stance, it remained the official position of the WPP for the first four years.

In 1919, the WPP reorganized as the United States section of WILPF. It continued to advocate nonresistance. However, the term used to describe this position became *nonviolent resistance* or *nonviolence.* Peace historian Linda Schott noticed that a slight shift in meaning also occurred. Unlike *nonresistance,* the terms *nonviolent resistance* and *nonviolence* no longer exclusively meant the refusal to commit or sanction violence. They included a commitment to eradicate the underlying causes of violence—political, economic, and social inequalities of all kinds. This broader definition of *nonviolent resistance* reflected the national board's effort to become more inclusive. This new stance later gained the attention of minority groups who were often victims of racist oppression.

The WPP's initial position of nonresistance and its adoption of non-violent resistance a few years later, for example, appealed to black women interested in ending racial injustice. Some African American women joined the peace group with the intention to purge America, and later, the rest of the world, of political, economic, and social inequalities. These women believed that they truly understood the significance of the WPP's (and later, WILPF's) mission and realized that it would not be easy to achieve. The WPP, they reasoned, needed all of the human power that it could muster. For that matter, so did the African American community.

No one knows how many black women were involved in WILPF between 1915 and 1975 because officials did not maintain membership records by race or ethnicity.[8] National WILPF workers in the Philadelphia administrative records office, however, have estimated that less than one percent of its membership was African American during the period of this study.[9] In 1940, Bertha McNeill alluded to WILPF's small black membership in her annual report of the national Committee on Minorities and Race Relations: "It is gratifying to note that more branches have organized minority committees. . . . More Negro women have been asked to serve on local and national boards and more have become members, though the number is still too few."[10] Years later, distinguished peace historian Carrie Foster observed that WILPF "remained a predominantly white-oriented organization internationally, and in the United States, because black women as well as working-class women of any race were always a distinct minority."[11] She added that, by 1964, WILPF had approximately "150,000 members with 7,000 in the United States."[12] On the basis of the 1-percent black membership estimate given by national WILPF officials, only seventy or fewer of these women were African American in little more than a quarter century after McNeill first complained of their virtual absence.

WILPF began with five African American members when it was first organized in 1915 and had approximately twelve times that many by the time America withdrew its last group of troops from Vietnam in 1975. Nevertheless, the African American membership did not increase steadily over time. Blacks experienced a periodic rise and drop in membership, as did white peace activists. Decisions rendered on issues of special concern to African Americans often influenced their decision either to remain in or leave the peace group. For example, in 1972, national executive officer Mildred Scott Olmsted reflected on the loss of African American members in the 1930s: "During the Italian conquest of Ethiopia, we lost black members who felt that we should go into active support of Ethiopia."[13]

Outside pressures took a similar toll. During World War II, black membership declined along with that of whites as both groups faced increasing hostility for their actions from friends and foes. By 1943, sixty branches had disbanded because of a loss of members. A year later, membership had dropped from a prewar high of fourteen thousand to only 4,708. At the war's end, only 3,789 members remained.[14] When white membership declined, that of African Americans became even smaller, especially since they composed only 1 percent or less at the outset.

Despite their small numbers, black peace activists were still able to exercise a considerable amount of influence because of the positions they held. Mandates on policies, goals, and procedures for various branches across the United States came from the national office. Hence, the power of the organization resided in its national executive board. The majority of black members of WILPF served as chair of a national committee, as an officer of the executive board, or as president of one of the many branches that placed them in direct contact with the national executive board. Serving in any of these positions enabled blacks to influence the policies and goals of the organization.[15]

Essentially two types of African American women joined WILPF. The first group became involved in the peace organization prior to World War II and either was very active or ascended to positions of leadership between 1915 and 1945. These women established community institutions and advanced the philosophy of racial self-help. They were activists at a time in America when most black leaders adopted accommodationist thought. Race uplift work, however, allowed then to move beyond the limits prescribed by the dominant society. Bertha McNeill, Addie Hunton, Mary Talbert, Dr. Mary Waring, Lucy Diggs Slowe, Charlotte Atwood, Helen Curtis, Mayme Williams, Mary Church Terrell, and Alice Dunbar-Nelson were among the black women who joined WILPF before World War II. All were employed professionals and came to WILPF through ideological positions. Mary Church Terrell, however, was the only one who also came to WILPF through volunteerism.[16]

A different group of African American women began to join WILPF between 1946 and 1975. Like their foremothers, peace and freedom meant more than simply ending or avoiding war. Social, political, and economic equalities for blacks were essential to their agenda as well. Unlike their predecessors, however, these African American women aggressively challenged racial discrimination in every aspect of American society. More important, they began to see a distinct difference between the ideology and goals of the peace movement and those of the African American community. It is this group of women that helped propel WILPF into national prominence as they publicly endorsed causes that previously had been given only lip service. Eminent African American activists who joined WILPF after World War II included Sadie Sawyer Hughley, Coretta Scott King, Enola Maxwell, Erna Prather Harris, Fannie Lou Hamer, Angela Davis, Shirley Chisholm, Bessie McLaurin, Eartha Kitt, Inez Jackson, and Virginia Collins. All these women were employed professionals as well, who, like their foremothers, came to WILPF because of their ideological positions.[17]

For African American women, peace work represented the continuation of the struggle against racial intolerance. They joined the organization, in part, because of its written position on racial justice and to ensure that WILPF made good on its promise. They soon discovered, however, that rhetoric did not necessarily lead to action. While some white League members wanted to eradicate racial injustice and violence in America, an even larger number believed that it was best to leave such controversial matters alone. Consequently, those peace activists who did not believe in racial justice refused to enforce policies designed to achieve that goal.

Almost from the outset, racism within organized pacifism became a public issue, as African American peace activists pointed not only to the secondary status of blacks in the movement but also to the difference in treatment of black and white personnel, both in this country and abroad. Faced with the discriminatory treatment of blacks in the movement and the world at large, black peace activists became even more committed to self-help activism. Consequently, some black peace activists believed it necessary to leave the movement altogether and work on behalf of blacks' rights full-time, while others opted to continue the fight within WILPF.

Racism and the lack of concern for racial injustices within the peace movement did not prevent blacks who remained in the organization from working with white women on an all-inclusive pacifist agenda. This cooperation occurred mainly because African American women peace advocates were so committed to achieving world peace and freedom that they did not allow their colleagues' attitudes to deter them. However, it also happened because white peace activists, like Jane Addams, Mildred Scott Olmsted, and Caroline Singer, expended a great deal of energy combating incidents of racial injustice within WILPF. It was these same women, sometimes after some prodding from their black peace activist colleagues, who often reminded other, less sympathetic whites of one of the peace organization's founding goals: to eradicate injustice and violence. After a rocky beginning, black and white women developed a relatively amicable working relationship. Hence the mere idea of black and white women attempting to work together, especially during the period of this study, attests to the significance of WILPF.

Numerous historians have superbly documented the activities of outstanding European-American WILPF members. But no scholars have focused on the collective role of African American women in the movement and the implications of their participation for the study of social activism, black history, and women's history. A quick historiographic survey bears out this observation.

One of the first full-length works to address the role played by black women in the peace movement is Harriet Alonso's *Peace as a Women's Issue: A History of the U.S. Movement for World Peace and Women's Rights.* The book is about the connection between women's issues and peace. According to Alonso, the main theme that defines the peace movement is the link that participants made between institutionalized violence and violence against women, whether the institution was slavery, the military, or governmental oppression. Alonso maintains that this linkage has been consistent from the days of the abolitionist movement to today. Women's rights peace activists protested not only the physical abuse of women but also their psychological, economic, and political oppression. In addition, they saw "male control in both the private and public spheres as the principal source of the abuse of women."[18]

Alonso also examines the role of maternalism in the peace movement. Women in the various peace organizations believed that they, as the childbearers of society, "had a particular interest in peace—namely, not wanting to see [their] offspring murdered either as soldiers or as innocent victims of a war." Women peace activists believed that "*only* women could experience maternal feelings," and those maternal "instincts" gave them an "edge over men in understanding emotions, in being compassionate, and in being able to envision peace."[19]

Alonso devotes only a small amount of space to the role of African American women in the movement. She discusses Jane Addams's efforts to recruit blacks in 1915 and the racism encountered by African American women in the New York branch of WILPF. However, black women are not included in the larger discussion of the connection between women's issues and peace. Nor does she explore the experiences that gave *maternalism* a different meaning for black women and gave them a different perspective on peace.

Another major study, Carrie Foster's *The Women and the Warriors: The U.S. Section of the Women's International League for Peace and Freedom, 1915–1946* is a story of "pacifism, Progressivism, feminism."[20] Foster shows how WILPF combined progressivism with feminism, presenting a story of interest group politics and power pursued primarily by white peace activists. As in Alonso's study, black women receive little attention in this provocative study.

Of all the notable studies of women and peace, Linda Schott's *Reconstructing Women's Thoughts: The Women's International League for Peace and Freedom Before World War II* examines most fully the peace activism of African American women by devoting a subsection to WILPF's commitment to racial and economic justice. In doing so, she is able to include black peace activists Mary Church Terrell, Addie Hunton, and Bertha McNeill, arguing that they believed that "peace and racial justice went hand in hand." It was this belief that compelled black women in WILPF to devote a great deal of energy to race-based issues, including antilynching legislation and economic imperialism in nations inhabited by darker peoples.[21] However, even in this study, black women have been marginalized. The author introduces them only when she turns to the issue of how race became a peace issue. Moreover, Schott focuses only on the African American national leaders, the so-called women worthies. She does not mention black women such as Lucy Diggs Slowe, Mary Talbert, Mary Waring, and Charlotte Atwood, who were making a difference in their respective branches.

While these three studies make an effort to mention black female peace activists, the majority of published works on WILPF and the peace movement have virtually ignored African American women. *Pioneers for Peace: The Women's International League for Peace and Freedom, 1915– 1965,* by Gertrude Bussey and Margaret Tims, uses published and unpublished records of WILPF to provide a moving story of the League's first fifty years. Nevertheless, the authors barely mention black female activists and, even then, the reader has to determine their race and ethnicity. Catherine Foster's *Women of All Seasons: The Story of the Women's International League for Peace and Freedom* is a collection of interviews that examines WILPF's history from 1965 (when Bussey and Tim's work ends) to the 1980s. It, too, focuses primarily on white peace activists.[22]

Although many studies about WILPF have either marginalized or completely ignored African American women, they remain pioneer studies in the field of peace history. They should be commended for attempting to fill a void in peace history, women's history, and American history. However, to have a fuller understanding of the United States peace movement, the experiences of African American women should also be included. Rescuing African American women from invisibility has several benefits.

First, it allows the reader to see more clearly how each race, black and white, defined peace and freedom. African American women's unique burdens of sexism and racism shaped their participation in the peace movement. For them, peace and freedom meant much more than ending war and ensuring that all humankind received civil liberties by law. While global issues undoubtedly concerned pre–Cold War era black peace activists, they believed that WILPF first had to deal with the home front. Specifically, race matters were essential to both domestic and international peace. They argued that it would be hypocritical for WILPF to engage in intensive debate with representatives from other countries about eradicating oppressive conditions when America was routinely ignoring racial injustice. Perhaps peace activist Inez Jackson best summed up what African American peace activists wanted when she stated, "The civil rights and peace movements are closely related because when people are being discriminated against it's violence." When asked the role of black women in the peace movement, Jackson asserted, "You couldn't work for peace and freedom without working against discrimination . . . freedom for *all* people and peace."[23]

Second, African Americans' involvement in peace activism provides a window into the world of interracial cooperation, its benefits as well as its drawbacks. Throughout America and in numerous foreign countries, black women joined white women in establishing hundreds of local WILPF branches that served as auxiliaries to regional and national organizations. A handful of white peace activists spent countless hours and a great deal of energy encouraging black women to join the movement. Despite enthusiastic responses from whites and an unquestionable commitment to peace and freedom by African American women, occasional outbursts of racist behavior or the more pervasive effects of racial indifference at times prevented full and equal cooperation between the two races. Such barriers ranged from a shortsighted vision of activists' goals to the outright exclusion of African Americans from certain WILPF-sponsored activities and branches for fear of alienating unsympathetic whites.

Third, an examination of the role of African American peace activists in WILPF offers proof that the organization was in the vanguard in race relations for most of the twentieth century. This finding is significant when one considers the relationship between blacks and whites in America between 1915 and 1975. WILPF was founded during the nadir of the black experience in America, when lynching and race riots were commonplace and de jure and de facto segregation were deeply entrenched throughout the country. Issues of segregation and racial injustice continued to plague the country in the early 1970s. Sometimes the League mirrored societal race problems as blacks and whites clashed and struggled over difficult ground. However, it also differed from the larger society in that some of its black and white members were determined to work together despite pervasive racism and racial indifference in America.

Finally, placing black women at the center of a study of peace activism reveals the extent to which they helped shape the League's goals and ideology. African American women played a far more significant role in the peace movement than has been previously acknowledged. They were crucial to broadening the public arm of WILPF, and it is in large part due to their efforts that the League became an effective vehicle for black peace activists' struggle against racial violence and oppression.

Previous studies of WILPF have focused primarily on peace activists in the urban North. Most peace activity did occur on the East Coast and in an urban context, which is not surprising considering that a large number of middle-class blacks lived in large American cities. This study, however, concentrates on the peace activism of women not only in northern areas but also elsewhere in the United States, focusing especially on well-known centers of peace agitation. These centers include Philadelphia, the District of Columbia, New York City, Atlanta, Berkeley, San Francisco, San Jose, Tuskegee, Chicago, Chapel Hill (North Carolina), Montgomery, Wichita (Kansas), Tulsa (Oklahoma), and Gary (Indiana). Although each city had its own unique characteristics, most were sites of well-known institutions of higher learning—which were also centers of peace agitation.

The major goal of this study is to fill large gaps not only in the enormous body of scholarship on the peace crusade but also in African

American and women's history. Beginning in the mid-1970s, scholars became interested in researching the experiences of African American women. For example, Hazel Carby published *Reconstructing Womanhood: The Emergence of the Afro-American Woman Novelist.*[24] Furthermore, Paula Giddings's *When and Where I Enter . . . The Impact of Black Women on Race and Sex in America*[25] appeared, as did bell hooks's monumental *Ain't I a Woman: Black Women and Feminism,*[26] Joyce Ladner's extraordinary *Tomorrow's Tomorrow,*[27] and Gerda Lerner's timely *Black Women in White America.*[28]

In the 1990s, other scholars of women's history published studies that addressed issues ranging from black women's experiences in the national suffrage movement to their agency in various local communities. For instance, Rosalyn Terborg-Penn examines the role of black women in the suffrage movement in her recent study *African American Women in the Struggle for the Vote, 1850–1920,*[29] Stephanie Shaw focuses on the lives of the African American professional class in her book, *What a Woman Ought to Be and to Do,*[30] Deborah Gray White explores the contours of black women's history in the twentieth century in *Too Heavy a Load,*[31] Tera Hunter addresses the activism of domestics after emancipation in *To 'Joy My Freedom,*[32] and the prolific writer Darlene Clark Hine explores various issues relevant to women in several studies.[33] Conspicuously absent from this flurry of publications is a book expressly devoted to the peace activism of African American women.

A study of the experiences of black female peace activists is necessary for several reasons. For one, it confirms that African American women were not one-dimensional. Their experiences encompassed more than slavery or service in some subservient role after emancipation. Likewise, even when they exercised agency, they focused on more than domestic issues. Consequently, African American women developed an international consciousness. Their concerns transcended America's boundaries.

Second, an examination of black peace activism provides insight into how such activists were able to connect or link race to issues that were often considered irrelevant to the African American experience. Furthermore, it not only reconceptualizes black peace activism but also points the way toward a comprehensive analysis of the very nature of power itself.

Third, an exploration of the peace activism of African American women offers a much-needed account of their experiences in an interracial organization. While many studies have examined the roles of black women in various organizations and movements, few have focused on their experiences in an interracial organization.

Finally, this study of black female activism clearly confirms the claim of feminist theorist Patricia Collins that "every culture has a worldview it uses to order and evaluate its own experiences." Collins further adds that "black women's grounding in traditional African American culture fostered the development of a distinctive Afrocentric women's culture."[34] Herein lies another major value of this study. It illustrates how an "outsider-within stance functions to create a new angle of vision,"[35] with African American peace activists offering a different perspective of peace and freedom from that of their white colleagues.

African American peace activists' experiences suggest that black women as a group understood a world different from that of their white colleagues. These concrete experiences "stimulate[d] a distinctive Black feminist consciousness concerning the material reality."[36] Hence, the African American woman's activist tradition offers a new model for examining African American political activism overall.

Therefore, to fill these voids in scholarship on African American, women's, and peace history, I analyze ideas and arguments advanced by black women activists for peace. I also ascertain the extent to which the rationales that these activists developed issued from a concern for the rights of blacks. I also dispel the myth of black apathy toward pacifism, suggesting that black women had to be able to directly link peace to racial justice issues.

What factors united these two groups of women? Certainly, each group's desire to eradicate social injustices not only in America but throughout the world joined them. However, this shared belief, which was necessary, was not sufficient. Also important is that despite their many differences, black and white peace activists shared important attributes. They were middle-class, college-educated, and, if employed, professional. Furthermore, most unemployed activists from both groups were married either to entrepreneurs or to college-educated professionals.[37] In other words, black and white peace activists had similar class backgrounds.

Most black peace activism occurred on the national level, for two reasons. First, during the first twenty-five years of the study period, most black women became "members" of WILPF only after joining either its local or national interracial committees. The national Interracial Committee later became the Committee on Minorities and Race Relations. The committee, designed to recruit black women, consisted mainly of women of color and, for many years, was the only way that most black women could have any kind of association with WILPF. Most local WILPF branches did not have interracial committees. Second, white women in local WILPF branches were not as supportive of the organization's policy on racial justice as those in the national office. Most local white women seemed to have mirrored the rest of society when it came to racial justice and desegregation. It took them much longer than their colleagues in the national headquarters to adopt these peace causes.

This study, which focuses on African American peace activism mainly in the United States between 1915 and 1975, attempts to move forward to show change and continuity. However, the multitude of issues has forced me to examine the topic thematically as well. For instance, when African American activists worked with their white colleagues to recruit black women, they also became members of and subsequently became involved in the controversy surrounding the Interracial Committee. Moreover, at the same time that black women were establishing links between race and domestic peace, they were doing the same with international peace issues. In these two situations, in particular, I have devoted separate topics to each and attempted to show how the two issues were being addressed at the same time.

For African American WILPFers, peace and freedom were linked to worthy goals—goals that they struggled to obtain for themselves and their peers between 1915 and 1975. Untold millions of men, women, and children of all races and ethnic groups suffered and died for these goals, which still elude us today.

Peace . . .

Freedom . . .

Black peace activists maintain that these two states of being are as important to human existence as are air and water, that human life is meaningless in their absence. Peace and freedom are inextricably bound together. As African American members of WILPF have maintained since the organization's founding in 1915, there is no freedom without peace and there can be no lasting and just peace without freedom.

Part One

1915–1945

Bold Beginnings

The First Ten Years

1915–1925 By February 1915, a leading American peace activist, Carrie Chapman Catt, had repeatedly asked her colleagues what more could be done to end the war raging in Europe. Little more than six months previously, Austria had unleashed its terror on Serbia, subsequently bringing most of Europe into what became known as the Great War. Angry, and perhaps with little hope, Catt penned a letter to the *New York Times* in which she warned men that if they did not end the war, women would. She wrote,

> They tell us men were told [*sic*] off for war, women to care for homes and children, and in time of peace, war, the man's business, gives way to politics, the man's business.
>
> The politics of men have embroiled the world in the most wholesale slaughter of the sons of mothers the world has ever known.... Hundreds if not thousands of women have been forced to bear children by soldiers of their country's enemy all along the war zone.... When war murders the husbands and sons of women, destroys their homes, desolates their country and makes them refugees and paupers, it becomes the undeniable business of women.[1]

The women whom Catt was referring to were members of a rapidly growing female peace movement.

Female peace activists believed that they had sat on the sidelines, helplessly observing the events unfolding in Europe, long enough. When it seemed as though World War I was spinning out of control, they politely and respectfully tried to impel their male colleagues to adopt measures to end the conflict. But their entreaties fell on deaf ears, as male peace activists continually refused to oppose the war publicly or privately. Women pacifists initially were baffled by the inaction of their male colleagues. They finally concluded that men who had once supported peace reform now feared America's wrath and did not want to become a casualty in the nation's own private war against dissent.

Most female peace activists had firsthand experience in opposing the Great War. For instance, in mid-December 1914, after several conversations about how the existing peace groups were "exclusionary in leadership and ideology," eminent social worker Jane Addams invited interested American women to a peace meeting to be held on January 10–11, 1915, in Washington, D.C. Addams had mentioned in the invitation that Carrie Chapman Catt was a co-organizer of this new group, the Woman's Peace Party (WPP). Feeling uneasy about her name being used, and perhaps worried about the pervasive intolerance of opposition to World War I, Catt wrote Addams a letter in which she stated, "I wished only to support your effort in an inconspicuous way."[2] Although Catt offered a reason for her hesitancy, I suggest that she was afraid of the unfavorable repercussions during an era known for its intolerance.

Not long after the WPP was officially organized, its members began to receive vicious attacks and threats from war proponents in America—attacks that would continue long after World War I had ended. During the war, the national office was broken into more than once and files were destroyed or examined. Jane Addams once recalled how even mail that "protruded from the door . . . was frequently spat upon" and the office door "often befouled in hideous ways."[3] Furthermore, WPP members learned that they were under surveillance by the Department of Justice. While some women left the WPP because of these external pressures, many others remained and fought harder for world peace and an end to the Great War.

The remaining peace activists became proactive, initiating antiwar action. As though deciding to remain in the WPP weren't enough, peace activists demonstrated amazing courage as they tackled peace and freedom issues. For example, many opponents of war dissenters, as well as critics of the WPP and its agenda, were virtually speechless when Jane Addams "testified before a House Committee against proposed increases in military spending." They believed that female peace activists had finally gone too far. Addams had agreed to testify before a group of men, many of whom she had accused of not "treasuring human life" and therefore saw no moral or ethical need to end the conflict in Europe.[4] Who was she to make such bold accusations about a conflict of which she, a woman, knew so little?

What her critics failed to realize is that Addams and the handful of women who remained in the WPP during the Great War did not care what others may have thought about them or the peace movement. Dressed in winter clothes that perhaps unintentionally concealed their identities, the slightly more than three thousand middle-class white women who traveled to the nation's capital in January 1915 were interested only in "bring[ing] about an early end to the war."[5] They wanted the world to know that there were some in America who owned their souls and were determined to preserve the rights of innocent war victims, no matter what the cost. Therefore, amid a devastating war, the resistance to the expanding roles of women, the growing intolerance of antiwar proponents and minorities, and an emerging Communist menace, a group of courageous women dared to challenge an era marked by intolerance, hatred, and exclusion. For most Americans, it was a time of great social and political upheaval. The major cause of this agitation was deep-seated racism.

Although urban progressives had helped bring about many reforms in the two decades before Woodrow Wilson's first administration, most of those long-awaited changes were exclusively for whites. Despite the economic, political, and educational gains enjoyed by African Americans, they were, for the most part, small compared with those made by whites. For example, residential segregation ordinances were springing up all over the country. Lynching and other forms of violence against blacks increased. Furthermore, many African American men had not been able to exercise the right to vote since the 1880s. Disillusioned and disheartened, many blacks began to migrate to cities all over the country in search of much-needed jobs and housing. White Americans, fearing that the new immigrants would take jobs and housing away from them, retaliated, often with violence. African Americans defended themselves in major race riots, first in East St. Louis, Illinois, and Houston, Texas, and later in Elaine, Arkansas; Chicago, Illinois; and Tulsa, Oklahoma. Between 1908 and 1919, race riots became commonplace in America as whites and blacks clashed over jobs and housing.[6]

As Darlene Clark Hine and other scholars have noted, pseudoscholars fed into this fear. Several wrote allegedly scientific treatises that strengthened the cause of white supremacy when they claimed the black man's inferiority and called for the separation of races at any cost. For example, Lothrop Stoddard, along with others during the late 1920s, accurately captured the prevailing view of white Americans during World War I when he observed, "We know that our America is a White America. 'America,' in the traditional sense of the word, was founded by White men, who evolved institutions, ideals, and cultural manifestations, which were spontaneous expressions of their racial temperament and tendencies. And the overwhelming weight of both historical and scientific evidence shows that only so long as the American people remain White will its institutions, ideals, and culture continue to fit the temperament of its inhabitants,—and hence continue to endure."[7] Such thinking created a more hostile atmosphere for African Americans, as whites did whatever was necessary to keep blacks in subordinate positions in society.

Several books and films also conveyed inflammatory racist messages that aroused fear and hatred of African Americans by whites. Studies such as *The Leopard's Spots: A Romance of the White Man's Burden, 1865–1900* and *The Clansman: An Historical Romance of the Ku Klux Klan,* both by Thomas Dixon, helped create a Negrophobic atmosphere in World War I America. Both books promoted a "theory of racial retrogression." The fundamental principle of the theory was that not only were African Americans "inferior to whites but also as they became further removed from the taming influences slavery had provided, they were actually retrogressing to an even more bestial state that made their very presence a threat, particularly sexually to white society."[8] Since whites believed that blacks could not be "rehabilitated" or treated as equals, the only option available was complete segregation. After all, most whites conceived of blacks as "silly, simpleminded brutes" that lusted after "white women, grasp[ed] white property, and refus[ed] to accept their preordained status at the bottom of the social order."[9] Americans who held such beliefs took action to protect themselves, often resorting to extralegal violence when they believed it was necessary.

In an atmosphere of fear, hatred, violence, and deliberate exclusionary practices, one of the most controversial films in American history was released. Like the many books on the subject, the film also sent a well-constructed message of "Negro inferiority" and the need to "keep the Negro in his place." Written and directed by D. W. Griffith, *The Birth of a Nation* first appeared in 1915 and immediately caused a stir. Many whites, including President Woodrow Wilson, supported the film. They heeded its ominous warning against giving African Americans power and agreed with its proposition of a new Ku Klux Klan to control the "slothful and inferior race."[10]

In that same year, the modern Ku Klux Klan was organized and its members immediately spearheaded most of the violence and intimidation against blacks that followed. The Klan vowed that it "would not rob the colored population of their rights," but it "demanded that [blacks] respect the rights of the white race in whose country they [were] permitted to reside."[11] Hence the revival of the Klan, coupled with *The Birth of a Nation,* signaled the continuation of violence and terror in World War I America.

Although Griffith denied it, William Joseph Simmons, the chief initiator of the new Ku Klux Klan, headquartered in Stone Mountain, Georgia, alleged that he organized the secret order to "herald the coming of the film." Simmons related in 1928, "There was good reason, as I have said, for making Thanksgiving Day [November 25, 1915] the occasion for burning the fiery cross. Something was going to happen in town [Atlanta] the next week [*sic*] [the premiere of *The Birth of a Nation*] that would give the new order a tremendous popular boost."[12]

When *The Birth of a Nation* opened in Atlanta, the *Atlanta Constitution* printed alongside an announcement of the film an "advertisement announcing the Ku Klux Klan revival." Maxim Simcovitch also notes in his article on the subject that when "Simmons was interviewed in 1928 and asked if there had been no film, could he have pushed his new order forward as quickly as he did? Simmons' reply was 'no. *The Birth of a Nation* helped the Klan tremendously.'"[13] Perhaps Simmons was telling the truth. Nine days after he and others assembled on Stone Mountain and erected a fiery cross, the state of Georgia granted a "charter" for the "origination" of the Ku Klux Klan. Two days later, December 6, 1915, *The Birth of a Nation* opened to the public in Atlanta shortly after it began showing in Boston, New York, and Chicago. The African American community for the most part was outraged. Represented by the National Association for the Advancement of Colored People (NAACP), African Americans and other critics of the film insisted either that the film be banned or that certain parts offensive to blacks be cut. They also demanded that the New York Film Review Board "let Negroes preview the film."[14] The board agreed to allow NAACP officials to preview the film as long as they were not African American. This request was not unusual, since during this period of intolerance, some of the most liberal whites refused to share a table, or even room, with the most promising black citizen. In an effort to close the case, "Jacob Schiff, Jane Addams, Lillian Wald, and other [white] NAACP members" were approved by the New York Film Review Board to "privately view the motion picture."[15] All of them adamantly opposed the film.

The NAACP and others who had attended the private showing initiated criminal proceedings against the New York Film Review Board. They demanded that the "New York Commissioner of Licenses stop the film as a nuisance."[16] The New York Film Review Board's initial response to the NAACP was an offer to edit the film. After further consideration, the board decided that the film would be released without the proposed modifications. Reactions to this decision were mixed. On one hand, rioting and violence occurred in some cities where the film was shown. For example, an enraged white man in Lafayette, Indiana, killed a black man after seeing the film. In Houston, Texas, during a scene in which a white actor in black face pursued the film's white star, Lillian Gish, viewers shouted, "Lynch him!"[17] Some news presses and individual citizens thought the film was a depiction of reality and praised Griffith for such a fine work of art. Even worse, the film gave rise not only to the Ku Klux Klan but to other vigilante organizations such as the Knights of the White Camellia and the Red Shirts. In some towns, it was dangerous to be around African Americans or, even worse, to be an African American. It became impossible for blacks to escape the white man's vengeance. Virtually no white or black was left untouched by the pervasive racism in America.

A second issue that divided Americans was a fear of Communism. The country resented the success of the Bolshevik revolution in Russia in 1917. This fear was stimulated somewhat by "acts of violence on the part of radical individuals and by a series of [labor] strikes" in the United States. The result was pervasive anti-red hysteria, led by the U.S. attorney general, Mitchell Palmer. Although the real danger was small, anti-Communist raids took place in scores of cities. The police were ordered to arrest hundreds of people with or without warrants. Before the Red Scare was over, "more than six thousand [people] were arrested and held for six days or, even worse, without any opportunity to know the charges against them." Furthermore, "hundreds of suspects were deported." By the time the hysteria subsided, many Americans had suffered irreversible damage to their personal and professional lives. For example, "the New York legislature expelled five Socialists who had been legally elected to seats in the Assembly."[18] This pervasive fear did not abruptly disappear after World War I. The Red Scare, which had begun in 1919, continued until 1924. By then, however, it had become more specific in its victimization, targeting mainly those groups and individuals who either were unrelenting critics of the status quo or had behaved in ways that were historically unacceptable. This situation explains why female peace groups were blacklisted and unfairly targeted.

Many of these peace dissenters were also part of the emerging "New Woman" phenomenon. Jane Addams, in particular, was regarded by several scholars as "exemplify[ing] the New Woman of the 1890s, who integrated Victorian virtues with an activist social role." Such historians further maintain that women like Addams "transformed" themselves into figures "of national repute."[19] Hence the roles of women were changing because of a changing society. The women's world "expanded visibly" when scores of women stepped outside the private sphere by engaging in work that traditionally had been considered men's work. Women began to build institutions, wage a more aggressive campaign for suffrage, and become increasingly involved in voluntary associations, often after graduating from college. Their special mission in public life was to "purify, uplift, control, and reform; to improve men, women and society; [and] to extend the values of the home."[20]

However, as women crossed the extremely rigid line that separated the private and public spheres, controversy ensued. Questions were raised about the role of women. Should a woman be allowed to vote? Should she be allowed to attend college? If she attends college, would it not ruin her health or cause her to lose her mind? If she is allowed to pursue a career, how will it affect her identity as a woman? Would she be considered female? Should she be allowed to speak in public or to attend meetings? These questions lingered in the minds of many opponents of public women for years. While society tried to answer these questions, the New Woman continued to pursue a college degree, a profession and, essentially, her own identity. Society was indeed changing, as evidenced by urbanization and industrialization. The New Woman was a product of these societal changes. Despite this connection, most people were not ready to accept the New Woman, making the issue another one to divide Americans.

Racism, the Red Scare, and the "Woman Question" contributed to the volatile atmosphere in World War I America. From this environment, female peace activists emerged and fought to express their views. For the most part, they persevered and moved forward with their agenda. After all, they were the "new" women that America had come to both love and hate. They were determined to take charge of their own lives, and the WPP provided them with the opportunity by allowing them to be independent of male control in the peace movement. Moreover, these courageous women were not deterred by the backlash from their actions. Their bravery was most evident in how they dealt with both the Red Scare and African Americans.

Various groups, including the U.S. War Department, critically attacked the Women's International League for Peace and Freedom (WILPF) in particular and the peace movement in general. By the time of the first Red Scare in America, the WPP had reorganized and become WILPF, with several local and state branches.

During the Great War, WPP members suggested that leaders engage in arbitration to settle their differences. This unpopular position later provoked the labeling of WILPF members as Communists—an earmark no one wanted during and immediately after World War I. Some historians maintain that opposition to pacifism grew from a postwar conservatism led by right-wing groups. At least that appears to be the reason.

After World War I, many Americans wanted to protect the country from future attacks by anyone. One way to ensure such security was to adopt a policy of military preparedness. Congress concurred. In 1920, the House of Representatives and the Senate passed the National Defense Act, which provided for a peacetime army and a National Guard.[21] Of course, WILPFers opposed this act on the same grounds they had during World War I. They believed that instead of spending money on military armaments, the government's policy and spending should be directed toward international arbitration and promotion of world peace. Once again WILPF was attacked by nationalist groups as being un-American as soon as it made public this position.[22] This time its members were labeled not only as Communist but also with the hated terms *radicals* and *socialists.*

Secretary of War John Weeks was the first public figure to speak against the women's peace organizations. To counter opposition to the National Defense Act, Weeks began "a public campaign designed to increase the visibility of the army, convince the public of its importance, and counter the headway that peace groups were making in opposition to the War Department's national defense policy."[23] He also began to monitor more closely WILPF's activities in particular and ordered that certain members be followed. The organization's members first learned of this surveillance at their annual national congress in Washington, D.C., in 1924. This shocking revelation enraged them. One member, who wanted to remain anonymous for fear of repercussions, wrote a letter to Weeks in which she denounced his actions and demanded to know his reasons for monitoring WILPF. She wrote,

> I am advised by various peoples that the War Department is much opposed to the forthcoming Congress of the Women's International League for Peace and Freedom to be held in this city early in May and that the Department has expressed definite hostility to certain speakers on the agenda of the Congress. I am further advised that the Bureau of Investigation of the Department of Justice is to place certain of the Delegates under surveillance during the Congress and that some speakers may be prevented from addressing the meetings. . . . I shall be obliged if you will advise me of the precise theory on which any action by your Department along the lines indicated is contemplated.[24]

This anonymous letter is worth recounting in its entirety because it is so revealing. For one, the peace activist's decision to remain anonymous implies that she might have been horribly afraid. More important, it gives some sense of how perilous the period was for dissenters. Second, the letter clearly shows that post–World War I America was a time of intolerance and repression. Also, peace activists were being observed twenty-four hours a day by the U.S. government and were subjected to potentially lethal retaliatory acts for their "un-American" behavior. Finally, it is obvious that the government wanted to suppress any and all opposition. This powerful threat certainly created a hostile and dangerous atmosphere for anyone who opposed the status quo.

WILPF saw this increased activity by the War Department as a threat to its survival. Therefore the peace group publicly condemned the National Defense Act. Its members also sent letters to those who accused them of being Communists and refuted every slanderous claim made against them.

For instance, when Brigadier General Amos H. Fries, director of the Chemical Warfare Bureau, claimed that WILPF members took an oath against any involvement in war, the leaders of the various peace groups immediately defended themselves. Lucia Ames Mead, chair of WILPF's

Committee on Education, wrote Secretary Weeks a letter in which she made it clear that the alleged "slackers oath" was "simply a proposal made by one member and rejected." She emphasized that WILPF required "no [such] oath." She continued by maintaining that WILPF was not guilty as charged by Fries. She then suggested that he apologize to the organization, and ended her letter with a personal criticism of Fries and the governmental department in which he worked. Mead maintained that Fries had done WILPF and the National Council of Women a "[grave] injury" and therefore, she reasoned, the department should "rectify it." Mead noted that Fries should have said that his statement was his opinion, since he could not prove it. "But," Mead retorted, "when he [Fries], however unwittingly, libel[ed] patriotic, well-meaning people and [said] they took a pledge which they rejected, and when he decline[d] to withdraw his statement when shown in falsity, it [brought] discredit on his profession which is supposed to be composed of gentlemen. Therefore," she added, "if it [were] possible for Fries to have a wrong rectified," then hopefully he would "see [his] way clear to have it done, without in any measure curtailing everyone's right to an expression of his opinions."[25]

Others falsely claimed connections between the peace movement and Communism. One lady, Francis Ralston Welsh, likened WILPF to a Communist Party and claimed that it was "founded in the interests of Germany and taken over by the Communists in their own interests and controlled by them."[26] WILPFers were also referred to as a group of "ultra-pacifists, propagandists of un-American sentiment," who "represented Sovietism" in America.[27]

WILPF's membership and image suffered because of the unwarranted attacks. For instance, in 1923, Dr. Robert Tucker, the minister of Cass Avenue Methodist Episcopal Church in Detroit, supported pacifism but could not persuade some of his church members to support WILPF because of how the organization was perceived. So Tucker wrote WILPF's national board a letter to obtain clarification on the organization's purpose and agenda. He shared with board members that, when he tried to recruit some of his parishioners for peace work, they rejected his invitation because of the negative press that WILPF had received. He then urged WILPFers to make an effort to improve their image because "all manner of charges [were] being made in the public press which [were] influencing many people." Tucker closed his letter to the board by asking whether the peace organization was "prompted by the Bolshevist regime in Russia."[28]

That same year, when WILPF members attended the Cause and Cure of War Conference in Washington, D.C., a pamphlet, *Peace at Any Old Price,* was circulated that depicted WILPF as the "most subversive, . . . the most insidiously and cleverly camouflaged, thoroughly anti-American and un-American group."[29] The authors of the pamphlet also denounced WILPFers at the conference for openly "boast[ing] of 'slacking' during the war," when some of them "claimed that they refused to buy bonds, to roll bandages or to participate in any of the relief work" which was of so much aid to the soldiers in the trenches overseas. They then concluded that the entire conference was "dominated by a spirit of Russian Communism" and, in the process, peace activists were working against their own government for "internationalism." When the pamphlet was circulated among America's citizens, it caused many of these "faithful, law-abiding, loyal Americans" to denounce WILPF's activities as un-American.[30]

Despite the persistent acidic attacks, which WILPFers believed were unsubstantiated, they continued to wage their battle for world peace and freedom. Most attacks leveled at WILPF were based on the belief that as an international organization, it had to be un-American. Therefore WILPF's various responses to the disparaging remarks were designed to discredit this assumption. WILPF basically issued the following simple statement when responding to critics: "Belonging to an international organization, the American members [WILPFers] are concerned with common, human interest and are loyal and patriotic American citizens."[31]

The attacks continued through 1924. The most damaging criticism was in the form of the famous spiderweb chart, which first appeared in Henry Ford's newspaper, the *Dearborn Independent.* This chart, which originated in the Chemical Warfare Bureau of the War Department, linked numerous women's organizations and their members to communist and socialist doctrines. The chart was given its name because the various lines "linking individual women to organizations" resembled a spiderweb. On the chart, the names of many leading WILPFers were highlighted in colors from red to violet. For instance, peace activists Madeline Doty, Jane Addams, Emily Greene Balch, and Belle LaFollette "were all underscored in red on the original chart."[32] The color red was used to signify WILPF on later versions of the chart.

Many of the accused were outraged by the chart and expressed that anger. After learning of the chart's origin, Maude Wood Park, chair of the Women's Joint Congressional Committee, wrote a letter to John Weeks, Secretary of War, in which she maintained that a great injustice had been done to the committee by the circulation of the chart. She further added that the publication of such false information was "exceedingly irritating to the organizations comprising the Women's Joint Congressional Committee and to the twelve million voters comprising these organizations."[33]

No one really knows the extent of the government's involvement in the red-baiting of WILPF and several other women's groups. But records of WILPF affirm that various members were often followed by investigators from the Military Intelligence Division of the War Department throughout the 1920s. However, the majority of the surveillance occurred prior to 1925.

Furthermore, the organization's national office, directly across the street from the War Department, was raided periodically. The military, much to the surprise of many peace reformers, stole files, destroyed important documents, and wrecked the filing system.

In addition, the Military Intelligence Division collaborated with patriotic groups like the American Legion to maintain records about radicals believed to be threats to national security.[34] Furthermore, as previously alluded to, the national WILPF office in New York City was frequently vandalized and its files stolen or disrupted in the search for information about members.[35] WILPF officers graciously accepted the criticism. For the most part, the peace organization's national officers never revealed to their contemporaries all of the tactics of espionage that the intelligence division employed against them.

Despite public opinion, peace activists were determined to take charge of their lives and decide their own agenda in the newly formed WILPF. As WILPFers weathered the storm of criticism for their many unsolicited actions, they began to take the peace movement in a different direction. A major shift was the acceptance of African American women into an organization that once prided itself on being, for the most part, an all-white, middle-class group.

After WILPF issued its initial call for black women in late 1915, members of the national executive board boldly stepped forward and publicly recruited African American women who would adopt the peace cause. In response, a few equally courageous black women agreed to join the peace group despite an environment less than friendly to the Negro.

African American peace activists demonstrated bravery in several ways. For one, they were willing to work in an interracial organization with women who clearly were not free of racial prejudice. For instance, the New York branch, perhaps the most liberal thinking of all branches, would not speak to or engage in conversation with its lone black recruit, Helen Curtis.[36] This kind of behavior was characteristic of many white peace activists in local branches across the nation. Furthermore, African American women were willing to work in an organization that publicly denounced the war and America's involvement in it. They did so at a time when blacks were enduring racial injustices on a daily basis, and any challenge to the status quo was regarded as an act of Communism. Also, black peace activists were women who challenged the prevailing view that the woman's place was in the home. Finally, the first blacks to join WILPF were women who courageously fought for female suffrage. Thus black peace activists placed themselves in an extremely precarious position as they crossed certain boundaries and seemingly "forgot their place."

However, they were not overly concerned about the danger that they put themselves in by stepping forward and calling for an end to a major war or advocating world peace after the Great War. Instead, while most of America waged a fierce battle over the Negro's rightful place in society, black peace activists joined white WILPFers, like Jane Addams, Carrie Chapman Catt, and Emily Greene Balch, in their campaign to make WILPF a color-blind peace organization determined to end all forms of inequality.

After a series of heated debates on the meaning of *nonresistance*, WILPF's executive board still could not agree on a definition appropriate for World War I. Even when they traveled to Zurich in 1919, U.S. delegates to the International Congress of the Woman's Peace Party could not agree among themselves on a suitable clarification. In Zurich, the American delegation tabled the discussion to address other issues on the agenda. Instead, they joined women all over the world in adopting resolutions that they hoped would prevent another major war. They also agreed to change the name of the Woman's Peace Party to the Women's International League for Peace and Freedom, with each country having a national office and local branches in each state or district. After returning to America with a name change and new agenda, WILPF's executive board revisited its nonresistance position.

After much discussion, the assembled members agreed to continue to advocate nonresistance. However, *nonresistance* was replaced with a newer term, which was more broadly defined. The phrase used to describe the group's new position became *nonviolent resistance,* or *nonviolence.* This shift in position was accompanied by a slight variation in meaning. While *nonresistance* meant the refusal to commit or sanction violence, the terms *nonviolent resistance* and *nonviolence* were broadened to include a commitment to eradicating "the underlying causes of vio-lence—political, economic, and social inequalities of all kinds."[37] This change in WILPF's position in 1919 was another significant and bold step for the organization. The peace group's national leadership decided to publicly promote a policy of racial tolerance at a time when most white and black Americans knew only racism in its various forms. WILPF be-lieved that much of the violence that resulted from the existing racism was due to institutionalized racial and social attitudes.

This position caused WILPF to become embroiled in internal and external struggles. Two factors contributed to this conflict. For one, the acceptance of African American women into the peace group and aug-mentation of the definition of nonviolent resistance created problems within WILPF. Some white WILPFers had difficulty accepting black women as peace activists and behaved as the women in the New York branch did when black peace activist Helen Curtis joined. Others refused to commit themselves to fighting for economic, political, and social equality for all people. Meanwhile, the peace group began to lose a few members, who did not want to be labeled as Communist or endure constant sur-veillance by various prowar groups and the American government.

To make matters worse, WILPF leaders, who did not knowingly sup-port Communism, refused to denounce Communists or their activities. Unfortunately, WILPF suffered at the hands of those who led an anti-Communist crusade in America. First, the U.S. government went so far as to publicly ridicule some of the organization's leaders. In January 1919, a New York lawyer employed by the Military Intelligence Division testi-fied before the Overman Senate subcommittee and produced a list of sixty-two names of people whom he "labeled dangerous, destructive and anarchistic."[38] Both Jane Addams and Emily Greene Balch were on the list. Second, some peace activists, like Balch, lost their jobs for being a part of the controversial WILPF. Finally, others, like Addams, were ac-cused of using both the national and international peace organization to promote their "socialistic views."[39] For many women, being a mem-ber of WILPF was the least of their goals during the organization's first ten years. Women who elected not to join WILPF did so either out of fear or because they, too, believed that the group's willingness to embrace black women and to oppose the war was un-American.[40]

Pervasive racism, the Communist scare, and the "woman question" created a volatile atmosphere for peace activists, who usually were con-nected to each of these issues. But they persevered and moved forward, determined to take charge of their lives and decide their own agenda. Did they not boldly step forward and form their own peace group when men prevented them from making decisions in traditional peace groups? As they weathered the storm of criticism for their many actions, WILPFers who stayed the course courageously took the peace movement in a different direction. And they paid a price for doing so.

The attacks were expected and understandable. They also confirmed that WILPF had dared to be bold at a time when conservatism characterized most of U.S. political policy. Most Americans still were grappling with the notion of changing their foreign policy position from isolationism to internationalism. The mere thought of adopting an internationalist approach to resolving America's foreign policy and domestic issues made most of its citizens cringe. The United States was not ready to move in that direction. Thirty years would pass before the majority of Americans embraced internationalist thought and policy, and even then, acceptance of that policy would be done reluctantly. WILPF was indeed ahead of its time.

By 1925, WILPF had begun to recover from the attacks by anti-Communist groups in America. Even the U.S. government no longer closely monitored their activities. However, although fewer members were leaving the organization in the mid-1920s than in previous years, no black women were joining. To rectify this problem, WILPF's executive board decided to seek more aggressively women who were not traditionally middle-class, middle-aged, and white. Adoption of this position forced them to recruit African American women more vigorously.

When the executive board decided to reach out once again to African American women, it was not out of touch with its white membership on this issue. National officers knew that many of their members, especially in local branches, had difficulty accepting black women as equals. This problem had been proven by the attitudes exhibited when the first few blacks were admitted in 1915. But when the board agreed to seek additional members, WILPF's survival was of the utmost importance. Consequently, WILPF made the search for black women who believed in the peace cause a high-priority item on their agenda. What black women would answer the call for peace and freedom?

In Search of the Perfect Black Peace Activist

1915-1945 After dining with her traveling companions, Mary Church Terrell returned to her cabin on the ship so that she could finish her resolution for the International Committee of Women for Permanent Peace (ICWPP) Conference in Zurich, Switzerland. She sat at her desk and began to write, "We believe no human being should be deprived of an education, prevented from earning a living, debarred from any legitimate pursuit in which he wishes to engage, or be subjected to humiliations of various kinds on account of race, color or creed." As the night faded into day, Terrell continued to craft a document that revealed her basic philosophical beliefs about world peace and racial justice.

It was late April 1919, less than a year after World War I had ended, when Terrell and fourteen other American delegates en route to the global conference agreed to draft resolutions that would ensure postwar peace and justice. They further agreed that the resolutions would be presented at the conference. However, before arriving in Zurich, the women decided to share what they had written. Terrell was the only American delegate to link world peace with racial justice. Needless to say, she was surprised when her colleagues suggested that she delete some of her references to America's alleged racial prejudice. She was even more shocked that they thought their recommendations would only "improve" the resolution.[1]

Terrell believed that America's race problem was a peace issue and, for that reason, needed to be addressed. Therefore, she adamantly opposed any suggestions that her white colleagues offered. Terrell's peace activist friends continued to pressure her to change her text, but she refused. Emily Greene Balch and her other white peace associates were equally determined to prevent Terrell from discussing America's race problem. Consequently, they ignored Terrell and made the changes anyway.

Just before their riverboat docked in Zurich, Balch informed Terrell that the text of her resolution against racism had been altered. Terrell was angry and told Balch, without mincing words, that she disapproved of such arbitrary actions. Terrell was deeply offended by her colleagues' actions, which, she felt, amounted to a lack of respect for her and any of her opinions. She was determined, however, not to be ignored or disrespected so easily. Besides, she really did not understand what was so problematic with her resolution. After all, WILPF was rapidly earning the reputation of being linked to the protection of life, liberty, and property of all human beings. However, Terrell learned for the first time the truth about WILPF's position on racial justice. She was disappointed that some WILPFers were not as concerned about racial and social justice as they had so publicly proclaimed. Terrell would become the first of many African American peace activists to point to this gap between rhetoric and action.

Terrell exposed this contradiction to the world when supporters outside America invited her, at the eleventh hour, to represent the U.S. delegation by delivering the keynote address at the main conference of the ICWPP. Although her colleagues had improperly changed the text of her resolution, they had no control over what Terrell talked about a few days later at the opening session. Her text was a well-organized oratory, which kept the crowd on its feet.

Terrell's first sentences, spoken fluently in German, expressed her belief that "the race problem" was inextricably linked to world peace. In her speech, Terrell emphasized the progress blacks had "made as a race along all lines of human endeavor in spite of almost insurmountable obstacles" and appealed "for justice and fair play to all the dark races of the earth." She also emphasized that "white people [possibly would] talk about permanent peace until doomsday, but they could never have it till the dark races were treated fair and square."[2] When she left the stage, Terrell felt better than she had in a while, and rightly so. She had managed to launch her indictment of the status quo and demonstrate how racial injustice made a mockery of the logic on which WILPF's specific brand of peace activism was based without suffering public criticism or ridicule from the listening audience outside America.[3]

Years later, Terrell eagerly recalled the audience's response to her speech. She proudly noted, "There was such an outburst of approbation as I had not heard since I addressed the International Congress of Women which had met in Berlin fifteen years previously."[4]

Not all of her listening audience felt the same way. The American delegation in particular was critical of Terrell for addressing the race problem after they had advised her against doing so. They privately condemned her speech as nonpacifist because they believed that Terrell had "glorified the Civil War as a means of liberating her people."[5] The American delegates failed to realize that Terrell really did not care how they felt about her speech or her denunciation of racial injustice. She had already made her point. She deemed that her white colleagues would never fully understand her position. After all, they only had to look around to see the racial disparity in the room where they were all seated. Although there were millions of colored people in the world, Terrell was the only black delegate at the conference. Because of that, Terrell believed that she was "representing the women of all the nonwhite countries in the world."[6] Many of her white colleagues did not realize that her unfortunate experiences with racism had shaped her peace politics and subsequently highlighted a major difference between her and them over its definition. These differences of opinion often led to conflict, which was first evident at Zurich. Nonetheless, while black and white peace activists had different views about WILPF's goals, they shared a similar socioeconomic status. In the end, it was their shared sense of self and background, not a definition of peace, that united them.

Terrell's life stood in stark contrast to those of the twentieth-century white women who assembled in Zurich that year. Race had been the absolute determinant of privilege and opportunity in late-nineteenth- and early-twentieth-century America. To be of color was a mark of degradation. In other words, being black in America between the late 1880s and the 1920s was difficult regardless of one's socioeconomic status or educational level. Terrell knew that better than anyone in that room. She was a member of the black elite and had the benefit of a college education, yet racism was as much a part of her life as the air she breathed. Regardless of where she traveled or with whom she came in contact,

Terrell knew that she would experience racism on some level. She had no idea, however, that she would encounter racist behavior within WILPF—an organization that initially appealed to her because of its pro–racial justice stance.

Jane Addams first reached out to African Americans in 1915, as a way of making WILPF more racially diverse. According to peace historian Carrie Foster, Addams, Carrie Chapman Catt, and a host of other national leaders wanted to open WILPF's doors to nonwhite groups to address racism internally and to broaden the group's constituency.[7] Two issues seem to have motivated this significant move. For one, several peace historians maintain that WILPF had always been concerned about equality for all human beings and therefore was impatient with every policy that discriminated against any persons because of their race, gender, religion, or ethnicity. According to scholars writing on the subject, WILPF promoted the belief that such injustices were morally and legally wrong.[8] Therefore, in an effort to end such practices wherever they existed, WILPF adopted as part of its peace initiative a policy against racial injustice. It seemed as though WILPF's charter members wanted the world to know that they would not tolerate racism or discrimination of any kind.

Second, charter members evidently realized that the mere adoption of such a racial justice clause would seem hypocritical if they excluded blacks from the very organization that promoted such ideology. Therefore, the national board decided to open its doors to African American women. Unfortunately, many members were reluctant to accept, and an equal number adamantly opposed to acceptance of, black members. But the decision had been made.

While it may be true that national board members believed that the organization could benefit from racial diversity and a broader pool of potential peace workers, most were not prepared for what such a move would do to their overall peace agenda or to women within the peace organization. Once WILPF opened its doors to African American women, its agenda changed and the most liberal of its white membership were forced to reexamine their own feelings about race relations. While some members reluctantly welcomed black women, others separated themselves from the Negro.

As black women became more involved in WILPF, they learned that its membership faced a dilemma. How could the organization continue to present itself as a peace-loving group who detested injustices of any kind while privately it was engaged in a struggle to come to terms with the racist feelings of many of its own members? The members did not want to appear hypocritical. So what could they do? How could they conceal the race prejudice among members? Surprisingly, charter members unknowingly revealed their race prejudice when they began their search for black women who would adopt the peace cause.

White leaders established the criteria for black peace activists. What qualities should a black peace activist possess? To answer this question, white members looked at women already in the organization, that is, themselves. They believed that black women should possess the same qualities as white peace activists.

Jane Addams, for instance, born September 6, 1860, grew up in the small community of Cedarville, Illinois. Her father, John Huy Addams, was a wealthy miller who eventually became a state senator. Jane Addams's mother, Sarah, who died when she was two, was regarded by many in the community as a "kind and gracious lady." Her father remarried six years later to Emma Haldemann, who took care of the family of nine.

At an early age, Jane seemed to be different from her three older sisters. While they were content with the traditional women's role of domesticity, Addams was much more ambitious. She decided to attend Rockford Seminary in 1877, becoming one among the first generation of college women. In 1881 she graduated and eventually became a leading figure in the settlement movement occurring in America at the time. By 1889 Jane Addams had settled with a school friend, Ellen Gates Starr, in a shabby old mansion on the West Side of Chicago. Their neighbors were people of a dozen races who called the place "the old Hull House" after its builder, Charles Hull. Eventually *Hull House* was adopted as the name for what was to become the most famous social settlement in America and which made Jane Addams a household name.

Over time, Addams's charitable efforts increased. So too did her political ones. Instead of devoting all of her time to taking care of the poor, Addams directed her efforts at the causes of poverty. She was able to secure the aid of people who would help her persuade the state of Illinois to revisit laws regarding child labor, factory inspection, and the juvenile system. Addams also wanted to help immigrants and women, subsequently demanding legislation to protect immigrants from exploitation, limit the working hours of women, mandate schooling for children, recognize labor unions, and provide for industrial safety.

All of this work eventually led Addams and her supporters to demand women's suffrage. These causes made Addams a controversial figure. She faced even more criticism during World War I when she became a well-known peace activist. Eventually, the once beloved Jane Addams became a pariah, labeled as a socialist, an anarchist, and a Communist.[9]

A close friend of Addams, Carrie Chapman Catt, also became a part of the peace movement. Her life was similar to that of Addams.

Born on January 9, 1859, in Rapon, Wisconsin, as Carrie Clinton Lane, Catt was the second of three children of Lucius Lane and Maria Clinton Lane. At the age of seven, her family moved to rural Charles City, Iowa. She later graduated from the Iowa Agricultural College and model farm in Ames at the top of her class, in which she was the only woman. After college, she worked in Charles City as a law clerk and, later, in nearby Mason City as a schoolteacher and a principal. In 1883, she became one of the first women in the nation to be appointed a superintendent of schools.

In February 1885, Carrie Lane married Leo Chapman, editor and publisher of the *Mason City Republican.* The following year, Leo died of typhoid fever in San Francisco, California, where he had gone to interview for a job. Carrie Chapman then went to San Francisco and decided to remain there and work as a newspaper reporter. In 1887, she returned to Charles City and joined the Iowa Woman Suffrage Association.

In June 1890, Carrie Chapman married George Catt. At about the same time, she began working for the National American Woman Suffrage Association (NAWSA), speaking in 1890 at its Washington, D.C., convention. Catt eventually became a leading suffragist. In 1900 she succeeded Susan B. Anthony as the NAWSA president. From then on, her time was spent primarily in speechmaking, planning campaigns, organizing women, and gaining political experience. By the time World War I began, Catt divided her time between the suffrage and peace movements. As a peace activist, Catt became one of the founders of the Woman's Peace Party. Like her dear friend Jane Addams, Carrie Chapman Catt was honored and praised by many for her work. That adulation changed, however, when she became an opponent of war. Like Addams, she too spent her last years defending herself against critics who claimed she was unpatriotic and a Communist.[10] Catt also realized that it was virtually impossible for her to devote equal time to both the suffrage and peace movements. Therefore, when forced to make a choice between the two, Catt chose the suffrage cause.

A third member of WILPF's first executive board who reached out to black women was Emily Greene Balch. Her background was similar to that of Addams and Catt. Born in Jamaica Plains, Massachusetts, she was the daughter of a successful lawyer. Balch was a member of the first class to graduate from Bryn Mawr in 1889. She went on to study economics and social sciences in Paris from 1890 to 1891, then at Harvard, the University of Chicago, and Berlin in 1895.

From 1896 to 1915, she taught economics and sociology at Wellesley College, heading the department in 1913. Her work in Boston was greatly influenced by that of Jane Addams. Balch worked in a Boston social center and studied the background of Slavic immigrants in America and Europe.

In 1915 Balch was a delegate to the International Congress of Women at The Hague, where she helped found WILPF. She became a devout pacifist and consequently lost her job at Wellesley. Undeterred, she joined the staff at the radical *Nation* magazine and wrote her book *Approaches to the Great Settlement.* Meanwhile, she continued to work for WILPF. In 1946 Balch received the Nobel Peace Prize for her lifelong dedication to the cause of peace and justice.[11]

So when the leading peace activists searched for black women who would adopt the peace cause, they used themselves as examples of the ideal peace reformer. It never occurred to them that their criteria limited the number of black women eligible for peace work or for membership in WILPF.

White women like Addams, Catt, and Balch wanted only those African Americans who were "cultivated, preferably professional" women because they believed that such ladies "set the pattern for the others."[12] As far as they were concerned, only certain black women were intellectually and culturally prepared for membership in WILPF.

These women did not find their criteria for black women appalling. However, many African American women thought that their selection process was horrendous because it seemed so classist and arrogant. Nevertheless, the founders of WILPF initially believed that club women possessed the qualities they were looking for; therefore they aggressively recruited such black women. White members who supported the campaign to recruit black women either directly approached such women wherever they might have been or urged fellow peace activists to identify and actively pursue them.

The first African Americans to join WILPF, therefore, were virtually mirror images of white pacifists. The groups shared similar interests, vocations, educational levels, forms of activism, and socioeconomic status. But despite their shared characteristics and experiences, white peace activists wanted African American women who also understood "their place" in America. In late 1915, Jane Addams and some of the earliest members of WILPF eagerly welcomed their first recruits, Mary Church Terrell, Mary B. Talbert, Charlotte Atwood, Dr. Mary Waring, and Addie Hunton.[13] For the next decade, various women's clubs were the main recruiting grounds for white WILPFers. By 1928 WILPF began looking for "representative Negro women" in places other than women's clubs. All black organizations and sororities, the Young Women's Christian Association (YWCA), public school systems and universities, and various civil rights organizations became major recruiting grounds for WILPFers. During this period, prominent black women in the organization included, among others, Vera Chandler Foster, Vivian Carter, Helen Curtis, Marian Anderson, Thelma Carter, Thelma Edwards Marshall, Dr. Flemmie Kittrell, Alice Dunbar-Nelson, Sadie Daniels St. Claire, Lucy Diggs Slowe, Mayme Williams, Addie Dickerson, and Bertha McNeill.

Many of these African American women, although activists and staunch supporters of racial justice, seemed to accept and continue to perpetuate WILPF's dominant belief that only a few black women were ready for the organization. They believed that still far too many members of their race were not as cultured or as well bred as they should be. These black peace activists, like so many of their other middle-class African American contemporaries, considered white middle-class values and morals to be the benchmarks of an urbane and socially acceptable culture. For some of these black women, that belief meant the complete and often emotionally painful rejection of any semblance of their African heritage. While they believed strongly that the enslavement of Africans and the racism inflicted on the descendants of slaves were unjust and unworthy of America's democratic goals, some pre–World War II peace activists held the same views as many of their black middle-class contemporaries. They never questioned the white assumption that African Americans should conform to the standards and behavior of middle-class whites as a prerequisite to social acceptance by whites. Consequently, the views of black pacifists buttressed the perceptions of African Americans by many white middle-class peace activists.

Black peace activists who held such views believed that they were more culturally advanced than the black masses; therefore they had a responsibility to bring other members of their race within white society's desired elevated sphere. Part of their work included serving as ambassadors from their group. They aimed to impress on their white colleagues through their actions that there were black people who were similar in all other ways but their race to the best of white people and that, given the chance, those blacks who had not reached this level would do so as well. Peace activist Addie Hunton, for example, was both angry and insulted that whites regarded all women of color as the same. She once stated, "Those who write most about the moral degradation of the Negro woman know little or nothing of the best element of our women."[14] Hunton, like most of her black peace activist colleagues, wanted her white pacifist friends to recognize class differences among African Americans.

Even Mary Church Terrell, arguably the most radical and race-conscious pre–World War II black peace activist, exhibited condescending and paternalistic behavior toward those of her race whom she vowed to help. Terrell was a charter member and the first president of the National Association of Colored Women (NACW), an organization of club women charged with the task of racial uplift. In *A Colored Woman in a White World,* Terrell details comments made about the Association's members by whites who attended national and regional conventions of the NACW between 1896 and 1920. All accounts given by Terrell demonstrate a deep-seated desire to meet white approval and gain subsequent acceptance.

While noting "[i]t was a great honor and satisfaction to be elected president of the National Association of Colored Women," for instance, Terrell felt that her greatest honor and satisfaction actually came from the publicity given to the organization and its programs by the "biggest and best dailies" in the country. She took delight in recounting news reports of the association's biennial national conventions between 1897 and 1917. Terrell maintained that the editorials in "several leading [white] newspapers bestowed unstinting praise on the meetings, the officers [of which she was one] and the delegates."

The *New York Daily News,* she noted with pride, believed the association's meetings "exhibited wide and appreciative knowledge of conditions confronting colored people." In commenting on the delegates, Terrell stated that the *New York Times-Herald* admitted, "These women were a continual revelation, not only as to personal appearance, but as to intelligence and culture." Terrell found even greater delight in sharing with her readers that the editor of the *Times-Herald* felt that "if by a bit of magic the color of their skin could be changed white, he would have witnessed a convention of wide-awake women, which in almost every particular would compare favorably with a convention of white-skinned women."[15] She seemed especially proud to have been favorably compared with white women.

Terrell makes similar observations elsewhere in her autobiography. In one instance, she informs the reader of comments made by these same dailies about a meeting she and other prominent blacks attended with whites. While at the biennial convention in Chicago in 1909, Terrell and other officers of the NAACP were invited to lunch with Jane Addams, a charter member of WILPF. In commenting on this event in her autobiography, Terrell said that the *Times-Herald* wrote that "the color line was given another good rub yesterday by Miss Jane Addams of Hull House who entertained at a luncheon a party of colored women. . . . 'We were impressed,' said one of the residents later in the afternoon, 'with the intelligence of these colored women. They inspected the settlement understandingly and poured in upon as many questions as we could answer.' This is the first time," continued the *Times-Herald,* "that colored women have been given recognition in a social way by a woman of lighter skin."

Of the same historical event, Terrell told her audience that the *Chicago Tribune* said in an editorial

> that within a single generation since the war which gave freedom to the race such a gathering as this should be possible means a great deal. Could Abraham Lincoln have looked in upon [these people] and have seen the representatives of the race he emancipated and listened to the addresses said to have been so admiringly spoken by the president of the convention, Mrs. Terrell, and others, and observed their essential dignity, evident refinement of manner and noted the breadth of their outlook for their race and country, it is not difficult to imagine some of the emotions which would have stirred him, especially in view of their so clear apprehension of the real conditions of the problem before them.

Terrell further noted that a "distinguished white woman" had said, "After watching these capable colored women three days" in Chicago, "I never want to hear another word about their [*sic*] being no hope for the Negro. Another thing, if the Lord helps him who helps himself, these colored women will have a good, long pull with Providence."[16]

By selecting these accounts, Terrell encouraged her readers to believe that they could rise above oppression, discrimination, and racism. Terrell and her colleagues undoubtedly evaluated their lives on the basis of what was proper and acceptable behavior for middle-class white women. Their efforts to assume responsibility for their own lives would be futile, black peace activists such as Terrell believed, if they were not validated by whites.

What these activists failed to realize is that they, like other black elites, had unconsciously internalized racism. They blamed African American men and women for failing to measure up to middle-class white America's value system and, in the process, seemed to have momentarily forgotten it was racism, as well as the violence that too often accompanied it, that prohibited countless African Americans from realizing the American dream. Hence Terrell and other black peace activists were wrongfully blaming blacks for "supposed weaknesses branded into the race's moral fiber by slavery."[17] For them and countless other middle-class blacks of the period, race uplift signified "the struggle for a positive black identity in a deeply racist society." Historian Kevin Gaines explains the behavior of the black middle class as "turning the pejorative designation of race into a source of dignity and self-affirmation through ideology of class differentiation, self-help, and interdependence."[18] Conversely, Terrell's editorials and public lectures indicated that some African Americans had reached these standards much to many whites' surprise. These accomplished blacks were clearly an unusual group of people of color, those who had somehow managed to acquire a good education and make a respectable living despite the obstacles. This group, of which Terrell was a member, represented those African American peace activists whom white pacifists would acknowledge and, perhaps, accept *on almost equal terms*. For each of these women, therefore, socioeconomic factors loom large in determining their worthiness as peace activists.

Terrell, for instance, was the most respected of all black peace activists during the World War I era. She was also the most economically secure. Terrell's father, Robert Church, who was born a slave in 1839 in Holly Springs, Mississippi, eventually amassed considerable wealth after the Civil War. He used money inherited from his white father to purchase a hotel. The income received from the hotel business was used to build institutions that provided "entertainment, cultural enrichment, and improved living conditions for African-Americans."[19] By 1900 Church was considered the richest black man in Memphis and was frequently described as the first African American millionaire in the South.[20]

The Churches' family lifestyle was exemplary of their financial status. The family lived in a two-story house with servants in the suburbs of Memphis. The two children, Mary and Thomas, attended private schools, and Mary spent her leisure time reading, participating in community benevolence and reform, and studying music, Latin, and German—all symbols of financial achievement.

Unlike most African American women, Mary Church's mother, Louisa, devoted much of her life to social causes without the daily worries of providing for her family. Furthermore, she hosted African American friends, who made regular visits to her home to socialize and discuss race uplift work. With so many reform-minded friends in their midst, the Church children received an early education in social and political activism, an experience shared by most of her white peace activist contemporaries.[21]

In 1884 Mary Church received a bachelor's degree from Oberlin College, and a few years later, she received a master's degree from the same institution. After teaching for a while at Wilberforce University, Church met and married a Harvard graduate, Robert Heberton Terrell. The Church-Terrell marriage allied two prominent families.

Robert Terrell's father took him from Virginia, his birthplace, to Washington, D.C., when he was ten years old. He attended the public schools of the District of Columbia. Terrell was popular, and black people often spoke with pride of the "first colored boy who had graduated from the high school in Washington" and subsequently "taken a degree at Harvard University."[22] In Washington, Terrell eventually became well known as a lawyer and judge. Presidents Theodore Roosevelt, William Howard Taft, Woodrow Wilson, and Warren Harding appointed him to a judgeship in the Municipal Court of the District of Columbia. Each time, the appointment was for four years and required confirmation by the U.S. Senate.[23]

While her husband served as judge, Mary Terrell was appointed by the commissioners of the District of Columbia to two terms on the board of education as the only black and the only woman. She had been recommended by Dr. C. B. Purvis, son of the well-known African American abolitionist Robert Purvis, who reasoned that Mrs. Terrell was "well-qualified by education and training to represent the colored people of the District."[24] The Terrells met many prominent black and white people in their respective positions. Many of these people were guests in their home over the years.

Mary Church Terrell's socioeconomic status prepared her for WILPF and certainly made her an excellent choice for peace work. Long engaged in social justice work, Terrell had no difficulty engaging in conversation or working daily with people outside her race. Hence her background was similar to that of most white peace activists of that period. She had been reared in a household of activists and had grown up observing the comings and goings of whites in her house. Even more important, Terrell was wealthy. WILPF's work required its members to be able to attend conventions and other important meetings both in America and abroad at the member's expense. Like most of the more active white peace activists, Terrell could afford to travel. Furthermore, she had gained the respect of most of her white colleagues in the peace organization. Each of these factors, her white colleagues reasoned, would help Terrell function in the predominantly white WILPF at the turn of the twentieth century.

Other African American peace activists recruited by white pacifists also came from respected families. They were not, however, as well off as the Churches and Terrells. In spite of this relative lack of wealth, their families were prosperous compared with most African Americans of the period. The Marshalls and the Fosters, for example, maintained a comfortable lifestyle as long as all adults in the family brought home a steady income.

In Wharton, Texas, the family of black peace activist Thelma Edwards Marshall enjoyed the comforts of a well-to-do household. Her middle-class parents were leading African Americans in their community and were engaged in several social reform activities. Marshall's parents instilled in her, while she was growing up, a sense of responsibility to African Americans. Once Marshall became an adult, like her parents before her, she became involved in several social reform projects and chose a profession that allowed her to assist those of her race who needed such.

Born August 13, 1899, to Horace Ferdinand Edwards and Anna Belle Johnson Edwards, Marshall received her earliest formal education in the public schools of Texas. After moving to Gary, Indiana, she taught in the public schools for ten years. She later married Dr. Vereen Marshall, and they had one son, William.[25]

The Marshalls enjoyed financial success in the steel-manufacturing town of Gary. While her husband was the town's only African American dentist in an age of segregation, Thelma Marshall received recognition as the first African American social worker to hold the rank of supervisor in the state of Indiana. She eventually became a vital resource within the black community.

After graduating from high school, Marshall studied at Fisk University. Upon graduation from Fisk, she was hired as a social worker. While holding this position, she also participated actively in civic leadership. In the early 1940s, she took personal initiative in the campaign to bring federally supported low-rent housing to Lake County, Indiana. The administrators of the conservative, heavily industrialized city of Gary were opposed to federal intervention to provide local housing, asserting that there was no need for it, that existing housing was adequate, and that the occupants were satisfied. To counter the opposition, Thelma Marshall traveled over the city and surrounding areas with camera and notebook, taking pictures of slum dwellings and interviewing slum families. She showed her slides before church groups, civic organizations, professional societies, and all other interested groups to educate the community about existing conditions. As a consequence, federally supported low-rent housing became a reality.[26] Marshall proved her commitment to social justice again at the close of World War II. By then she had been recruited by white peace activists into the local WILPF and had begun to make her presence felt within the organization. Yet she still found time to fight for social and human justice. In 1945, while most citizens of Indiana were preparing for the eventual return of soldiers and a world without war, Marshall continued to be concerned about the injustices that some people were experiencing, especially the discriminatory hiring practices of some employers not only in Gary but throughout the entire state of Indiana. She believed that of all the ostracisms, exclusions, and double standards that had beset African Americans, the most hideous discrimination was in the field of employment. Most blacks had depended on employment by whites for their entire existence. In view of that fact, Marshall believed that she could not give mere lip service to such an important brazen act of social injustice. Accordingly, for six months, she worked in Washington, D.C., under the direction of black labor activist A. Philip Randolph, as a lobbyist for the National Council for a Permanent Fair Employment Practices Commission.[27] Although it took a while, the Fair Employment Practices Commission was formed to address employment discrimination and other labor-related issues. People of Gary and from across the state of Indiana lauded Thelma Marshall for her efforts to bring about justice and equality in housing and employment. In addition, as a social activist, Marshall often opened her doors to activist friends. As the wife of a prominent dentist, Marshall met many of the city's black and white elite, often hosting parties and meetings for other prominent African Americans and interested white citizens to discuss race work.

Marshall's experiences and socioeconomic status made her a perfect candidate for membership into WILPF. A well-educated woman with a long record of social activism, she knew all too well the type of commitment peace work required and, more important, felt quite comfortable in an interracial organization such as WILPF.

Marshall first joined the Gary branch of WILPF in the late 1930s. White peace activists who saw her as the ideal black peace activist had aggressively recruited her. She was persuaded to join WILPF after hearing its mission statement and goal of achieving racial justice at a recruitment meeting at the local YWCA.

Another black peace activist, Vera Chandler Foster, also shared a common background with white peace colleagues. Respectable members of the black community in Tuskegee, Alabama, both Foster and her husband, Luther, were race leaders and social activists in the southern city that was widely known for its racial prejudice and violence. Unlike many of her African American neighbors and friends, Vera was as well educated as many of her white peace activist colleagues. Prior to moving to Tuskegee, Vera Chandler lived in Nashville, Tennessee, where she grew up in a middle-class suburban neighborhood. Upon graduation from the local public high school, she enrolled in nearby Fisk University. She graduated from Fisk in 1936 with a bachelor's degree in sociology. Four years later, Foster, who had married by then, earned a master's degree in social work from the University of Nebraska. She was an outstanding student at both universities and earned a fellowship to study at the University of Minnesota. After completing further study as a Rosenwald Fellow at the University of Minnesota in 1941, Foster received a second master's degree in social work from the prestigious University of Chicago.

Prior to earning her graduate degrees, Vera moved to Tuskegee, where she met and later married Luther Foster, the president of Tuskegee Institute. The first few years of their marriage were difficult ones. Between two pregnancies and weeklong commutes to Nebraska, Chicago, and Minnesota to continue her studies, Foster shared responsibility with her husband for the success of the family economy. Between 1939 and her retirement in 1980, Mrs. Foster held various positions: secretary to the president of Virginia State College, Petersburg, Virginia; dean of women and instructor of sociology at Langston University, Langston, Oklahoma; and medical-psychiatric social worker at John A. Andrews Hospital at Tuskegee Institute and the Tuskegee Veterans Administration hospital.

In addition to holding a full-time job, Foster found time to accompany her husband on business trips to various parts of the world and to hold active membership in several organizations. Her involvement in the service sorority Delta Sigma Theta, Inc., the Tuskegee Women's Club, the

National Association of Social Workers, the American Association of University Women, and the advisory boards of both the YWCA and the Young Men's Christian Association of Tuskegee illustrate her commitment to the community.

Even more amazing, Foster found time for her children, Adrienne and L. Hilton, as they became older and more involved in school and community activities. She was an active member and one-time president of her children's school parents-teachers association and head counselor at Camp Indian Brook in Vermont, where her children were enrolled. Like so many of her African American peace activist colleagues who were married to prominent men, Foster served as hostess to various groups and visitors at Tuskegee Institute while running a busy household.[28]

Although Foster had an incredibly busy schedule, she believed that time had to be made for any cause that proved worthy. This was the case for WILPF. Her first encounter with the peace group occurred while she was visiting a relative in Washington, D.C., in early 1938. Foster was introduced to the group by her close friend, peace activist Bertha McNeill, who had invited her to a meeting of the D.C. branch.[29] McNeill had been asked by white members to help find qualified black women for peace work. Some of the pacifists had heard about Foster's work with the Tuskegee Women's Club and thought that she would be an excellent person to organize a branch of WILPF in her hometown. Therefore they invited her to one of their meetings to introduce her to peace work. Foster was so impressed with the goals, programs, and more important, the pacifists of the D.C. branch of WILPF that she quickly agreed to try to form a branch once she returned home.

By December of that same year, while studying for a graduate degree and trying to be the perfect first lady, Foster had persuaded several of her close friends in Tuskegee to organize a branch of WILPF there. Because of her many responsibilities, Foster's first few years of involvement in the newly formed WILPF branch were not easy ones. However, she refused to give up. Instead she continued to wear her many hats until her studies were completed. Realizing how important she was to the peace movement in Tuskegee, white pacifists agreed to assist her wherever they could to retain her as a member. To many white peace activists, Vera Chandler Foster was indeed the perfect black woman for peace work. Therefore she was too important to lose.

Several other black women were involved in peace work prior to World War II. Like Marshall, Foster, and Terrell, they too were mirror images of their white colleagues. For each of these black peace activists as well, economics was the principal factor shaping their activism and influencing white activists' selection of them as potential peace candidates.

Although the black women recruited for peace work were decidedly middle-class, most of them, like many Americans who relied on limited resources while enjoying prosperity, could easily fall on hard times. For some black women, their socioeconomic status changed after becoming involved in the peace effort. For example, sometimes the death of a spouse or family member permanently altered economic circumstances.

For the well-known peace activist Thelma Edwards Marshall, hard times came when her husband died. Upon his death, the family lost a valuable source of income from his dental practice. Mrs. Marshall, who participated in various organizations, did not want to resign from her position. The work of these organizations was too important for her to renounce. As far as she was concerned, the Gary, Indiana, League of Women Voters needed her, and so did Goodwill Industries, the National Urban League, the local YWCA, and WILPF. Fortunately, Marshall did not have to sacrifice any of her voluntary positions so that she could work another salaried job. To make certain that his mother would continue her lifestyle as usual, Marshall's only son, William, brought in the family's main source of income as a stage, screen, and television actor.[30] Unlike the majority of black youth in 1930s America, Marshall's son had received the benefits of a college education and contacts with people who had a positive influence on him.

There were other black peace activists who had not always been financially secure. The stories of two heavily recruited middle-class African American peace activists, Lucy Diggs Slowe and Inez Jackson, illustrate particularly tragic endings.

Slowe, the daughter of financially secure parents in Lexington, Virginia, saw her financial status deteriorate when both parents died in 1891. Orphaned at six, Slowe was reared by a paternal aunt in Baltimore, Maryland. For the next ten years, she watched her aunt struggle to support the two of them.

Since Slowe wanted to continue her education beyond high school, she helped supplement her aunt's income when possible. By the time she graduated, Slowe had earned enough money to pay her tuition at Howard University in Washington, D.C. While there, she helped found Alpha Kappa Alpha, the first sorority of black college women. After receiving her undergraduate degree at Howard and a master's degree at Columbia University, Slowe taught English at high schools in Baltimore and Washington, D.C. Furthermore, she became an accomplished tennis player—a winner of seventeen cups—and a talented contralto.[31]

In the end, Slowe turned adversity into success. It is this same determination and dedication that made her appealing to certain WILPFers, who had frequently noted her commitment to various social causes. Eventually, her involvement in a wide range of activities often allowed her to interact with white pacifists, some of whom were extremely interested in promising black peace candidates. In March 1938, Bertha McNeill invited fifty-three-year-old Slowe to a meeting of the local District of Columbia branch of WILPF. It was the same meeting to which Vera Chandler Foster had been invited. Slowe eagerly listened to their mission statement and was impressed with the various issues on the agenda. She began to think seriously about peace in the context of racial justice. Before the meeting ended, Slowe prepared to join the organization. It seemed as though she had come full circle in her life, from a childhood of potential poverty to an adulthood marked not only by success but the ability to give back to her community so that another black child might overcome oppressive conditions.

Another black peace activist, Inez Jackson, experienced a different mishap. She, her husband, and their six children had lived in Oklahoma all their lives. In early 1944, her husband, a self-employed barber, was required to enter military service or relocate to California and work in the shipyards for the U.S. War Department. Mr. Jackson chose the shipyards, leaving his family in Oklahoma. Inez Jackson could not leave because she taught school and had another five months remaining on her current contract. Once the school year ended in June, Mrs. Jackson and her six children immediately moved to California. Jackson had planned to teach in San Jose, but much to her dismay, the local board of education had a policy against hiring black teachers. She then sought work through the local employment office. The only job the agency offered was domestic work. Although her family greatly needed the money, Jackson angrily admitted, "I wasn't going to do it. I told the woman at the employment office that I would see my children starve and die before I would do domestic work."[32]

Jackson was a proud woman and rightfully so. She had invested much time and energy in a formal education so that she could avoid domestic work. Ultimately she did avoid it. As an alternative, she worked at the local cannery, harvesting prunes, apricots, and pears.[33] This action, however, had an unfavorable effect on the family's financial status. Although a teacher's salary had afforded the Jacksons few material luxuries, it was a necessary part of the family economy and had provided respectable status in their Oklahoma community.

In the interim, Jackson and several of her close peace activist friends, as well as colleagues of the local NAACP, continued to confront the San Jose School Board. They urged the board to hire her and publicly denounced its racial discriminatory policies. Regrettably, the board remained indifferent. So Jackson's friends then rallied around her family, providing much-needed support.[34] Before long, the Jacksons were "back on their feet." When President Harry Truman gave permission for African Americans to take the civil service exam, Inez Jackson did so. Although she passed the test, the local post office refused to hire her. It was only after Jackson and her friends inundated the local post office's personnel division with telephone and written inquiries and personal visits was she hired as a postal clerk. Once again her friends, several of whom were active peace workers, came to her aid.

Six months after relocating to San Jose, Jackson had become involved in peace reform. She had joined the local WILPF at one of its many meetings. Her involvement highlighted the fact that she was no patsy, apathetic to the chain of events occurring in her life. She had spent countless hours demanding justice while also working for peace and freedom. It is at this point in her life that Jackson first realized the link between peace and racial justice.

Another trait that black peace activists shared with their white recruiters was the ability to divide one's time among household duties, jobs, community activism, and peace work. While peace was a priority, it was not necessarily the single most important issue in the life of a pacifist. Dr. Mary Waring best illustrates this kind of peace activist. An extremely busy and committed physician, and president of the NACW's Department of Health and Hygiene, Waring desperately wanted to spend more time on peace and freedom issues. But she simply did not have enough time in her busy schedule to devote herself exclusively to peace reform. Waring was troubled by her inability to become more involved in as many peace activities as possible. She subsequently became her harshest, and perhaps only, critic. In time her white and black colleagues convinced her that her inability to devote a significant amount of time to peace reform was not unusual. Several other committed peace activists had the same dilemma. They assured her that a committed activist had to balance peace work with other forms of social and political activism. Eventually, Waring also realized that she had to juggle her race, women's, and peace advocacy work.

While actively involved in peace work, Waring continued race uplift work through the NACW. She was always traveling around the country and abroad, lecturing and leading seminars on a wide range of health issues that confronted the black community in general and black women in particular. Her principal work, however, was in the area of universal woman's suffrage, a passion she shared with most of her white colleagues early in the movement. Waring believed that for women to be effective activists, they had to be politically empowered.[35] The ballot gave women that power.

In their quest for perfect black peace activists, white women also welcomed single black women into WILPF. Bertha McNeill was one such woman. Even as a single woman, she was extremely involved in the community, yet she found time to devote to peace politics through WILPF. McNeill's spunk and energy, coupled with her middle-class status and sophistication, made her an ideal candidate for WILPF membership.

Prior to joining WILPF, McNeill taught in the District of Columbia public school system. She was also an activist, a journalist, a member of the Alpha Kappa Alpha sorority, a founder of the College Alumnae Club, Inc. (affiliated with the National Association of University Women), a charter member of the Howard University Women's Club, and an active member of the Lincoln Congregational Temple, United Church of Christ.

Addie Hunton was the first to approach McNeill about joining WILPF to work for its twin goals of peace and freedom. In 1934, while serving as the chair of the Interracial Committee, Hunton was given McNeill's name as a potential worker. In her quarterly report to the various branches, Hunton indicated that she had met with several interracial committees and strongly urged each of them to submit to her names of possible peace candidates. "Correspondence has been held with most of our Interracial Committees," Hunton wrote. "Dr. Crooks has given me the name of . . . Mrs. Vivian Cook, a colored high school teacher to help us in any way nationally in our interracial work. Miss Margaret Jones has sent the names, that of Miss Blanch Wahl, Miss Bertha McNeill and Georgia Bond [mother of Julian Bond] for a like service at Washington, D.C."[36]

Not long after circulating the report, Hunton asked Bertha McNeill to join the District of Columbia's branch of WILPF. McNeill accepted the challenge, approaching her peace work the same way that she did her other obligations. Her commitment to peace reform eventually resulted in her successful election as president of the D.C.-area WILPF.[37]

A year after joining, McNeill aggressively recruited other African American women for peace reform. Involving more black women in the peace movement was McNeill's primary concern. "I have been thinking constantly of what can be done and how to do whatever seems possible or feasible," she once stated. McNeill then identified specific women she deemed ideal for WILPF's work. She stated,

> You will be glad to know that Mrs. Wharton has indicated continuing interest in the work [peace work], but that substitute work she has been fortunate enough to secure has kept her busy both day and night. She is one who has promised membership dues, and attendance whenever possible. She is also trying to interest others. . . . On December 26, I asked Mrs. Vivian Cook of Baltimore to arrange a meeting. She is already a member of the W.I.L. and intensely interested in the growth of the peace movement among us. She promises to call together early in January a number of colored women for a discussion of their views on peace. . . . I went to Baltimore Saturday and took advantage of the trip to make several inquiries and concerns, [sic] Miss Juanita Jackson . . . she has made the same impression upon many—that of sincerity and force.[38]

Two years later, McNeill attended the 1937 International Congress as an American delegate. In 1946 she was a delegate to the Luxembourg Congress. McNeill also served as second vice president of WILPF that same year. Each of these positions allowed her to help shape the peace agenda both at home and abroad.

Dr. Flemmie Kittrell was equally committed to peace politics. Like McNeill, Kittrell, single also, became adept at balancing her peace and social activism. White peace reformers were intrigued by Kittrell's international consciousness. She had traveled on several occasions to West Africa and India to improve the living conditions of the indigenous peoples. This goal was among those of the white peace activists as well. Therefore they were ecstatic to count among them Kittrell, who had earlier gained recognition as an educated Pan-Africanist.

After receiving a doctorate in home economics and human nutrition from Cornell University in 1935, Kittrell worked as a professor and the head of the Department of Home Economics at Howard University. A Fulbright scholar, Kittrell published several articles in noted journals on health and human nutrition. She also conducted nutrition studies in

Africa and India. As a result, the U.S. State Department employed her as a lecturer in East and West Africa and as a data researcher in Bangladesh, Zaire, and India for a family ecology study. Kittrell also taught home economics to women in the Congo.

She was convinced that America's "best plan for cementing international friendships [was] an enlarged teacher exchange program." She further added that the "key to world peace [lay] in better understanding among people and nations. And [therefore it was] up to the women of the world to help bring this about . . . through enlarged teacher exchange programs and higher education for women."[39] For this reason, Kittrell spent her available time developing research programs for food and nutrition in various countries. Her extensive involvement in this lifelong endeavor left little time for social life, or anything else for that matter. But because her work was directly linked to world peace, Kittrell was able to become involved in peace politics.

WILPF's executive board immediately recognized Kittrell's commitment to improving conditions in Africa. When the peace group created the Committee on African Affairs several years later, Kittrell became the only choice of the WILPF nominating committee. They were ecstatic when Kittrell agreed to chair the newly formed committee. Writing on behalf of the national board, Mildred Scott Olmsted stated, "It was very glad news to hear through the Nominating Committee Chairman, Mrs. Woodruff, that you had agreed to accept the chairmanship of our new Committee on African Affairs. I am happy to welcome you to this work and also to membership on our National Board."[40]

WILPF's national board decided to form the Committee on African Affairs to support the human rights position adopted by the United Nations in San Francisco three years earlier. Moreover, WILPF's leaders believed that "Africa, as a continent, [was] becoming increasingly important" and that "Africa was taking a larger place in world affairs and [was] very little understood by [their] own members or by the general public." Therefore, WILPF peace activists asserted, Kittrell would be expected to "keep [them] informed of action" WILPF should be taking and why. Kittrell was also expected to "point out material which [their branches] should be studying so as to be intelligent about conditions on this great continent."[41] She did not disappoint her peace colleagues.

By the 1930s, Kittrell was the most visible African American peace activist in WILPF. She served on the national board from 1958 to 1962. During that time, she represented the world WILPF organization at the

Second Conference of the United Nations Committee Against Discrimination in 1959, and served as the American delegate to the Stockholm WILPF Congress.

Any married peace activist whose husband also supported the cause was aggressively recruited. White peace reformers realized how significant to their own individual commitment to peace work was the approval of family and friends. This support was extremely important during the two world wars, when family members could persuade the most dedicated peace activist to leave the movement until the war was over.

Vera Chandler Foster's marriage to Luther, for instance, proved to be a positive catalyst for her activism. Her marriage to the Tuskegee Institute president enabled her to obtain an education, travel abroad, and participate in peace activities. In the early 1940s, she traveled extensively, stopping in Hong Kong, the Philippines, Indonesia, Liberia, Nigeria, and China to study their different welfare programs. She also went to India to examine the welfare of women and children. Her findings were revealed years later at the 1955 and 1958 WILPF international congresses.[42] When Foster traveled to these areas, she often went with her husband. In most cases, she had arranged to visit a particular region after she realized that her husband would be going there for a meeting on behalf of Tuskegee.

Furthermore, Terrell's husband unconditionally supported his wife's peace work, as well as her other forms of activism. Robert Terrell never criticized her for becoming a public woman. Instead, he supported her with encouraging words and a warm disposition.[43] Terrell's husband was unusual, however, in comparison with most of his male contemporaries. Perhaps this difference was because Robert Terrell had excelled in his own right and did not feel threatened by his wife's success. Other possible factors for his support were his life experiences with activists and his own commitment to his chosen causes. Robert Terrell was only one of a handful of black and white men married to peace activists who supported their public activism. He too was committed to issues of social justice.

White women pacifists continued to search for female black peace activists who were decidedly middle-class and thus financially secure, demonstrated the ability to overcome difficult obstacles, were committed to social justice, and had the support of loving friends and relatives. Such black women had to be mirror images of white pacifists. In their search for this so-called perfect specimen, white women visited all-black organizations, attended conferences and other meetings hosted by black or interracial organizations, and relied on other African American peace activists. But despite their ongoing efforts and determination to recruit black women, WILPFers were not successful. Few black women joined WILPF after that first group of five. In fact, by 1925, WILPF's leadership was still concerned about its small black membership, which continued through the interwar years.

Bertha McNeill attributed the small percentage of black women in the organization to a lack of funds among black women. Therefore she suggested a group membership to the Washington, D.C., branch. McNeill was convinced that many groups whose members could not join WILPF because they lacked the necessary funds could be interested in peace work. She recommended that such groups finance one representative who would keep the entire body aware of WILPF's agenda, suggest activities for implementing various programs of the peace group, and bring suggestions before the larger body for consideration. McNeill even recommended a few African American women for membership, namely Lucy Diggs Slowe, a dean at Howard University; Mary McLeod Bethune, a leading black educator; and Charlotte Hawkins Brown, a founder of a finishing school for girls in Sedalia, North Carolina.[44]

Of these three women, McNeill expressed a preference for Slowe.[45] Although white WILPFers extended invitations to Jackson, Slowe, and Bethune, records show that only Slowe finally joined the peace group. In Slowe's case, it took her at least a decade to agree to join WILPF, only after the insistence of Bertha McNeill, a longtime friend.

White peace activist Caroline Singer suggested that perhaps black women did not join WILPF in record numbers because of the white women involved in peace work. Therefore Singer urged white pacifists to "first educate [themselves]" if they genuinely wanted to "win the confidence of representative Negro women." She believed that the white woman's peace work should

> include an intensive—and a continuous—study of Negro affairs . . . inform themselves about Negro history and achievement . . . [compel them to] cooperate consistently with the National Urban League and the National Association for the Advancement of Colored People. . . . In the end, the barrier, separating [white women] from Negro women, that barrier which, denied by the law of [American] Democracy, nevertheless exists, will have been dissolved. The extension of peace work among Negroes can then be accomplished, as it should be, with the counsel and active cooperation of those best fitted to it.[46]

It was clear that white women wanted only "certain" black women to join WILPF. But to suggest that the white woman's own racist behavior prevented black women from joining was difficult for them to accept.

There were other reasons for little interest by black women in peace work between 1915 and 1945. For one, the majority of black Americans were poor or working-class, and a disproportionate number of them were illiterate. Furthermore, "the bleak economic circumstances in which most" African Americans lived during the period of this study "made sheer survival an imperative that hindered the vast majority of black women from working for any social or political issue, regardless of how strongly any individual may have felt about it."[47] Wage differentials were such that even the employed professional woman or the wife of a professional man in the black community had much less to spend than a white woman of the same social level.

Caroline Singer, who was probably more tolerant of blacks than most of her white colleagues in WILPF, believed that she indeed understood the black culture. She also realized that the peace organization relied on its members' monetary contributions for operation and therefore could not afford to accept members who could not offer some kind of financial support. Moreover, members often used their personal funds to finance travel across America and abroad for conferences, congresses, and other peace reform activities. Because they lacked funds, black women, as Singer observed, "hesitate[d] to pay even the $1 membership dues since they . . . [knew] that, once members, they [would] be pressed to pay for dinners, etc." Singer even admonished her white colleagues to be cognizant of racial differences in what constitutes class. "Do not be deceived by the look of prosperity among upper-class Negro women," she exhorted. "Their fastiditiousness [sic] is inspired by pride and, nearly always, the result of shrewd planning and sacrifice. I have had difficulty in convincing several W.I.L. members that the appearance of prosperity does not denote an ability to give or spend."[48] Consequently, the socioeconomic status of most black Americans prevented them from either joining WILPF or being approached by WILPFers as potential members.

Second, for most of the period of this study, de facto as well as de jure discrimination made the maintenance of a low profile the better part of wisdom for black Americans. African Americans were even less likely to become involved in a cause that most perceived as being not only irrelevant to their plight in America but also controversial. Most African Americans were trying to secure their civil and political rights in an all too hostile environment. They could not afford to have their loyalty questioned.

Third, because the majority of black women worked, it was extremely difficult for them to attend meetings other than those held on Sunday afternoons. Singer best summed up the black woman's condition when she stated in a letter to one of her white colleagues, "Working for less pay, [black] professional women often work longer hours than white women on the same jobs. Housewives generally have heavier burdens—families of their own or dependents. Those who rise [such as the women noted in this study] carry unbelievable burdens. . . . [T]hey have innumerable underprivileged relatives" for whom they are responsible.[49] Most WILPF meetings across the country were held on weekday mornings or early afternoons. Regardless of their socioeconomic status, few African American women were available for weekday meetings.

Fourth, between 1915 and 1928, in particular, most African American women believed it was too dangerous to join an organization as controversial as WILPF. In response to the 1917 Bolshevik revolution in the Soviet Union, the General Intelligence Division of the U.S. government aggressively conducted an ongoing investigation of any persons who might be enemies. African Americans were especially targeted during this first Red Scare. As the government conducted an aggressive monitoring campaign against radical blacks and any militancy that was considered Communist-inspired, fewer engaged in activities that might have seemed subversive. Hence African Americans who spoke out forcefully for the race were "likely to be investigated by a network of federal intelligence agencies."[50]

In addition, many white Americans feared that the Bolshevik revolution might mobilize peoples of color worldwide into revolutionary action. As these same whites realized that Russia saw America as a fertile field for "creating revolutionary cadres out of disaffected minorities, the fear of black radicalism mushroomed."[51] Several African Americans were incarcerated or deported for advocating social, political, and economic equality for blacks. Many who rejected the subordinate place assigned to African Americans were labeled with the hated word *Communist*. Blacks interested in peace work could not risk imprisonment or deportation. Nor did those black women interested in peace politics want to be labeled as Communists. Becoming involved in a controversial organization such as WILPF would jeopardize their "freedom." Moreover, embracing racial justice as part of their peace and freedom activities was even more perilous for African Americans. Therefore most blacks refused to join radical organizations or become public opponents of the status quo in the decade following World War I.

Finally, many black women simply did not feel comfortable interacting with white women. The different historical experiences of black and white women made it extremely difficult for them to engage in mere social conversation with one another, much less to work together without some degree of friction. Most black women, especially those who were middle-class, did not want to be in such an environment. After all, they had to cope with racism almost daily. The last thing they wanted was to experience racism within an organization that publicly promoted racial justice and human equality.

Even for those black women who had decided to join WILPF, life experiences were often difficult as they battled racism daily. While it may be true that charter members of WILPF, as well as successive white members, wanted black peace activists who shared common experiences with them, there was one experience that black peace reformers constantly fought against and that the most liberal of the white pacifist would never know—racism. Regardless of their economic circumstances, racism was as much a part of black women's lives as the air they breathed.

Peace activist Inez Jackson's intimate connections to prominent blacks and whites that helped her seek employment in San Jose, for example, did not alter the reality of racism in her life. After finally securing a position as a postal clerk, Jackson and her husband searched nearly in vain for affordable housing in San Jose. They finally found a house out in the "Mexican Valley" off Jackson Avenue in an integrated neighborhood. The homeowner, however, sold the house to the Jacksons as an act of revenge against his neighbor. Inez Jackson recalled the incident many years later in an interview.

> The man who sold us this house did it to get even with his neighbors and his neighbor happened to be my boss at that time. I had gone to work for the post office. That morning when I started to go to work and I came out, he didn't [know] who had moved in. He had seen my husband and my kids, but he didn't know it was me [sic]. I went out to go to work and we'd go at the same time and ride up to the post office. I came out of the house and he came out of the door and he said, "Inez, is that you?" he said, "Are you the person that's trying to get even with me?" I said, "What

are you talking about?" He said the man who lived here was about to lose the house and he tried to borrow some money from him and he wouldn't loan it to him. He said, "I'll get even with you. I'll sell it to some niggers." Those were his exact words.[52]

Obviously Inez Jackson never forgot that encounter with racism. She was constantly reminded that despite her socioeconomic status, education, and profession, she could not escape being called the odious "N" word. Like Mary Church Terrell and other black peace activists, Jackson's skin color was her badge of inferiority in white America. Regardless of how much she and other blacks had accomplished as law-abiding American citizens, they could not escape racism.

Famed peace activist and singer Marian Anderson knew this truth better than anyone else. She experienced racism in the most unlikely place. Born in Philadelphia, Anderson had performed privately for various heads of state, including President and Mrs. Franklin D. Roosevelt. She had also traveled around the world on behalf of the American government, championing peace and freedom while experiencing success as an internationally acclaimed opera singer.

By 1939 Anderson had received rave reviews for her concerts all over the world. When her agent tried to rent Constitution Hall for April 9 of that year, however, he was rejected. The Daughters of the American Revolution (DAR), whose lease had a clause that prohibited blacks from performing there, owned the hall. The world was shocked to learn that Marian Anderson had been refused admission. Public officials, religious leaders, writers, and private citizens from all walks of life protested. Leading musicians canceled their concerts at Constitution Hall. Even Eleanor Roosevelt, a member of the DAR, protested. Furthermore, some peace activists expressed their disapproval of Anderson's treatment. Caroline Singer, WILPF's Intra-American Committee chair in charge of issues pertaining to American citizens, commented that Anderson's "pigmentation was unimportant." She was a successful artist, Singer remarked, and therefore should have been allowed to give her concert.[53] Despite criticism, the DAR refused to change its mind. Anderson instead sang at the Lincoln Memorial.[54]

Perhaps it was their daily encounters with racism that prompted some African American peace activists to join WILPF. For instance, Inez Jackson claimed that she joined the peace group because its members "worked against discrimination." She further added that when she first went to San Jose, where racism was pervasive, WILPF seemed to be the only organization willing to "eliminate some of [the] discrimination [in the city]." This realization forced Jackson to revisit her own definition of peace politics. She finally concluded that there was an undeniable link between peace and racial justice. She once told an interviewer, for instance, that "the civil rights and peace movement [were] closely related because when people [were] being discriminated against it [was] violence." She finally affirmed "civil rights and peace [were] connected" and further acknowledged that even the act of "conquering nations [was] discrimination and violence."[55]

This powerful connection between peace and racial justice is undoubtedly the reason many black women activists joined WILPF and committed their lives to fighting for peace and freedom. Like their ancestors before them, these women believed they could not be truly free as a race until the shackles of racial, human, and class oppression were completely removed. For many black American women interested in peace and freedom for all humankind, WILPF seemed like the perfect forum in which to rid America and the world of this dreadful blemish. But as black women began to join WILPF with racial justice in mind, they painfully learned that no place and no one in America was immune to racism or racial indifference.

Some of these same black peace activists were amazed at remarks made by their white colleagues in WILPF. For instance, Caroline Singer lambasted her colleagues in the 1930s for the way in which they perceived blacks and subsequently treated them in the organization. Singer assured them that their belief that "work with Negroes will involve close association with a culturally backward group" had no basis and therefore blacks did not need WILPF's white members to "go forth [among Negroes], like missionaries," supposedly "nobly bearing enlightenment to" them because they were clearly not "heathen."[56] The observations made by Singer were part of the prevailing stereotypes of black Americans held by many whites. Even the black women who had been so carefully selected for membership into WILPF were regarded as "Negroes" first and then as peace activists. Although white WILPFers tried to detach themselves from the average white American, who espoused racist beliefs and endorsed racist acts, many of them were also victims of a race-conscious and race-driven society. In fact, in some branches, whites openly opposed mixing of the races. This prejudice was most evident in branches where black women were active members. For instance, in the Manhattan branch, which had a larger number of black women than most others, whites were extreme in their opposition to race mixing. According to Singer, although African American Thelma Carter had been a member of the branch for more than a year, her white colleagues treated her "with little more than a pleasant courtesy." No board member had been interested in her as a "desirable person to engage her in conversation. . . . [S]he enjoyed no social benefits from her first attempt to cooperate with a white organization." In one meeting, Singer recalled, when Carter seated herself, "the white W.I.L. member next [sic] her made a point of turning her back." She observed that such rude behavior caused much personal discomfort and both shocked and enraged her.

However, Singer also offered an explanation for the behavior of some white peace activists. She maintained that white women who disliked black women did so out of "ignorance." In a memo to a couple of her white colleagues, Singer alleged, "I have found that the average white W.I.L. member—even the one undertaking racial work—[is] unspeakably ignorant of the history of American Negroes and, particularly, of Negro intellectual achievement. This ignorance makes for an appalling lack of tact upon the part of white members in their dealings with Negroes. Also it makes for a great deal of awkwardness in the relations between white women and Negroes." She then suggested that WILPF should abandon interracial work until it had an opportunity to educate its white members. Once that had been accomplished, Singer added, white peace activists would realize "that they [had]—in many instances—more to gain than to give in forming friendships with Negro women." Singer ended her memo with a plea that white WILPFers who were genuinely interested in black members try to "secure the cultivated Negro woman."[57]

Again Singer had made clear the type of black woman white WILPFers were willing to accept. Not just any black woman would be accepted. They had to be members of the black elite. More important, this particular plea from Singer demonstrates that even the most liberal-thinking white peace activists could harbor, perhaps subconsciously, racist beliefs about African Americans. It also explains, in part, why blacks who had joined WILPF repeatedly questioned WILPF's sincerity about blacks as members. Bertha McNeill, for example, once asked her colleagues whether a "conscious attempt" was being made by the organization's leaders to "include other racial groups in the peace movement."[58]

In the end, most white pacifists never really knew the black women that they invited into the peace group. While it is true that they searched for the socially elite black woman, the woman who was their mirror image, they still did not actually know anyone of this particular type. Perhaps Singer knew them much better than any of her white colleagues. She appropriately warned white peace reformers that most middle-class black women invited into WILPF had too much pride to allow themselves to be subjected to the "snobbishness" of white women.[59] She was correct about this particular group of black women. Although they might have internalized racism to some degree, they were still race-conscious enough not to tolerate racial injustice, not just in an organization that promoted its eradication but anywhere it might exist. They had devoted most of their lives to fighting for racial justice and would continue to do so as peace activists. This brand of peace activism shaped black women's peace politics and sometimes caused conflict with their white colleagues.

Nonetheless, was it really possible for WILPF's white members to be free of racial prejudice or racial indifference? Was it fair to anticipate such behavior from them? It certainly could not be expected during this particular period in American history, an era of intolerance, exclusion, repression, and severe racial hatred. It was difficult, if not impossible, to live in such an environment and not be affected by it. Some of these women arguably had no clue that they sometimes exhibited racist behavior. As a result, many were innocent victims of a society that thrived on racial, economic, and class oppression.

This lack of awareness also meant that an equal number of these women believed that only the privileged in America should be leaders. White peace activists undoubtedly believed it as they established the criteria for the ideal black peace activists. They used themselves as the paradigm for all activists interested in peace work. Consequently, the criteria may have been their own downfall. The desire of white peace activists for the "perfect" or "representative" (of them) black woman (a well-educated, decidedly middle-class community activist trained in the social graces) excluded most African American women in pre–World War II America.

While their criteria invited educated, middle-class black women into the traditionally exclusive WILPF, white peace activists did not truly understand their black colleagues' dedication to racial justice and the influence that strong commitment had on their definition of peace and freedom. For black women, peace would not and could not be possible without freedom, and freedom was unattainable without peace. If "qualified" African American women thought the twin goals of peace and freedom were unachievable through WILPF, they either refused to join the organization or left after becoming a member. A low retention rate, coupled with criteria that limited the number of black members, forced WILPFers to spend the greater part of the interwar years trying to determine how they could best increase their African American membership. They did not realize that the answer lay in self-retrospection.

Building a Coalition while Avoiding Confrontation

3

1928–1941 As she briskly walked up the stairway to her small, makeshift office, peace activist Caroline Singer seriously thought about the annual report she was preparing. She had recently finished her first year as chair of WILPF's Intra-American Committee and wondered what more could be done by her fellow peace colleagues to increase black membership. Twenty-two years after Jane Addams, Emily Greene Balch, and other national leaders opened WILPF's door to a select group of African American women, the organization could boast of only a small black membership. As Singer turned the key to unlock her office door, she decided that her report would list the committee's activities for that particular year, address the problem of the lack of a large black membership, and suggest how each member could recruit black women interested in peace politics.

Singer's frustration showed in her trembling hand as she penned a somewhat pessimistic narrative. Writing into the early morning hours of that cold December day in 1937, Singer reminded the organization's members that its constitution required the peace group to open its door to women of all races and ethnic groups.[1] She paused for a few minutes to reminisce about WILPF's long-standing policy of nondiscrimination. By then, however, Singer was too tired to finish her document, so she retired for the evening on the couch in the lounge next door. It was too late to make the long drive home. Besides, she had to be back in her office early the next morning to finish the document.[2] The next morning, well-rested and obviously more alert, Singer washed her face in the nearby sink, made herself a cup of coffee, and began to work on her report again. After finishing the draft, Singer wrote a letter to her fellow members in which she urged them to once again "make [more of] an effort to bring into its membership at the top a cultivated Negro woman, preferably a professional woman."[3] A few weeks later, WILPF's leadership revived the vigorous search for black women that the organization's controversial Interracial Committee had begun in 1928.

That year, frustrated with their own inability to appeal to African American women and wanting to disprove earlier implications by Bertha McNeill that they were not making a "conscious attempt to interest and include blacks," WILPF's national leadership decided to organize an interracial committee whose primary responsibility was the recruitment of African Americans for peace work.[4] There was a national Interracial Committee with local committees in those branches that wanted them.

When the Interracial Committee was formed, African American peace activist Addie Hunton, one of the national leaders on the planning committee, suggested that it be composed of four women, two white and two black.[5] For many others, the committee's composition did not matter. Regardless of how people felt or what they thought, once it became an official arm of WILPF, the committee became a haven exclusively for African American women. Furthermore, most branches that chose to establish interracial committees made them separate auxiliaries of WILPF, which suggested that many whites were not comfortable working side by side with blacks. Such blatant separatist practices also gave credence to Singer's allegations that her white colleagues were racists just like those in society at large. On a more positive note, however, the formation of the Interracial Committee indicated that WILPF was committed to making racial issues more central to its programs and policies regardless of who was to introduce them.

The idea of an interracial committee caused controversy within WILPF as soon as it was suggested. Peace historian Linda Schott, writing on the subject, noted that various members of WILPF asked many questions about the purpose of the committee. What did *interracial* mean? Did it mean cooperation between black and white Americans or among all kinds of racial and ethnic groups? Was *interracial* a code word for segregation? Was the Interracial Committee supposed to work on racial problems directly, or was it a sort of social experiment in which people from different races cooperated to further the peace movement? In an effort to answer these questions, black and white peace activists engaged in debates about the purpose and meaning of the Interracial Committee that became so intense they all but destroyed WILPF internally.

Many people believed that the Interracial Committee was a convenient way to segregate black women within the peace group. Others argued that it shifted the responsibility of working on racial justice issues from white women to black women, a clear indication that white peace activists were not concerned about issues relevant to African Americans. But contrary to what their critics thought, white pacifists believed that the committee created an opportunity for African American women to make racial issues a priority and provided a comfortable and supportive niche for black women who had decided to join the organization.

Controversy over the meaning and purpose of the Interracial Committee began as soon as it was formed. Jane Addams, WILPF's president, appointed Addie Hunton from New York as the group's first chair. A graduate of Spencerian College of Commerce (1889), Hunton joined WILPF at the age of forty-seven. She was known to many of her white peace movement colleagues as a social activist for the rights of women and African Americans. Before joining WILPF, Hunton was one of the charter members of the NACW, served as the YWCA secretary for work among African American women, and had volunteered with the YWCA in France from 1918 to 1920. Although working for peace proved exciting and worth the effort, chairing the controversial Interracial Committee was even more challenging and important to Hunton. The committee's mere existence, Hunton thought, held certain implications about the organization's position on racial justice issues. Therefore, Hunton felt that she had to proceed cautiously.

Hunton decided to rely on others for advice and support. After listening to mounting criticism, Hunton conferred with Mary Church Terrell, who had left the organization a few years earlier. She was certain her longtime friend and mentor could provide good advice about what was rapidly becoming a disputatious topic in WILPF. Hunton was one of the few black women excited about the Interracial Committee because she believed that it had unlimited possibilities.

The exhilaration Hunton felt about working with the Interracial Committee, however, was dampened after she talked with Terrell. What Hunton did not realize was that Terrell still harbored animosity against certain members of WILPF and therefore her advice might not be in the best interest of the organization or of blacks, for that matter.

Needless to say, Hunton was surprised when Terrell claimed that WILPF had been known in the past to segregate its black members. Terrell cited that assertion as one of the reasons she left the organization in 1921. After the two women discussed a number of other important issues, Hunton went home to think about all that Terrell had shared with her. She had many questions and few answers. If WILPF practiced segregation, why organize the Interracial Committee? What was the intended purpose of the committee? WILPF's members had always treated her with respect, so why did Terrell and others think that white women really did not want a racially diverse organization? Would WILPF use the committee to segregate its African American members?

Hunton could not believe that WILPF, an interracial organization commonly regarded as being at the vanguard of race relations, promoted segregation within its own organization. But even if the peace group condoned such practices, Hunton knew that she would never endorse any form of discrimination in WILPF. She decided to further investigate the matter, and if the alleged practices existed, she would wage a major fight to stamp out any known acts of racial injustice. Her decision to vehemently attack any form of discrimination was influenced by the wave of "black militancy" that swept across America during that time. A fervent black nationalist, Marcus Garvey, was accused of creating a new attitude among African Americans with his rallying cry, "Up you mighty race, you can accomplish what you will!" His movement and message of black pride attracted thousands of black supporters between 1916 and 1924. His message also appealed to Hunton. Like the Garveyites, Hunton was determined when she first heard Garvey's plea to confront bigotry wherever it existed.

A few days after her meeting with Terrell, a disgruntled Hunton wrote Mildred Scott Olmsted, the executive secretary and an executive board member who had been instrumental in securing her appointment as chair. Hunton told Olmsted that she had become convinced that it would be best to proceed cautiously in her new position. Realizing that Olmsted would want to know the reason for her wariness, Hunton simply added, "All colored women are more suspicious of the ordinary interpretation of interracial."[6] She even shared with Olmsted her conversation with Mary Church Terrell about the Interracial Committee. She then explained, in her letter, why Terrell and other "colored women" might believe that WILPF allowed its members to act on their racial prejudice.

Olmsted was concerned but also puzzled about what Hunton had told her. She wrote Emily Greene Balch, WILPF's national president, asking her to explain what Terrell meant when she alleged that WILPF practiced and condoned segregation. Olmsted also let Balch know that she wanted the matter resolved as quickly as possible before they lost or alienated the few black members already committed to peace work.[7]

Balch responded immediately to Olmsted's letter. Instead of offering the explanation that Olmsted wanted, however, she spoke disapprovingly of Terrell. Balch told Olmsted that Terrell might still have been upset with her and others for refusing to reelect her to the national board. But, she hastened to add, Terrell had not attended board meetings or "did the least thing." Balch ended her comments by suggesting that her observations about Terrell's inactivity as a peace activist might be inaccurate.[8] She conveniently had forgotten to tell Olmsted that she and Terrell had experienced conflicts in the past.

Balch then wrote to Hunton, insisting that Terrell's charge of segregation was untrue. She asked Hunton to obtain additional information from Terrell that would explain why she believed WILPF practiced separation of the races. Next, just as she had done in the letter to Olmsted, Balch tried to directly link Terrell's claims to her own disappointment at losing reelection to the board: "Perhaps this misunderstanding on her [Terrell] part may be the reason that, while she was nominally on the Board, she was, so far as I can recall, entirely inactive."[9]

As Balch requested, Hunton promptly wrote Terrell and asked her to cite specific examples of segregation in WILPF, since she had not personally experienced such behavior from her white colleagues.[10] Hunton told Terrell that while she believed that the accusations might have been indisputable, both Olmsted and Balch adamantly denied that WILPF ever practiced segregation. Terrell was livid when she read Hunton's letter. She could not believe that Hunton had shared confidential information with the very people that Terrell allegedly accused of such offensive behavior. But Terrell did not respond to Hunton immediately. She decided it would be in the best interests of both of them if she waited until she was calmer about what she felt was a betrayal.

A few days after receiving the letter, the Terrells attended a dinner party where Balch was also present. Before Terrell could say anything, Balch publicly confronted her about the charge of segregation in WILPF. Initially,

Terrell was at a loss for words. She could not believe that Balch would humiliate her in the presence of so many influential people. Also, Terrell believed that she had to be careful about how she responded to Balch, since she was one of the few persons of color in the room. While she wanted to demean Balch just as Balch had demeaned her, Terrell knew that neither she nor her husband could benefit from the potentially dangerous repercussions. It was 1928. Mary Church Terrell was quite aware of the movement to "keep the Negro in his place," regardless of whom and where he might be. So she remained calm and exercised much dignity and restraint in her tense exchange with Balch. Balch later told Hunton that Terrell said that evening, "The WILPF never stood for segregation or anything like it."[11]

After the dinner party, Terrell wrote to both Balch and Hunton, indirectly addressing her earlier claims about racism within WILPF. Terrell let Balch know in no uncertain terms that she disliked the way in which she was approached at the dinner party. She reminded Balch of each of the instances in which she had insulted her. Terrell wrote, "I realize that I have always rubbed you the wrong way, so to speak. From the day we first met many years ago you have given me indisputable evidence of the fact that there are many things which I do and say which you do not like."

For example, Terrell wrote, the first incident occurred while "you [Balch] were still teaching at Wellesley and others had occurred while [I] served on the national board."[12] The most recent incident had happened when Balch questioned her in front of a large number of guests at the dinner party.

Terrell insisted that Hunton had misunderstood her comment. She claimed that when Hunton asked her about the Interracial Committee, she told her that she "hoped the W.I.L. would never segregate" its black and white members. Furthermore, Terrell maintained, it was not uncommon for her to make such a comment whenever she discussed a group that "had never adopted segregation as a policy." Finally, Terrell assured Balch that she was no longer angry with her and could either forget or remember the incident. It really did not matter to her one way or the other.[13] At no time did Terrell admit that WILPF had indeed practiced segregation. Instead she tried to shift the blame by implying that Hunton's allegations were based on her own misunderstanding of their conversation. Regardless of what Terrell may or may not have told Hunton on the subject, Balch seemed satisfied with her response.

In her letter to Hunton, Terrell expressed her feelings of betrayal by her longtime friend and peace colleague. She told Hunton that if she had indeed accused WILPF of practicing segregation and Hunton had dis-agreed, then Hunton should have told her instead of asking either Olmsted or Balch. She then reprimanded Hunton for not having the courage to challenge what she perceived Terrell's views to be on the subject and ac-cused her of harming race relations within WILPF. Terrell then "played the race card," accusing Hunton of being disloyal to her race by reveal-ing to white peace activists a private conversation between the two of them. "It seems to me that a colored woman who was earnestly trying to tie colored women up to work white women are doing," she passionately penned, "would not go to a white woman to report to her what a colored woman had said unless she had tried to show the colored woman she had made a mistake and convince her that she was wrong." Being more cau-tious than ever about what she would tell Hunton, Terrell then closed the letter by emphasizing that she "love[d] the women who [stood] at the head of the W.I.L." She affirmed, "I owe a great deal to Miss Jane Addams and her co-workers which I shall never be able to repay. I would not say anything which would injure the organization [WILPF], if I could."[14]

Terrell's last statement was an obvious contradiction. It implied that she had experienced some problems within the organization and they were severe enough to cause her to continue to view WILPF unfavorably years after she left the organization. Her last remarks were more reveal-ing about her feelings than she realized. Hunton did not respond to Terrell's letter. After the incident, the two women went their separate ways, crossing paths only when working on certain race-related projects. Meanwhile, the Interracial Committee, chaired by Hunton, began its first few months as an auxiliary of WILPF amid a great deal of controversy.

Balch and Olmsted tried to make sense of the conflict that almost single-handedly destroyed relationships within WILPF. Both women felt that Terrell had overreacted, although they could understand her reason for doing so. As Olmsted put it, Terrell had experienced more than her share of "slights in her life." Balch, on the other hand, acknowledged that segregation could potentially destroy decent, law-abiding people.[15] In other words, both women believed that Terrell was a victim of segrega-tion. As Linda Schott so aptly stated, although Balch and Olmsted could arrive at numerous reasons for Terrell's alleged accusation, they never once thought that they might have offended Terrell.[16] However, despite their feelings and whether or not Terrell charged WILPF with segrega-tion, the issue was on the table and continued to plague WILPF for the next few years.

Ironically, Addie Hunton eventually became a major critic of WILPF's decision to establish an interracial committee whose main goal was to recruit black women. As chair, she began to receive an increasing number of reports from branches that confirmed that their committees were being used to segregate the races. Hunton was greatly disturbed by these revelations. She had long ago openly opposed a separate organization within WILPF for black women for any reason. She immediately sent a letter to all branches to learn their position on this issue and how they intended to resolve the problem if their particular committee indeed promoted segregation within WILPF.

The incoming annual reports addressed issues ranging from the composition of the interracial committees to their purpose and official role in WILPF and the peace movement. They even recounted their struggle with the term *interracial*. Hunton, for instance, noted in the 1932 annual report of her Interracial Committee that such committees were flourishing in seven local branches of WILPF: Boston, Cleveland, Detroit, Newark, New York, Philadelphia, and Washington, D.C. These bodies had pursued interracial work in various ways.

The branches in Cleveland and Boston seemed to have interpreted *interracial* to mean cooperation among all races and ethnic groups focused on furthering the peace movement. Branches in Detroit and Newark dealt more directly with race relations. The Detroit branch found it "somewhat difficult for [WILPF] to hold [their] aim of being strictly a peace committee with interracial members, because inevitably race relations [had] come [up] for a short time at each meeting." Newark's experience was similar. Although this branch believed in "the broader interpretation of the word interracial," it was frequently asked to help other organizations promote better race relations. It had divided its work between arranging for speakers on peace and holding meetings with the primary purpose of discussing and improving race relations.[17]

This confusion over the nature and purpose of interracial work hampered WILPF's efforts to recruit black women. Hunton wrote in 1933, "The claim cannot be made as yet that any great number of colored people have come to a recognition of the deeper implications of the peace movement, and so it has not yet won their first and deepest loyalties." Hunton believed black Americans were too busy struggling just to survive to devote much time to the peace movement. However, she continued to hope that "when they [were] able to visualize their own relations to this new world of peace and realize how their strivings and yearnings

[were] bound up in it, they [would] seek to be a part of it." Hunton concluded that it was up to WILPF to explain the connections between peace and racial justice. "To me," she wrote, "it seemed that the [WILPF] is challenged by its basic principles to meet the need of this particular group for larger knowledge and participation in the movement."[18]

Two years later, Hunton expressed her lack of confidence in WILPF's sincerity about interracial work. She told her dear friend and peace colleague Dorothy Detzer that while she admired her courageous efforts to work for good race relations, for the last year or so, she had not believed that WILPF was really ready for an interracial program.[19] A short time after this letter was written, Hunton resigned from the committee and became less active in the peace organization.

Hunton's successor, newly recruited Bertha McNeill, was also disappointed with the small number of African American members in WILPF. Critical of WILPF's predominantly white Emergency Peace Campaign, McNeill made a plea for WILPF and its subcommittees to make a special effort to include African Americans, whose unique peace perspective could enhance WILPF's overall program. Furthermore, she argued, the number of blacks in the peace movement should accurately reflect the percentage of blacks in America.

Pointing to the African American women in the Emergency Peace Campaign Council, McNeill asked their white colleagues whether they thought that number "sufficient to represent 12,000,000 colored women." She suggested that no fewer than four or five should be included for effectual results. McNeill was equally concerned about the message being sent to the African American community by such a small black membership. She contended, "The inclusion of fewer [black women] would seem too much like a mere gesture and furnish in itself an excuse for failure to arouse the warm support of colored people."[20] McNeill then ended her letter by asking the Emergency Peace Campaign Council members what they, in particular, had been doing along interracial lines. The members did not respond.

For the remainder of the 1930s, however, WILPF's national Interracial Committee, as well as the various branch committees, continued their search for African American peace activists. Because of their efforts, prominent black women like Dr. Flemmie Kittrell of Washington, D.C.; Marian Anderson from Philadelphia; Thelma Marshall of Gary, Indiana; Vera Chandler Foster of Tuskegee, Alabama; and Thelma Carter and Helen Curtis from New York joined the organization. Over the next decade and a half, these middle-class professional women, along with several others, became involved in peace work in their respective local communities, and one in particular, Bertha McNeill, soon became a WILPF leader.

In addition to seeking black women for peace work, the national WILPF continued to struggle with the composition of the Interracial Committee. In 1934, under the able leadership of Addie Hunton, this committee reported that although WILPF originally had wanted members of the branch interracial committees to represent a variety of racial and ethnic groups, the committees had remained largely biracial, with only African Americans and European Americans represented.

In most branches, however, the interracial committees were composed exclusively of black peace activists. White pacifists were not joining the committees for various reasons. Some white peace activists could not link peace with racial justice. For that matter, nor could some black women, as Hunton previously alluded. Many white women assumed that the committee was formed to address racial justice issues that were of no interest to them. The national board finally publicly condemned the practice. It issued a one-sentence statement that "there should be no separate organization of these [African American] women, nor should they be restricted to the work of the Interracial Committee, but should serve on any or all of the committees of the branch."[21] Although the national office issued this mandate to all branches, several local officers continued to segregate their members. On the other hand, some WILPF branches decided that the best way to ensure integration was to disband their interracial committees. The Massachusetts branch took this step in 1936, replacing the committee with the commitment to "take up more seriously the study and understanding of the interracial problem, and have one meeting during each season truly integrated with a free discussion of interrelated subjects." When notified of this change, Hunton, who was serving her last term as chair of the Interracial Committee, expressed her approval. Writing to her successor, Bertha McNeill of Washington, D.C., Hunton said, "It is a fine move and I hope our group will join."[22] Although the national Interracial Committee had condemned the practice of segregating black women in 1934, its black members were still confined to peace work exclusively on the committee.

In 1937, Bertha McNeill stepped into the middle of this debate when she assumed leadership of the national committee. While McNeill could effect change in the committee's policy on the national level, she realized that it would not be as easy to do so on the local level. Although McNeill wanted to follow the traditional WILPF policy of allowing state and local branches a great deal of autonomy in making decisions, she was still apprehensive about how the different branches had handled the issue of interracial committees so far. McNeill expressed her disapproval of the fact that in some branches, black women were members of the Interracial Committee without being members of WILPF. This practice would not promote integration, and McNeill reminded branches that individuals needed to be members of the larger organization to serve on a committee.

After several months as chair, McNeill gave her unsolicited opinion on the dissolution of interracial committees. She was not sure that it was a good idea. She feared that instead of integrating African American women and a concern for racial justice into the larger WILPF, dissolving interracial committees would effectively exclude those women and limit the discussion of racial issues. For example, in Massachusetts, the secretary of the state branch, Doris McElwain, believed that disbanding the Interracial Committee there had been a mistake. "Not very many of that group joined the League, as had been hoped," she noted. Furthermore, even McNeill knew that the only discussion of racial issues held by the branch since disbanding the committee had been a meeting about anti-Semitism.[23]

McNeill's observations corroborated what black peace activists all over America had alleged. WILPF had long advocated a policy of racial justice. However, although its leaders had reached out to African American women soon after the organization's inception and had adopted a policy of racial justice, their commitment to both blacks and the policy was influenced by the social milieu. WILPF undoubtedly needed more members, especially during World War I, when membership drastically declined, and in the 1920s, when the Red Scare frightened members away from the controversial group.

WILPF's leaders also realized that the majority of white women in the organization harbored racist feelings toward black women. Therefore, in an effort to increase its membership, retain its most loyal white members, and improve its public image, WILPF's leadership reached out to black women who shared similar socioeconomic backgrounds. Although the criteria they used in the selection process excluded most black women, it ensured a pool of women that most whites would not spurn. Even if they did, the greater issue of low membership would be resolved. Meanwhile, some reasoned, black women could be recruited to the Interracial Committee so that they could work exclusively on racial justice issues without making the organization appear racist. This arrangement was misleading for those on the outside, because it led them to believe that the organization as a unit was committed to racial equality, not a specific group within WILPF.

Some black peace activists realized that racial separation was the leadership's goal and complained that the committee promoted segregation. But these same critics continued to work for peace and racial justice. Like McNeill, many of these women believed that dissolution of the Interracial Committee before another was put in place with the same mission would probably mean an end to work on racial justice issues.

Meanwhile, national leaders realized that the women they had so carefully selected for peace work also had a commitment to race work. Therefore, they reasoned, such women would continue to work for racial justice even in less than favorable conditions. For that reason, many sanctioned an interracial committee. Unfortunately, white peace activists failed to realize that the black woman's commitment extended beyond society at large—they were determined to eradicate injustices everywhere, even in WILPF, if necessary.

Hence, to many black women, the interracial committees were symbolic of racial inequality. For that reason, they had to be disbanded. As a result, black women felt compelled to continue their struggle for racial justice as members of the Interracial Committee and spent countless hours campaigning to dismantle the very auxiliary that represented what they most despised.

McNeill was also concerned about the purpose of the committees in those WILPF branches that had gone against the national office's mandate and instead retained them as separate entities. She asked whether the interracial committees were indeed separate from the local WILPF branch. McNeill quickly learned that "the answer depend[ed] on the membership of the individual branch." For instance, "in the District of Columbia," where McNeill lived, "a person who join[ed] the Branch had the choice, according to her interests or time, of working with the office, the Lobbying, the Interracial, the Publicity or the educational committees." However, in "Baltimore, members of the Interracial Committee were not members of the W.I.L."[24]

That this conception of an outside authority or entity was not confined to the Baltimore group astounded McNeill. In Boston, the Interracial Committee as a separate group disbanded and the members were being asked to join the main organization. Before the disbanding, "Negro women" were allowed to join the interracial committees only. McNeill was surprised by this type of behavior from peace activists. "After all these years," she remarked, "there were still white women who were not ready to accept Negroes as full members."[25]

While some branches regarded their interracial committees as separate, others were totally opposed to segregation of any kind within WILPF. The New York branches, in particular, expressed their disapproval of such committees. According to white peace activist Caroline Singer, the New York State board member in charge of such local matters, it was discriminatory to have special committees for recruitment. The less racist path was to include women of color in the regular membership committee as the New York City women were doing. Singer reproved her white colleagues for believing that black women were culturally and innately inferior and therefore should only gradually be allowed to perform peace work. She believed that forcing black women to work for peace through the controversial Interracial Committee until they were ready for work alongside white women was a callous act that went against the policies and philosophies that WILPF embodied.[26] Rather, Singer believed that peace activists should educate themselves about blacks and advocate racial cooperation.

Singer even suggested that the "drive for Negro members be carried on in the logical fashion by the regular membership Committee, with a representative Negro woman on every Board," unless the organization's interracial work was to be no more than a "pious but ineffectual gesture." She maintained that WILPF was a democratic organization in which women of "all types" belonged. Finally, Singer prophesied that peace work could be extended only to "Negroes" who were "best suited to it" until white peace activists knew more about black women. She felt that once whites became better informed about blacks, black women would become better pacifists. Singer alleged, "By virtue of our education we will have become that much better equipped to live individually as pacifists. In addition, we will have formed friendships with women who, having survived the barbarities of discrimination, without bitterness, have learned to live as pacifists."[27]

Singer added that a separate committee for African American members was a "perpetuation of Jim Crowism."[28] She reminded leading WILPF officials in New York and the executive board that the organization, according to its constitution, had no right to practice segregation. She further expressed concern that if WILPF segregated one racial group, it would segregate every group. If that happened, they would be "merely sustaining, rather than putting down a situation" that Singer thought was "vicious and undemocratic."[29] Singer opposed racial discrimination and segregation and used her position as chair of the Intra-American Committee to try to eliminate all vestiges of discriminatory practices within WILPF.

Yet Singer harbored a belief in the racial inferiority of some blacks even as she worked first with Hunton and later with McNeill and others to end discriminatory practices within the organization. Much of her belief in the inferiority of some blacks could be seen also as class prejudice on her part and a perception common among whites that all African Americans were inferior. Singer once noted, "[M]any members [had] requested advice on securing outstanding Negro women for local boards." Because of their preconceived racist notions about blacks' intellectual and physical inferiority, Singer suggested that white WILPFers become better informed about blacks, since so many were wholly unaware of the vast numbers of cultivated African American women.

Singer asked whites who were uninformed or misinformed on the subject of blacks to read more books about African Americans. She believed that if they were ever truly to understand the black person's position, they needed a mental picture of race problems in general. Demonstrating her supposed mastery of the subject, Singer shared with her colleagues that "few know that in history no other racial group has come forward culturally centuries in a generation. The sons of primitive African slaves are doctors, researchmen [sic], air-conditioning experts, architects."[30] She then suggested that her colleagues subscribe to *Opportunity* magazine, published by the National Urban League, for news of black life.

Although Singer meant well, like her white colleagues whom she criticized, she also had misguided and condescending notions about African Americans. She believed that "despite blacks' lowly beginnings," a few had succeeded in becoming model citizens.[31] It was the black women of this group whom Singer and some other white pacifists targeted for membership in WILPF.

Some of their colleagues, however, had a problem with blacks joining the peace group. In fact, in some branches, whites were openly opposed to intermixing of the races. This prejudice was most evident in branches where black women were active members. For instance, in the Manhattan branch, which had a larger number of black women than most others, whites were extreme in their opposition to race mixing. They refused to be near, talk to, or sit in the same room as black women.[32]

Of course, some black peace activists refused to tolerate such behavior. For example, Thelma Carter, already serving on the national executive board, refused to serve as chair of the national Interracial Committee because she believed the very term *interracial* stood for separation and threatened to remove herself from the board if it continued to use the word. According to Singer, Carter believed that *interracial* was acknowledgement of a separate problem and added, "American Negroes [were] no more a minority problem than [were] Jews." Carter then politely reminded her peace colleagues that if they treated "Negroes" as a minority, then they were out of order.[33] Her plea fell on deaf ears. For the next two years, at least, remaining interracial committees continued to seek blacks for peace work and, for the most part, restricted their work to that particular committee.

For the remainder of the 1930s and into the early 1940s, WILPF's members continued to debate the meaning of interracial work and the role of interracial committees. Meanwhile, members of the virtually all-black Interracial Committee continued to work for racial justice. Under the leadership and guidance of first Hunton and later McNeill, the committee fought for an antilynching law, an end to the jim crowism not only within WILPF but in society at large, an increase in the African American's presence in WILPF and the development of their leadership skills, the awakening of an international consciousness in African Americans by creating a network through which women of color all over the world could join white women for peace reform and an end to racial injustice in the America. Addie Hunton best summed up the committee's twofold goal: "to bring about a fuller understanding of the program of the League" and "to [provide] a [greater] opportunity for participation and engagement" in WILPF's activities by African Americans "heretofore not reached."[34] She further noted that in "seven large centers, [interracial] Committees [had] been organized with the specific purpose of spreading peace ideals and making a careful study of international affairs."[35] Consequently, while fighting to disband all interracial committees, WILPF's black members also worked on racial justice issues, as well as other peace goals.

In June 1934, an antilynching law was debated in Congress. It appeared that once again the law would not gain the approval of American congressional members. WILPF's executive board, which decided mandates for all American branches, initially refused to take up the antilynching cause. However, its black members did not allow WILPF's unwillingness to embrace the antilynching cause prevent them from doing so and immediately made their views known. Interracial Committee chair Hunton, for instance, sent a letter to WILPF national secretary Dorothy Detzer that articulated the committee's position on the antilynching cause. Hunton wrote, "In acting as chairman of interracial work for the coming year I would be glad to be more closely identified with any efforts along the line [antilynching] at our National Office and would be glad to make any financial sacrifice possible to participate in any such effort—it is this point of my greatest interest."[36] Because the antilynching cause was important to Hunton on a personal level, she was expected to make it a major issue for the Interracial Committee. And she did. Working within both the controversial Interracial Committee and various all-black organizations such as the NAACP and the Alpha Kappa Alpha Sorority, Hunton tried to push through Congress an antilynching bill. In a second letter to Detzer that same year, Hunton maintained that she knew that countless "colored people, especially . . . colored women, [would] be used for the next few months in collecting funds to be spent for publicity and lobbying for the passage of the bill."[37]

Hunton even internationalized the antilynching cause when she traveled in late 1934 as a delegate to the National Counsel Convention in Paris. She believed that a lot of money would be needed to pass the law. So, while in Paris, Hunton promoted the bill and asked for monetary support from European sympathizers.[38] Her efforts paid off when various members of international WILPF made generous donations and went on record as supporting a federal antilynching bill in America. Despite support from Europeans and Americans alike, the antilynching bill did not pass in Congress in 1934. WILPF's members, however, refused to give up. The national Interracial Committee spent most of the 1930s trying to push an antilynching bill through Congress. By 1936, WILPF's national executive board had joined its interracial committees in the antilynching campaign and various leaders began to publicly denounce the heinous act.

The antilynching issue was one of several that dominated the national Interracial Committee's agenda in the 1930s. The committee also focused on eradicating jim crowism, within both WILPF and society at large. Committee members first began working on segregation within WILPF in 1934. They believed that all peace members needed to work together if they were going to achieve their goals. Therefore, as previously noted, both Hunton and McNeill, while chairs of the national Interracial Committee, waged an aggressive campaign against segregation within WILPF by demanding that such committees be disbanded. Finally, in 1941, the controversial interracial committees were replaced by the national Committee on Minorities and Race Relations.

However, before the interracial committees were disbanded, its members took advantage of opportunities to internationalize opposition to jim crowism within the organization and society at large. For instance, one of the key agenda items at the 1934 National Counsel Convention in Paris was segregation, the primary reason WILPF's executive board chose Hunton as America's delegate.

Hunton wanted to be taken seriously at the convention. Therefore, a month before leaving for Paris, Hunton asked Dorothy Detzer to write a letter about her [Hunton's] "appointment [as delegate to the National Counsel Convention], the importance of the meeting for many Americans and of a colored delegate." She further added, "This would help [her] very much in getting it over in an impersonal way."[39] But it was personal for Hunton. The convention delegates would decide whether to pass a resolution about segregation. If so, international exposure of such blatant racial injustice would help the cause in America. At least that is what Hunton hoped.

That same year, as the chair of the Interracial Committee, Hunton publicly denounced another racial injustice in America. Nine Scottsboro, Alabama, boys who had been falsely accused and subsequently convicted of sexually assaulting two white females in 1931 remained incarcerated three years later. Hunton had attended the *Herald Tribune* Conference and the Convention of the National Council of Women, at which the Scottsboro case was a main agenda item. At both meetings, Hunton joined African American and white women who decried the injustices in Alabama. Hunton later wrote a letter to national WILPF executive secretary Detzer in which she shared the views of her colleagues at both conventions and called on WILPF to take a position on the issue. In recalling the plea made by the first vice president of the Convention of the National Council, Estelle M. Sternberger, Hunton told Detzer that those assembled believed "the National Council and other similar groups could boast of extremely large memberships of women" and therefore were "in a position to speak out thunderously on the issues of the day." Furthermore, the delegates agreed that Scottsboro, "with its refusal to call a single Negro for actual jury duty, challenge[d them] to make to the State of Alabama a ringing appeal to recognize the Negro's rights and claim the liberties guaranteed to him under the Constitution." At this point, Hunton departed from her colleagues at the convention and made personal pleas to persuade her white peace activist friends to wage an aggressive campaign on behalf of the Scottsboro Nine. Hunton ended her letter with a direct declaration: "American womanhood needs a William Lloyd Garrison to end the Negro's betrayal. . . . [WILPF] along with the Council and other organizations should be able to turn the tide of Scottsboro."[40] A few months later, WILPF issued a public statement in which it denounced the wrongful incarceration of the Scottsboro Nine. In the end, the controversial Interracial Committee had achieved two of its many goals: fight for racial justice and create a network through which women of color could truly join white women for peace reforms.

Another goal of the Interracial Committee was to increase African American presence within WILPF. Under Hunton's leadership, the committee aggressively pursued "intelligent and understanding colored women" interested in peace.[41] In 1940 Hunton issued an annual report that proudly boasted of significant African American representation in WILPF. She credited the interracial department with providing African American women a "larger opportunity for participation in the activities of the League."[42]

In the same report, Hunton proudly alluded to a budding international consciousness among African American women. She noted that black women all over America were honing their leadership skills and had requested help in "enriching their knowledge in the study of international relations." She proudly wrote, "It has been a year marked by a real awakening of leaders among colored women to a responsibility of sharing in the many adventures for Peace." Giving WILPF credit for cultivating this consciousness, Hunton ended the letter on an even more optimistic note when she predicted, "[T]hrough the efforts of the Women's International League for Peace and Freedom, another year will no doubt bring much larger results in this interracial advance."[43] Hunton's prediction eventually became reality. By 1948 several African American peace activists were chairing committees that focused on peace reform outside America's borders. For instance, Dr. Flemmie Kittrell, who chaired the Committee on African Affairs, spent countless hours establishing links between the American peace reform movement and the economic, political, and educational development of several African countries. Kittrell did not have to be coerced into taking this particular leadership role. She had long been interested in ending imperialist colonialism in the various African countries and subsequently helping Africans develop their resources after regaining their independence.

Nonetheless, before black women could work on other WILPF committees such as the one on African affairs, their peace activism was restricted to work on the controversial Interracial Committee. As previously indicated, the national Interracial Committee was eventually replaced by the Committee on Minorities and Race Relations. This new committee, first chaired by Bertha McNeill, represented a merging of two committees, the Interracial Committee and the Committee on Minorities. Many WILPFers welcomed this structural and name change. The committee's aim was to inform WILPF's membership of the problems of all minority groups, including African Americans, Jewish Americans, Mexican Americans, and Japanese Americans. After identifying the problems, the committee was charged with securing action to bring about greater freedom for those groups that were being oppressed.[44] Although the committee would make WILPF known to minority groups all over the country, it was not responsible for recruiting these minorities to serve exclusively on that committee. These women, who had once been excluded from several WILPF branches, could now join the peace group as members with the same rights as everyone else.

Black peace activist Sadie Daniels St. Clair, who served as the first chair of the Committee on Minorities and Race Relations, applauded WILPF for such a significant move. For the first time since being admitted in 1915, blacks could expect to work alongside whites on peace issues. There were several reasons WILPF finally granted black women unconditional admission.

For one, by 1940, WILPF had lost 1,084 members. As peace historian Carrie Foster points out, at least one thousand of these women were dues-paying members, which hurt WILPF financially. In fact, Dorothy Hommel, WILPF's national chair, alerted a colleague to WILPF's bleak financial position when she noted, "We are faced with the danger of dissolving the U.S. Section for lack of financial support."[45] Hommel wrote that most prospective contributors refused to give because of WILPF's "radical stance on neutrality and aid to the Allies."[46] So, for the next year or so, WILPF struggled to remain an organization. At that time, the admission of black women into the organization unconditionally seemed like a viable option. WILPF leaders believed that many African American women had refused to join in the past because of the organization's alleged discriminatory practices; therefore, allowing them to join uncon-ditionally would prove WILPF's commitment to racial justice, increase its membership, and subsequently improve its finances.

Second, by 1940, Americans were more concerned about possible in-volvement in the war raging in Europe than they were about the poten-tial spread of Communism. Therefore, WILPF was not being as aggres-sively attacked for its "un-American" activities and political positions on issues. In the 1930s, the hysteria over "reds" resurfaced but not to the extent that it had between 1919 and 1924. Even when some people who still viewed pacifists with suspicion labeled them as Fascists, the label did not seem relevant because WILPFers had always taken a position against Fascism. For example, peace activist Hannah Clothier Hull emphasized that WILPF "opposed Fascism" because it was "directly contrary to ev-ery principle of freedom and American democracy."[47] Dorothy Detzer, another leading peace activist, later remarked that WILPFers fought against Fascism more than Communism because they had "first-hand knowledge of the Fascist threat to life and liberty whereas it "did not consider . . . Communism [to be] a menace" at the time.[48]

WILPF's decision to publicly denounce Fascism worked in its favor. In the 1940s, the peace group could concentrate on other, more impor-tant issues such as low membership, conscription, America's wavering neutrality stance, and the controversial Embargo Act. These were issues with which most of America's leaders were preoccupied. Therefore, in 1940, WILPF could open its door to black women without fear of ex-ecrable repercussions.

Third, WILPF clearly had broadened its membership to include other racial and ethnic groups, as illustrated by the creation of the Committee on Minorities and Race Relations. The committee's major responsibil-ity was to focus on the problems that minorities such as Jewish Ameri-cans, Mexican Americans, African Americans, and Japanese Americans encountered.[49] This move by WILPF heralded a desire to become more racially diverse. Although many of its members continued to show signs of racist behavior, the allowance of other minority groups to join WILPF made it virtually impossible for the group to confine African American women to a separate auxiliary without causing suspicion and generat-ing allegations of racism. WILPF had been successful so far in conceal-ing from the public its internal struggle with racism. Its members may not have been able to continue to discriminate blatantly against black women through separation within the organization. More important,

WILPF could not promote a policy of racial justice as part of its peace initiative and be taken seriously by the general public if Americans knew of its own members' problems with race relations.

Finally, although racism was pervasive, various government agencies, such as the Fair Employment Practices Commission and the Office of Civilian Defense, made a few concessions to African Americans in an effort to mask their problems with racism. However, for the most part, African American civilians endured daily economic discrimination, white racism, and housing segregation. In response to their condition, blacks fought back with a vengeance.

An example is A. Philip Randolph, the president of the Brotherhood of Sleeping Car Porters, who called for black people to unify their protests and direct them at the national government. He suggested that ten thousand African Americans march on Washington in January 1941 under the slogan "We loyal Negro-American citizens demand the right to work and fight for our country."[50] In the next few months, Randolph helped create the March on Washington Movement. It eventually became the largest black movement of African Americans since the 1920s movement led by Marcus Garvey. The March on Washington group demanded that the American president bar companies with government contracts from discriminating against its employees because of race and require the U.S. Employment Services to supply defense workers on a nonracial basis. The group made other demands and, unlike any other African American protest groups of the time, banned whites from taking part and encouraged the participation of the black working class.[51] Randolph was able to mobilize large numbers of African Americans who had never before shared in any of the activities of middle-class-dominated groups.

When President Roosevelt realized that at least one hundred thousand blacks would converge in the nation's capital in protest, he issued Executive Order 8802, which called for an end to discriminatory practices in the defense industry and government. Roosevelt was involved in a war to preserve the four noble freedoms—freedom of speech, freedom to worship, freedom from want, and freedom from fear. America could not very well be the arsenal of democracy if it denied any one of these precious liberties to its own citizens. African Americans of the 1940s also fought discrimination in organized groups. The newly formed Congress of Racial Equality, along with the NAACP, the National Urban League, and other existing civil rights groups, spent countless hours fighting discriminatory practices by white Americans. Furthermore, the bloodiest race riot in the nation's history gripped America in 1943, as relations between blacks and whites deteriorated. When the riot in Detroit, Michigan, ended, thirty-four people were dead and more than seven hundred injured. In the aftermath, the city created the Mayor's Interracial Committee to promote civic harmony and fairness.

By 1941 African Americans had unmistakably put white Americans on notice by saying they would no longer tolerate discrimination. For black peace activists, *white Americans* included WILPF as well. Bertha McNeill, chair of the controversial Interracial Committee and later the Committee on Minorities and Race Relations, best exemplifies this shift in African Americans' attitudes toward discriminatory customs. She led a campaign within WILPF to end the interracial committees' practice of segregating black women. McNeill was tired of the suppression of civil liberties and mob violence. She continued her crusade against blatant segregation in WILPF until the national board disbanded the contentious interracial committees and assured her of its commitment to fighting for racial justice.

Once the various interracial committees were completely disbanded in the early 1940s, black and white women could work more closely on peace and freedom issues. Until then, each group had to develop its own peace agenda. Consequently, black women interpreted world peace through the eyes of African Americans, in the images of African Americans, and with African Americans' needs in mind. Black women rooted peace soundly in race from the moment they were first invited to join WILPF in 1915.

4

Race-ing Domestic Peace

1915–1945 While peering out of her kitchen window to watch the colored children at play, Addie Hunton quietly hummed the first verse of the old Negro spiritual, "Swing Low, Sweet Chariot." She smiled as she thought about how the little children innocently engaged in play while the world around them was in a state of anarchy. As the war wreaked havoc in the lives of Europeans, and as countries like the United States positioned themselves for involvement in the conflict on some level, Hunton thought about how the children seemed to be the only persons not affected by it all. With that thought, she turned to prepare a cup of coffee and read the morning paper. However, just as she opened her cupboard to look for the sugar and coffee, someone knocked on her front door.[1]

"Who could that be?" she wondered and headed to the door, quickly examining her appearance in the hall mirror. When she opened the door, she was surprised to see a courier with a telegram. She nervously took it, gave a generous tip, and sat down to read the message. It was a personal invitation from Miss Jane Addams of Hull House to join the Woman's Peace Party. "Well, well," Hunton thought, with a broad grin on her face. "I can't believe this. Miss Jane Addams wants me to join her in the peace struggle. Well, well, well . . . peace, huh? Now, I don't know, with everything else that I have to do. Would fighting for world peace conflict with my race work? I must admit that things are out of control both here and abroad. In a world with so much violence and conflict, someone needs to work for peace. But how can I work for both peace and racial justice?"[2] Hunton later realized that peace issues and race issues were inextricably linked. Because Hunton and her black colleagues in WILPF defined peace in the context of race, they could not work for one without the other.

Hunton was not alone in her initial thoughts that perhaps there were too many important domestic issues to address before she could become involved in a conflict thousands of miles away. When war came in 1914, Hunton and many other Americans were unprepared even to stand on the sidelines and watch the world plunge itself into the madness and insanity of battle. They had been preoccupied with their own domestic problems. Woodrow Wilson's promise of a "New Freedom" had focused attention on the economic and social maladjustments that were the legacies of the extraordinary industrial growth of the previous generation. Hunton and countless Americans, both white and black, were victims of the unfortunate and unexpected consequences of the industrial revolution. Therefore they initially focused on these unfortunate circumstances instead of an oppressive war.

For African Americans like Hunton, the challenge that lay ahead was even more difficult. They were forced to deal with not only the problems caused by industrialization but issues of racial injustice as well. So while the war raged in Europe, most African Americans focused their concern on how Woodrow Wilson would address the race problem. Needless to say, they were disappointed with Wilson's performance. The first Congress of Wilson's administration, for instance, proposed a record amount of discriminatory legislation against blacks. At least twenty bills advocated segregation of the races on public carriers in the District of Columbia, the exclusion of blacks from commissions in the army and navy, separate accommodations for black and white federal employees, and the exclusion of all immigrants of African descent.[3] There were similar proposals in the next Congress. Although most of the legislation failed to pass, Wilson, by executive order, segregated the eating and restroom facilities of African American federal employees and phased most of them out of civil service.[4] This order mirrored the attitude of society at large, as white Americans expended a great deal of energy trying to keep the "Negro in his place." These problems for African Americans were compounded by the untimely death of Booker T. Washington. Washington's death left a major void in the emerging black movement—a void that controversial leaders W. E. B. DuBois and William Monroe Trotter competed to fill.

While DuBois met with prominent African Americans like Walter White and progressive-thinking whites like Joel Spingarn to determine the best course of action in dealing with the race problem, Trotter visited Woodrow Wilson and insisted that the administration address the concerns of blacks. Both men had essentially the same goals, but their efforts produced different results. DuBois, White, Spingarn, and several other black and white men and women founded the NAACP, whose major goal was to eradicate social and racial injustices in America. Conversely, the hot-tempered Trotter's behavior resulted in his being escorted from the White House by Wilson's assistants.

Hence blacks made few gains in the years leading to World War I. When the war began, however, they refused to turn against their country. Indeed they were still preoccupied with their own problems, but there was a shift in their priorities. For instance, the passage of the Selective Service Act on May 18, 1914, provided for the enlistment of all able-bodied Americans between the ages of twenty-one and thirty-one. Although more than seven hundred thousand blacks registered, most were not accepted. Before the end of the Selective Service enlistments, however, approximately 31 percent of all blacks that registered were accepted, while 26 percent of whites that registered were accepted.[5] This discrepancy was due to some draft boards discriminating against blacks in the matter of exemptions. African Americans, who comprised less than 10 percent of the American population, were being accepted into the American armed forces at a much higher rate than whites, who comprised more than 65 percent of the nation's population. Once again, this blatant discrimination did not prevent blacks from participating in the war. Even those who were opposed to the war because it was an imperialistic conflict answered the call of their draft boards.

Once allowed to enlist, black men wanted to become officers as well. They soon learned, however, that it would be extremely difficult to obtain such positions of authority. Consequently, the majority of African Americans were enlisted men who daily endured segregated facilities, assignments to menial tasks, and frequent insults from white officers. Even on leave, black soldiers often endured hostility from white civilians.

A few months after America declared war, the War Department began to deploy troops to Europe. Black combat troops were among the first to arrive in France, and many others were later sent to Germany and other parts of Europe where life was, for the most part, no better than it had been in America. Black men were confined to segregated units and subjected to the racist behavior of their white colleagues.

Despite the poor treatment, black men were determined to fight for their country at any cost. Some civilian blacks, who understood better than anyone else what black soldiers were experiencing, decided to assist the black troops once they heard about their treatment. Among this first group of black citizens were three WILPF activists, Addie Hunton, Mary Talbert, and Helen Curtis. When these women decided to travel to Europe to engage in war work, they became involved in a major controversy that dominated WILPF's agenda for a time.

As early as 1915, the peace organization had gone on record as opposing American involvement in war of any kind. When America entered World War I, WILPF asked its members not to engage in any activities that would either aid or give the impression that they were aiding the war cause. Several scholars of peace history suggest that WILPF had several reasons for taking this position.[6]

First, and fundamentally, WILPF was opposed to "aiding war, any war, by either direct or indirect service." Second, it believed that any energy spent on war work was energy no longer available for the positive work of fostering mediation and internationalism. Third, WILPF suspected that as international affairs became more pressing, the government would give less attention to domestic problems. Therefore, to ensure that the government would maintain its focus, WILPF believed the peace group should do all it could to help the government alleviate these problems. Finally, many WILPF members had worked to organize labor and refused to engage in volunteer work that they believed would lessen the amount of work available to paid workers.[7]

Hunton, Talbert and Curtis, like many of their white colleagues, were deeply troubled by the notion that war work directly contradicted the concept of peace, as well as WILPF's mission. They wondered how the two might be different. When they rooted peace soundly in racial justice, it made going to Europe to assist black troops all the more necessary, that is, an essential part of their peace work. Therefore Hunton and a few other African American activists decided to go against opponents of war work. They became welfare workers under the auspices of the Young Women's Christian Association (YWCA). Hunton, Talbert, and Curtis were among the twenty-two African American women who traveled to Europe with other YWCA members to conduct war work.

Having landed in picturesque Bordeaux, while en route to Paris, peace activists Hunton, Talbert, and Curtis believed that they "were crusaders on a quest for Democracy" who were "answering the call." As black women, they felt a responsibility to "represent in France the womanhood [of their] race in America—those fine mothers, wives, sisters and friends who so courageously gave their young men to face the ravages of war." They noted that African American men needed comfort and relief from those who understood their pain since "there were prejudices and discrimination often shown [exclusively] to the colored race."[8] Although black female war workers were to provide relief to all soldiers, Hunton maintained that African American men had different and, in many ways, greater needs. She and other black peace activists often spoke of the racism that black troops endured while serving the United States.

Hunton, Talbert, and Curtis vividly recalled how Col. Allen J. Greer, chief of staff of the Ninety-second Division, for instance, was alleged to have "systematically and unfairly attacked the courage, competence, and character of the troops, particularly their black junior officers." They further witnessed how high officials in the War Department condoned this kind of behavior.[9] Consequently, many people were not surprised to learn that morale among black troops was declining. For black peace activists, in particular, this kind of behavior further confirmed that black soldiers needed a support group. Therefore Hunton and other black peace reformers who engaged in "nurturing" as war work refused to apologize for their decision to go to France. Instead they immediately packed their personal belongings and joined nineteen other black women of the American Expeditionary Forces en route to Paris.

On arrival in France, Hunton immediately noticed that while the official heads of the YWCA at Paris "were in every way considerate and courteous to [their] colored constituency," the attitudes of many of the white secretaries in the field were to be deplored. They came from all parts of America," Hunton observed, "and brought their native prejudices with them. Our soldiers often told us of signs on YWCA huts which read, 'No Negroes Allowed' and, sometimes other signs would designate the hours when colored men could be served; we remember seeing such instructions written in crayon on a bulletin board at one of the huts at Camp 1, St. Nazaire; signs prohibiting the entrance of colored men were frequently seen during the beginning of the work in that section . . . sometimes, even when there were no such signs, services to colored soldiers would be refused."[10] The racist behavior encountered by both African American soldiers and welfare workers further convinced Hunton, Talbert, and Curtis that their services were greatly needed.

For the most part, few black women traveled to Europe as war welfare workers. Hunton once remarked, "The number of colored women was so small, few, if any, of the white Y.W.C.A. gave any attention to the colored group [soldiers] notwithstanding they were Americans just like the others."[11] In all, only twenty-two black women served with the American Expeditionary Forces in Europe during World War I. Of that number, peace activists Addie Hunton and her close friend, Kathryn Johnson, rendered the longest period of active service overseas.[12] They worked hard, visiting wounded soldiers in hospitals, teaching illiterates to read and write, listening to those soldiers who wanted to tell their stories of joy or sorrow, serving them food and refreshments, cleaning their huts and leave areas. Black women who engaged in "war work" were performing duties, Hunton contended, "for which women [were] peculiarly fitted."[13]

This last reason for war work offered by Hunton was part of the prevailing thought of most of her contemporaries in the peace movement. Women were "nurturers, lifegivers" and therefore it was only natural for them to nurture the physically and emotionally wounded soldiers. Whatever the reason, Hunton, Talbert, Curtis, and other advocates of such war work believed that they were obligated to assist the men of their race.

Therefore Hunton could not understand how some of her black colleagues in WILPF could oppose such valuable service. She knew that it had long been debated among white pacifists. However, when leading opponents of war work like Mary Church Terrell, Charlotte Atwood, and Dr. Mary Waring publicly denounced the activity, it was difficult for Hunton, Talbert, and Curtis to understand their reasons. African American men, they thought, needed as much support and as many friendly faces as possible.

Hunton and her supporters could not persuade Terrell and those who shared her position to agree with them. Instead, Terrell, Atwood, Waring, and others channeled their energy into ensuring that the rights of individuals in America were not being violated. They believed they were needed to fight for racial justice and freedom in America while the men of their race fought equally hard for the same lofty goals in Europe. In addressing the issue of war work in her autobiography, Terrell exclaimed,

> We verily believe that adherence to the teachings of peace is the rock upon which the colored people of America must build the superstructure of

their civilization for all their future. It offers the only sure solution for their many difficulties, although it must be accompanied by righteous and indignant protest against injustice. The colored soldier has in some measure removed the fetters from his soul. Approximately 150,000 soldiers, officers and men went to France to represent the colored race in America. Many of them were brigaded with the French, while other thousands had contact and association with this people, which resulted in bringing for the entire number a broader view of life; they caught the vision of a freedom that gave them new hope and a new inspiration.[14]

Black soldiers, Terrell thought, were experiencing freedom, albeit limited, and therefore did not need WILPF's help. Regardless of the reasons given by black and white proponents of war work, it was an unpopular and controversial issue among all peace activists in the early days of the Great War.

Eventually most WILPF members and leaders followed proponents of war work like Hunton, Talbert, and Curtis. By the time World War I ended, it was no longer a major WILPF issue. Two factors gave rise to this change.

First, during the intense debates engaged in by WILPFers on this controversial issue, Lucia Ames Mead, representing the national WILPF, recommended that each state branch perform some sort of public service so that their critics could witness their willingness to serve their country.[15] Such a policy should have been established long before then, since most of WILPF's members would have performed relief work anyway.

Second, some peace activists, like so many other social reformers, had performed volunteer and nurturing work for years in an effort to improve society. Therefore, when the national WILPF asked them to give up this kind of activity, peace historian Linda Schott maintains, it placed them in an ethical quandary. They had become involved in WILPF because they believed, like Hunton and others, that women valued human life and therefore had a special responsibility to prevent war. Thus they were surprised that WILPF expected them to abandon their nurturing function at a time when America seemed to be in the greatest need. Actually, women who did comply with WILPF's request often were accused of being inhumane because of their unwillingness to help America's soldiers.[16] Regardless of what pacifists generally believed, some black peace activists could not refrain from conducting war work. Their historical experiences with racism convinced them that black soldiers needed their services.

After the Great War, peace activists turned their attention to other concerns. Black peace reformers in particular focused on the problems faced by African Americans. They more blatantly linked race with peace and freedom.

In March 1921, for instance, Mary Church Terrell, who had been elected to WILPF's national board two years earlier, raised the race issue when she was asked, along with other board members, to sign a petition, whose origin was questionable, that requested the removal of black troops from occupied Germany. Because the other women were willing to sign it, Terrell's signature was important for unanimity, especially since she was the only black member of the board. When Terrell learned of the alleged "horrible crimes" committed against German women by black troops, she questioned the truthfulness of such stories and concluded, "I belong to a race whose women have been the victims of assaults committed upon them by men of all races." But, she went on, "I am certain that the black troops are committing no more assault upon the German women than the German men committed upon the French women or that any race of soldiers would probably commit upon women in occupied territory."[17]

Terrell also was told by a reliable source that the black soldiers were not guilty of such offenses and therefore decided that such allegations were "simply another violent and plausible appeal to race prejudice,"[18] to which she had become accustomed in America. For that reason, she refused to sign the petition. Instead she pointed to an incident in which black soldiers had been wrongfully accused of a crime.

Three years before, in early 1918, a document entitled "Secret Information Concerning Black Troops" was circulated among the French by Americans to warn the French against African American soldiers living in the area. Black soldiers had moved freely in France and developed an amicable relationship with French men and women. Nevertheless, the document in question asserted that it was necessary to maintain complete separation of blacks and whites if one wanted to prevent black men from raping white women.[19] However, Robert R. Moton, the president of Tuskegee Institute who had been ordered by President Wilson to go to France and learn the truth, had proved the rape charges false.

Terrell reminded her white colleagues that American whites stationed in France wanted to continue to perpetuate racism with false and inflammatory literature. She charged that the more recent accusation was just another ploy by whites to promote segregation and hatred of black troops in Europe. Terrell said she would be willing to offer proof that the more recent charges against African American troops in Germany were also false.

Proof was not necessary, however, for Carrie Chapman Catt had already investigated the matter and found the 1921 report to be erroneous.

Terrell was not surprised by Catt's findings. She first learned of the alleged accusations against black troops in early 1919 when she and fifteen other African Americans accompanied twenty West Indians and twelve blacks from outside America to a Pan African Congress cohosted by W. E. B. DuBois. DuBois had been asked by the NAACP to investigate, while at the congress, charges of alleged army discrimination against African American soldiers in the war.[20] The delegates actually met in February 1919 in the Grand Hotel in Paris. The meeting called the attention of the world to the fact that darker people in various parts of the world had material interest in the deliberations at Paris, and that they were seeking for themselves the democratic treatment for which they had fought. It also indicated the kind of treatment black soldiers were subjected to at the hands of Americans fighting for freedom and democracy.

When Terrell first learned of the alleged assaults by black soldiers on German women and that such attacks really did not occur, she did not imagine that her peace colleagues would be confronted with the issues almost two years later. Regardless, Terrell was willing to provide her colleagues on the board with proof.[21] Her colleagues insisted that no proof was necessary, however, and subsequently changed their position. Terrell later offered to resign, but Jane Addams refused to accept her resignation. Instead Addams agreed that WILPF's board should take action against the occupation of enemy territory—"not against any special troops."[22]

Terrell was relieved by Addams's response. "I was glad not to be forced to resign," she wrote; "I enjoyed working for peace, and the contacts with the fine women who were members were an education to me."[23] Terrell's actions on this particular issue illustrated the extent of her commitment to the African American community while working for peace and freedom.

Terrell, however, was not reelected to WILPF's national board after 1921, and WILPF records do not explain why. White board member Belle LaFollette warned her colleagues that failure to reelect Terrell certainly would be "interpreted as due to race prejudice." However, Mildred Scott Olmsted and Emily Greene Balch later claimed that Terrell was not reelected to the board because she had failed to attend board meetings on a regular basis.[24] The national board, consequently, was left with no prominent black member, a matter of some concern to those WILPF members trying to achieve racial diversity.

The black troops incident inspired WILPF to pass its first thorough condemnation of racism. In 1922 WILPF resolved that because "race prejudice [was] based on ignorance, [was] without reason or justice," and "create[d] distrust, suspicion, antagonism, and hatred towards the people of other nations, WILPF would condemn "race prejudice as un-American and unworthy of civilized human beings." Furthermore, the peace group would do all it could to "uproot and eradicate it from the minds of the people."[25]

According to peace historian Carrie Foster, this racial policy was first tested in March 1930, when WILPF members made plans to stay at the Grace Dodge Hotel in Washington, D.C., while attending the organization's annual meeting. Although they chose the Grace Dodge because it offered the best meeting facilities, was centrally located, and had reasonable rates for its meals and rooms, its policy did not allow blacks in the hotel corridors or as overnight guests. This policy created a larger problem for certain members. Blacks were allowed only to attend the meetings on the hotel's premises. While the hotel manager claimed the policy was designed to protect its black guests from attacks by segregationists, some black and white peace activists refused to accept such blatant discrimination.

Board member Bertha McNeill was the most outspoken critic of the hotel's new policy. She immediately made national leaders aware of her disappointment with the hotel's policy and insisted that convention participants not stay in a hotel that discriminated against blacks. McNeill also let her white colleagues know that if they insisted on staying at the Grace Dodge, she and other black pacifists would not attend and would "publicly question WIL's racial policy."[26]

When the board met in early April 1930, it decided to move its annual meeting sessions to the Friends Meeting House, which was also centrally located. WILPF also moved its annual banquet to the nearby YWCA. After making this decision, board members resolved to protest all hotels within the city that practiced racial discrimination. Although some board members retained their sleeping quarters at the hotel, they sent a letter to the hotel manager detailing their extreme displeasure with its policy of racial discrimination based on one's race and color.[27]

The action of WILPF on this issue gave its African American membership the impression that the organization was interested in achieving racial justice. After this incident, African Americans felt a little more comfortable linking race with peace and freedom issues and increasingly took the lead in doing so. Longtime NAACP member and national Interracial Committee chair Addie Hunton linked WILPF with the black community in the 1930s when she asked the national organization for its support on antilynching and the Scottsboro case, two issues critical to the black community.

Lynching, which had decreased steadily during the first thirty years of the twentieth century, was on the rise again with the beginning of the Depression decade. The increase can be attributed, in large part, to the bitter competition for jobs during the economic recession and World War II, to violent racism, and to growing intolerance. When African Americans were driven from traditional areas of employment, there was competition for scarce relief monies and open encouragement of racism by many who administered New Deal programs in the South.[28] Hunton also noticed a rise in violence other than lynching against the Negro during this period and suggested that the most horrific form of extralegal violence was rapidly gaining the attention of blacks and was caused by prior economic conditions. She noted, "The recrudescence of the lynching habit due to economic problems during the past few months has brought colored people to a state of strong feeling and agitation and is again commanding their first attention."[29] In response, she urged WILPF to publicly endorse a federal antilynching bill, adding that it was "probable that the best effort of colored people, especially that of colored women, [would] be used for the next few months in collecting funds to be spent for publicity and lobbying for the passage of the bill."[30]

Hunton was a leading member of the National Association of Colored Women, a well-respected black women's organization. Whether or not her white colleagues realized it, Hunton knew how the black community planned to deal with injustices that they endured daily. She was also putting her WILPF colleagues on notice that the antilynching crusade would dominate her time. She hoped they would support her in this important endeavor, given the League's goal of racial justice. She remembered quite well those WILPF leaders who had approached her during World War I and advocated nonviolence. Therefore, assuming the peace activists meant what they had said, Hunton urged the national office of WILPF to implore the various branches to write the president and their representatives in Congress and to hold special meetings on the bill.[31] Hunton also knew that the support of a politically influential organization such as WILPF would help her efforts.

Although WILPF had supported for years an antilynching bill introduced in Congress by L. C. Dyer in 1921, in the 1930s it now began to lobby forcefully and more aggressively on behalf of other such legislation. Claiming that "the recent lynching and burning of the bodies of Negroes [was] a blot on [their] civilization," national WILPF leaders resolved to step up their efforts to obtain congressional passage of the antilynching law.[32] They sent this message to all branches and received varied reactions. While some called for the enactment of a state antilynching law, others demanded prosecution of those committing the horrendous crime. A few branches refused to address the issue at all.

When the Costigan-Wagner bill against lynching was introduced in Congress in 1934 and subsequently failed to pass, WILPF's leaders again wrote President Franklin Delano Roosevelt to express, in a harsher tone, their disappointment. All League branches were again sent a letter and asked to take up the cause. The national office was clearly in accord with Addie Hunton when it noted the interrelatedness of racial prejudice and economic insecurity. "The economic tension between whites and blacks, when jobs are at a premium," wrote Dorothy Detzer, "has invariably been the real cause behind the violence of lynching. Lynching can so terrify the Negroes in a given community that they can easily be driven out or so intimidated that they will not attempt to hold jobs which can be filled by whites."[33] National WILPF then urged the various branches without interracial committees to become actively involved in the fight against lynching, so that everyone would know that all pacifists were equally committed to the cause.[34] Detzer assumed that the antilynching issue would be addressed in those branches with interracial committees, where black members actively served. After all, Hunton had warned her white colleagues that the issue was a priority among African Americans. The records are silent on the role played by various WILPF branches in the antilynching crusade. Most known activity originated from the national board.

Hunton praised national WILPF for its actions on the antilynching issue. However, in April 1935, when the antilynching bill again failed to pass through Congress, Hunton believed that it was because the various branches had not done enough. She quickly noted that while the executive board had asked the branches to join the antilynching crusade, few had done so.[35] Accordingly, even if national leaders genuinely supported antilynching legislation, many of their white colleagues in the various branches did not. Hunton knew this from firsthand experience.

A few weeks before the letter was sent to branch members, Hunton had engaged in a struggle with the New York City chapter over whether

to pass an antilynching resolution. It passed but only with much difficulty. Hunton's experiences taught her that not all of her colleagues felt
the same way about racial justice as did many in the national leadership.
She then paused to reflect on a conversation she had with her once good
friend Mary Church Terrell approximately six years before and, for the
first time, realized what Terrell meant when she stated that the organization had condoned segregation. WILPF's national board and various
branches could not adequately address racial justice issues until its members were completely free of racial prejudice. But Hunton did not allow
this fact to deter her from fighting for an antilynching law. She continued the struggle, both in WILPF and in the NAACP.

Hunton also campaigned to stop another racial injustice, the Scottsboro incident. In doing so, she once again linked a race issue with peace.

On March 25, 1931, nine African American boys and young men
jumped aboard a Memphis-bound train. Like many Americans during
the Great Depression, they were searching for employment. Their hometown, Scottsboro, Alabama, had been hit especially hard by the economic
downturn. En route to Memphis, the nine became involved in a fight with
a group of white boys on the train. When word of the brawl reached authorities, they stopped the train to arrest the black boys. In their search
for the African American hoboes, local police discovered two white females who had illegally jumped aboard the train as well. To avoid being
arrested, the girls accused the nine blacks of raping them. The black suspects, ranging in age from thirteen to nineteen, were immediately tried,
found guilty, and except for the youngest, given the death penalty. After
long court battles, charges against five of the nine youth were dropped;
of the remaining four, three were later paroled and one escaped but later
died in a Michigan penitentiary. Despite the eventual outcome, this was
an example of blatant racism.

Hunton maintained that she had "been deeply interested in a personal
way from the beginning of the case and [had] helped in all ways possible."
She further added that it was "one of the most strategic fights the Negro
[had] ever had in this country involving the whole question of human
rights." She urged WILPF to help in "free[ing] [those] boys who [had
been] proved without a doubt to be innocent."[36] Hunton based her claim
on eyewitness accounts and the contradictory statements of the alleged
victims. Although she believed that the evidence was sufficient, it was not
enough to persuade WILPF to become involved, at least at first.

National WILPF leaders became involved in 1937 after reviewing the evidence and hearing repeated pleas from Hunton for assistance. WILPF's executive board, at its annual meeting that year, resolved to ask that the governor of Alabama issue a full pardon to those of the Scottsboro Nine who had been wrongfully convicted of rape and subsequently incarcerated for a crime that never occurred.[37] This resolution came directly from the executive board and in no way could be considered an indication of how all WILPFers felt. The majority of branches never addressed the issue. Black peace activists were concerned with the lack of interest of local WILPFers. Once again they were reminded that WILPF had to address its members' own problems with race before they could truly adopt a positive racial justice position. This prejudice was evident in not only the issues that most WILPFers tended to embrace but also the organization's structure.

Twenty-two years after its inception and subsequent decision to admit a select group of black women, the organization continued to practice racial segregation. Furthermore, most racial justice issues had been introduced by chairpersons of the controversial national Interracial Committee and were expected to be addressed by the local interracial committees. After all, it was the Interracial Committee's first chair, Addie Hunton, who linked peace initially with lynching and then with the Scottsboro case. Bertha McNeill took up the cause when she replaced Hunton as chair of the committee.

In August 1937, the Ninth World Congress of WILPF met in Luhacovice, Czechoslovakia. By then the Scottsboro case had already received international attention, and America's race problem had become more evident to people outside its borders. McNeill used this visibility to her advantage. She was one of the first delegates at the Congress to express her outrage at the many injustices in this particular case and subsequently sought her colleagues' assistance in what had clearly become a global issue. In doing so, McNeill and some other American activists added an international appeal to the pressure on Alabama's governor. They hoped to have more success abroad in generating support for the case than they had experienced at home. Eventually the Scottsboro case was resolved, partly because of internal pressure placed on key officials by black peace activists, WILPF members in general, and all-black organizations interested in the case.

While McNeill, Hunton, and other peace activists continued to work to bring justice to the "Scottsboro boys," they also labored on behalf of another antilynching bill. When the House Judiciary Committee held hearings in early April 1937 on the issue of lynching, WILPF sent delegates to provide testimony. One peace delegate, Eleanor Fowler, underscored the international implications of the country's lynching problem by insisting that other countries would lose confidence in America's "good faith" once they learned that its leaders permitted the monstrous act. Another peace activist, Dorothy Detzer, commented that the House Judiciary Committee objected to an antilynching bill out of deep-seated "fear that federal intervention would interfere with the rapid progress which [had] been made in cutting down the number of lynchings in recent years."[38]

In mid-April 1937, the House of Representatives approved an antilynching bill. Nevertheless, the bill was not viewed as favorably in the Senate. Despite persistent pressure from concerned WILPFers and American citizens, Congress never passed an antilynching law.

Although WILPF could not persuade Congress to pass a law against lynching, its national leadership vowed not to end its fight for racial and human justice. While struggling to end racial and human injustice at home, WILPF was forced to face similar oppressions abroad. Fascism was rapidly gaining the attention of its members, especially among black peace activists, who were an important part of an emerging African American movement against the rise of Fascism in Europe. In fact, African Americans were among the earliest and most energetic U.S. citizens to condemn Fascism. Blacks quickly learned to hate Nazism and its Aryan doctrines. Adolf Hitler's *Mein Kampf* motivated these feelings. Some African Americans had read the controversial work and resented its defamatory comments about blacks. In 1938, public opinion in America generally censured Hitler's tactics in overthrowing Austria and dismembering Czechoslovakia, and blacks joined in the loud condemnation.

When Hitler's invasion of Poland in September 1939 plunged Europe into war, the position of America as a neutral nation became increasingly uncertain. Within two months, Congress, at the stern insistence of the president, passed an act permitting arms to be purchased by belligerent nations on a cash-and-carry basis. When Germany conquered Denmark, Norway, the Netherlands, Luxembourg, and Belgium in the spring of 1940, the American people became alarmed. The fall of France in June 1940 added to the panic. It looked as though Britain would be the next to fall. As Americans asked themselves what disposition Germany would make of the New World colonies of the conquered nations, they realized that the war had come frightfully close to them. It was time to prepare, and the following year witnessed a feverish effort to do so.

As America began to put itself on a war footing, African Americans wondered what consideration would be given them, both in the building up of a large fighting force and in the manufacture of the materials of modern warfare. When the Selective Service Act was passed in 1940, it was amended by a clause forbidding discrimination in the drafting and training of soldiers. For a time, however, some draft boards accepted only white men for training, because there was a lack of housing facilities for blacks at the camps. At the first signs of discrimination, African Americans began to protest loudly.

In September 1940, a group of black leaders, including A. Philip Randolph and Walter White, submitted to President Roosevelt a seven-point program that outlined the essential minimum consideration of African Americans in the defense program. The leaders urged that all available reserve officers be used to train recruits; that black recruits be given the same training as whites; that existing units of the army accept officers and enlisted men on the basis of ability and not race; that specialized personnel, such as physicians, dentists, and nurses, be integrated; that responsible African Americans be appointed to draft boards; that discrimination be abolished in the navy and air force; and that competent African Americans be appointed as civilian assistants to the secretaries of war and the navy.[39]

The policy of the War Department became clearer in the fall of 1940 when a statement was issued that African Americans would be received into the army on the general basis of the proportion of the African American population of the country. They were to be organized into separate units, however, and existing black units that were commanded by whites would receive no African American officers other than medical officers and chaplains. African Americans were furious and made known their indignation. To appease blacks, a few key appointments were made.[40] However, significant appointments and promotions of African Americans did little to quiet the voice of protest.

Despite blacks' protest, widespread discrimination in the armed forces and war industries continued. Blacks continued to experience segregation and other racial injustices both as soldiers and as civilians, a situation that made it difficult for America to serve as the arsenal of democracy. Americans, however, were not greatly concerned about how they were perceived by the larger world community in 1940. That changed a year later. On December 7, 1941, the Japanese bombed Pearl Harbor, precipitating America's entrance into the war. Japan and America had repeatedly vied for imperialist dominance in Asia. This war finally decided the issue.

When America declared war on Japan in December 1941, its industries had already converted to wartime production and thousands of civilians were working in war-related jobs. Just as African Americans flocked to war industries, they also rushed to recruiting stations, offering their assistance. Meanwhile, black peace activists once again established links between race and peace issues.

Meanwhile, Congress tossed around the idea of conscripting women. A bill had already been introduced in Congress in early 1942 calling for women volunteers for the army. While WILPF's leaders were concerned about such a bill, they were relieved that it was not a conscription measure. Before long, rumors circulated among WILPF members about a bill pertaining to female conscription that might be introduced in Congress. The bill, according to those who were close to the anonymous source, would provide for the registration of women, and a measure to follow it would call for their conscription. While some pacifists, led by Dorothy Detzer, supported such a bill, an equal number under the leadership of Mildred Scott Olmsted opposed such action.

Proponents of the bill, led by Detzer and approximately half of her white peace colleagues, believed that registration of women should not be opposed because it was in the same category as laws that required registration for marriage and automobile licenses. Furthermore, they reasoned, registration of women did not involve a question of conscience.

Conversely, the opponents of the bill, led by Olmsted and a significant number of white and black peace activists, argued that because registration was for the "express and definite purpose of preparing for conscription for war, it was part of the whole war system" and should be vigorously opposed.[41] This bill was passionately debated by both of these WILPF groups within the Committee on Conscientious Objectors for several months. Finally they voted on the issue and unanimously agreed to oppose both the registration and conscription of women for fear that if they did not, they would be compelled to adhere to the measure. Peace activists further believed that they should not be subjected to a five-year jail sentence and a ten-thousand-dollar fine for refusing to register.

After the peace activists agreed to oppose female conscription, they turned to Roger Baldwin, president of the American Civil Liberties Union (ACLU), as they had done in the past for legal assistance. Baldwin's organization could provide WILPFers with inexpensive attorneys who would be willing and able to successfully wage a fight against the conscription measure before members of Congress. And Baldwin did.

However, while assisting the peace reformers, Baldwin tried to calm their fears. He assured them that the U.S. government would not bring criminal charges against groups like WILPF if they did not register and further told them that they should not be "cajoled or scared into registering at this stage."[42] In the meantime, the ACLU petitioned the Justice Department for exemption of peace organizations, which is what WILPFers wanted.

After much debate and discussion, on March 18, 1942, the Baldwin bill was introduced in the House. It called for the registration of all female citizens and "aliens" between the ages of eighteen and sixty-five with the express purpose of providing for "complete information as to the capacity and availability of the registrant for service, civilian or military, in connection with the prosecution of war."[43]

After much discussion, WILPF's executive board, of which Dorothy Detzer, Mildred Scott Olmsted, and Bertha McNeill were members, admitted that it would be difficult to persuade citizens to oppose the Baldwin bill in Congress. The bill would not require women to kill, which meant that they would not have to go against their consciences in deciding to participate. The WILPF executive board, along with members of the National Service Board for Religious Objectors, finally decided to attempt to obtain an amendment of the bill that would exempt from registration all women "who because of religious training or belief [could not] participate in war in any form."[44]

Pacifists focused on the conscription of women for the remainder of 1942. However, Congress decided that it would not address the issue until December of that year or later. While the peace activists' spirits were dampened by Congress' decision, they tried to understand the body's position. They realized that while members of Congress continued to be interested in the matter, other issues needed their immediate attention.

Meanwhile, some peace activists continued their opposition to the proposed bill. For example, by December, Olmsted, one of the bill's most outspoken critics, was "determined to go to prison rather than register, should such a law pass." She added that it was her personal decision and in no sense represented the position or advice of WILPF, which never urged anyone to disobey a law or even be a conscientious objector. Olmsted finally reassured her supporters and critics alike that she had not reached this decision "lightly or quickly but only after long, long thought as to how [she] could best serve [her] fellow woman beings in a world of engulfing totalitarian ideas."[45]

Many women in WILPF seemed equally committed to the anticonscription cause. Therefore, in January 1943, they organized, under Olmsted's leadership, the Committee to Oppose the Conscription of Women.[46] By that time, black peace activists had been allowed to join mainstream WILPF, and several of them, such as Bertha McNeill, Vera Chandler Foster, and Thelma Edwards Marshall, who were active on the national level, comprised the committee's black membership. Needless to say, Olmsted, Detzer, and Mercedes Randall eagerly welcomed the support of black peace activists.

Within a month, the government provided the newly organized Committee to Oppose the Conscription of Women with a fresh focus. It also gave the executive board's black members another opportunity to link race with peace.

In early February 1943, Senator Warren Austin of New York and Congressman James Wadsworth of Vermont introduced a joint bill that called for the conscription of labor, male and female. Although pregnant women would be exempted, as could "any woman who [had] living with her and under her care a child or children under 18 years of age or other person who, because of illness or advanced age, need[ed] her care," all other women between the ages of eighteen and fifty would be "liable to contribute any personal service to the war effort in a *noncombatant capacity*."[47] The bill also included every man between eighteen and sixty-five, had no provision for conscientious objectors, and penalized failure to comply with a hundred-dollar fine or six months in prison.

WILPF argued that there was no need for such an act. From Olmsted's perspective, the Austin-Wadsworth bill was another example of "the tightening grip of the military upon every element of the population, in every phase of life." She commented, "It is curious how easily we copy the patterns which we think we hate and are fighting to escape and never notice that only labels are different. In one column our noblest orators denounce 'the enslavement of labor' or 'labor serfs' in fascist countries and in the next we are told that our own workers must be 'frozen' or 'ordered' or drafted to work in this or that war industry."[48]

Black peace activists expressed an additional concern about the Austin-Wadsworth bill. In her campaign to help defeat the bill, Bertha McNeill, as well as members of her sorority, Alpha Kappa Alpha, and the NAACP, "argued that the bill violated African-Americans' civil rights assured by the Thirteenth amendment." They were concerned that the bill contained "no adequate safeguards to protect workers from unrestrained and arbitrary action on the part of employers or local draft boards."[49] McNeill added that although the War Manpower Commission, through local draft boards, would administer the system of civilian war service called for by the bill, blacks would not be treated equally because the War Department had a record of discriminating against certain groups. McNeill contended that "aptitude tests and the training program provided by the Austin-Wadsworth Bill for the purpose of redirecting or stepping up skills would mean nothing to Negro selectees, or to any others whom private industry chose to ignore. Misuse of the bill's provisions for tests, training and qualifications, against which no safeguards [had] been provided, would result in wholesale discrimination on a scale yet to be seen, with members of racial or other minorities relegated to inferior jobs, . . . further exposed to fraud, intimidation and violence." The need, according to concerned blacks such as McNeill, was for a "national selective service act for civilians which would not violate civil rights," one with "specific non-discrimination clauses."[50]

Blacks were inarguably victims of flagrant discrimination in both the military and war industries. In June 1941, for example, President Roosevelt issued Executive Order 8802 because, as he stated, "needed workers [had] been barred from industries engaged in defense production solely because of considerations of race, creed, color or national origin." The order directed that all new defense contracts provide that the "contractors shall not discriminate against any workers."[51] In January 1942, America's Employment Service Act required that inquiries be sent to hundreds of industrialists with large war contracts to determine whether they would employ blacks. Government officials realized that they could no longer ignore the issue when "fifty-one percent of [the war industries] stated that they did not and would not employ Negroes and only half of the remainder stated without equivocation that they would use them as workers."[52]

After a year of war, McNeill, Walter White, and other interested blacks realized that the prejudice of employers against African American workers had not relaxed. A survey conducted by *Fortune* magazine of "5,000 ranking business executives" showed that 86.1 percent of them employed no Negroes, or Negroes constituted less than 10 percent of their personnel before the war."[53] McNeill questioned the result of such practices. She estimated that there were close to one million underemployed blacks in the United States. Yet the Austin-Wadsworth bill implied that workers were not volunteering for service in war industries, which paid much more than African Americans were receiving in their current positions. Also, McNeill reminded her WILPF colleagues, as well as friends in the NAACP, that "600,000 Negroes . . . [were] outright unemployed."[54] She once again maintained that the bill had already discriminated in the hiring of blacks and, if black men and women were conscripted, they would face additional discriminatory behavior from whites.

McNeill echoed other black peace activists and NAACP members when she questioned the constitutionality of the bill, claiming that it "savor[ed] dangerously to use of involuntary servitude."[55] Although McNeill was opposed to the war, she and others still believed that race prejudice was undermining the war effort. She noted, "Before even considering legislation to draft labor, this Congress could much more profitably direct its attention to the abolition of practices which prevent loyal American citizens from contributing or utilizing to maximum efficiency the training and skill which they eagerly wish to contribute to the winning of the war."[56] McNeill believed that it was critical to America's defense that African Americans be given the same opportunities as all other races and ethnic groups.

McNeill's comments illustrate the dilemma faced by African American peace activists. While she opposed war of any kind, McNeill understood, as an African American, that most blacks needed to be gainfully employed. Working in war industries was ideal for blacks, especially since the wages were much higher than what most African Americans were accustomed to receiving. McNeill and other peace activists, although antiwar, wanted blacks to benefit equally from the war. Therefore, they were not willing to tolerate racism or criticism from staunch opponents of war.

McNeill was also deeply concerned with the "implication of enforced servitude" noting that a major problem "in [contemporary] America [was] the unwillingness of employer and employee alike to accept the skills, actual or potential, which the Negro [had] and willingly offer[ed]. With this problem unresolved," McNeill made it clear that she "would not trust any man, Negro or white, with such sweeping power as the bill confer[red]. It virtually amount[ed] to bureaucracy and dictatorship."[57]

Both McNeill and White asked WILPF publicly to oppose the Austin-Wadsworth bill on these grounds. It was not difficult to convince WILPF that the bill was another example of "totalitarianism in kid gloves," as Detzer called it.[58] Many of WILPF's leading members had already articulated their opposition to the bill on these grounds. The claims made by McNeill and other interested African Americans only confirmed the fears of their white peace colleagues.

Meanwhile, Dorothy Detzer arranged for speakers to represent WILPF before the Senate Military Affairs Committee in March 1943. As one of those speakers, Mildred Scott Olmsted opposed the bill, using some of the same language McNeill had employed earlier. "The whole idea of conscription of labor," Olmsted said, "would create forced labor, which [was] in direct contradiction to the Thirteenth Amendment of the Constitution."[59]

Congress did not act on any manpower bill that spring. The Austin-Wadsworth bill was set aside that fall. "At least for the moment," McNeill wrote, "America is one step away from becoming a totalitarian country."[60]

The conscription issue continued to dominate WILPF's agenda for the remainder of the war years. Peace activists who had not submitted to the pressure of friends and foes to leave the organization fought with remarkable zeal and activity into 1945, given both their depleted numbers and financial resources. After the war was over, black peace activists, in particular, remained equally determined to keep WILPFers focused on racial injustice issues in America as they continually took the lead in introducing such incidents and demanding that WILPF use its power to influence those who could effect change. Hence, whether serving on the controversial interracial committees or the more powerful national executive board, black peace reformers repeatedly wielded their influence and used their connections with prominent people in both the black and white communities to pressure WILPF into achieving its racial justice goal.

After V-E Day, new issues began to take center stage for WILPFers. Horrified that the War Department had dropped the atomic bomb on Japan, concerned WILPFers immediately launched a critical attack of the government. Although the atomic bomb ended the most destructive war in human history, it was symbolic of what it might portend for the postwar world. Many peace activists believed that America's action violated every instinct of humanity. America's moral authority, they maintained, had been shattered.[61]

For black women engaged in the peace struggle, the bomb held other significant implications. It proved what many had thought for decades. Violence and oppression were not imposed exclusively on people of color in America. Nonwhite people all over the world were subject to unjust acts by the majority. Black women bolstered this claim by tracing the direction of America's foreign policy interest as it gradually shifted from isolationism to internationalism. It seemed that America followed the color line as it engaged in economic and political imperialism in Haiti, Liberia, and Ethiopia between 1915 and 1945. Black peace activists followed America's carefully drawn color line as they both articulated and fought to end economic and political oppression in the three black nations. They hoped that freeing the citizens of these nations from the yoke of oppression would ensure a society based on the twin goals of peace and freedom.

5

Race-ing International Peace

1915–1945 As the train pulled out of the Washington, D.C., station, most of its passengers gripped their seats and held their hats to stem the bodily jolts resulting from its frequent and abrupt stops. After the train had traveled a few miles, the mostly white group settled down and engaged in quiet, polite conversation with each other. No one seemed to notice the lone black woman sitting in the rear seat, unnecessarily burdened by a myriad of luggage.[1]

No one bothered to ask her name or where she might be traveling. If so, they would have learned that she was Dr. Flemmie Kittrell, a Howard University professor, en route to a port in Annapolis, Maryland, where a ship waited to take her to West Africa.

On that muggy June day in 1938, Kittrell was beginning her third trip to the continent. She had long been interested in the conditions of Africans and therefore had decided to take the steps necessary to help them cope with the postcolonial period, thus the purpose of her trip. Armed with a suitcase full of literature on nutrition and health care, and with a wealth of her own knowledge, Kittrell planned to spend the summer in several West African villages conducting workshops that ranged from child care to good health care. She believed that if the indigenous peoples continued to rely on imperialist powers, their nations eventually would become colonies again. The mere idea of a return to colonialism for those countries that had managed to gain their independence created mental images of violence for Kittrell.[2] Hence her peace philosophy about Africans hinted of Pan-Africanism, because she believed that as a black American, she had a responsibility to assist Africans both during and after colonialism.

Dr. Flemmie Kittrell was not the only pre–World War II African American peace activist whose activism extended beyond America's borders. Other such blacks included Mary Talbert, Mary Church Terrell, and Bertha McNeill, to name a few. These women and their black colleagues linked international peace issues to race just as they had done with domestic peace issues. They believed in an important and undeniable link between international oppression and world peace. It is within this context that we first witness an emerging international consciousness among black peace activists.

Before joining WILPF, many African American peace activists had joined the International Council of Women of the Darker Races (hereafter referred to as the Council), which was organized in 1920 by a group of women of color who wanted to broaden their understanding of international affairs and the conditions under which certain peoples lived. The Council emerged from the Pan-African consciousness that followed World War I. It brought together women of color to examine global issues of race, gender, class, and peace. Peace activists Mary Church Terrell, Mary Talbert, Dr. Mary Waring, Addie Hunton, and Bertha McNeill were among the first members of the organization. Lucy Diggs Slowe, Vera Chandler Foster, and Thelma Marshall joined later.

The stature of the first elected officers attests to the significance of the organization: Margaret Murray Washington, widow of Booker T. Washington, president; peace activist Addie Hunton, first vice president; peace activist Mary Church Terrell, second vice president; Lugenia Burns Hope, wife of Morehouse College president John Hope, third vice-president; and Adelaide Casely-Hayford, fourth vice-president for West Africa. Other officers included Elizabeth Carter, secretary; Marion Wilkerson, president of the South Carolina Federation of Colored Women's Clubs, treasurer; and Nannie Burroughs, founder of the National Training School for Women and Girls in Washington, D.C., chair of the executive board.[3]

The Council was initially composed of fifty American women of color and fifty foreign women of color. To ensure that all of its members were as well informed as possible, the Council encouraged the development of study groups. Under the Council's education section, "committees of seven" were formed in 1924 to "study conditions of darker races of the world." Each community was to form a committee to study problems of people of African descent in America, as well as the indigenous peoples of Africa. Educational, social, religious, and industrial concerns were suggested as broad areas from which specific topics could be selected. It was also recommended that the women read books about Africa and schedule visits from native Africans and missionaries.[4] Articles, letters, and minutes of club meetings show that the local committees took the suggestions seriously and worked to complete the recommended tasks. In a letter to Margaret Murray Washington, Jane Porter Barrett, for instance, founder of the Locus Street Settlement in Hampton, Virginia, wrote that evenings were spent on discussions about the women of Haiti, China, Africa, and Japan.[5]

Although the Council never moved beyond gathering data and proposing solutions during its early years, its members were able to expand their knowledge of peoples of color. The women also pressured school superintendents in America to order books about people of the African diaspora. The Council was especially concerned that African American youngsters, as well as its own members, become exposed to and understand the history and literature of their people.[6]

As it became evident, however, that the Council was not going to take a more active stance, most of its members began to turn their attention elsewhere. Such members were usually those women truly committed to helping the indigenous people of the black diaspora. Some of them joined WILPF when they heard that its members had decided to wage a battle against economic and colonial imperialism in several countries either inhabited by people of African descent or that had been acquired by America after the Spanish-American War.

America's gains after the Spanish-American War exposed many African Americans for the first time to the oppressive conditions of people of color outside America and Africa. The Spanish-American War of April 1898 marked the emergence of America as a world power with colonial possessions in the Caribbean and the Pacific. During the war, America won quick victories in Spanish colonies. In December, Spain agreed to a peace treaty that gave America control of Puerto Rico, as well as the Philippines and Guam. America ruled Puerto Rico directly through an American governor and an American-appointed executive council.

Cuba then became a protectorate of America. When Cubans drafted a constitution in 1900, however, America forced them to add a document known as the Platt Amendment. The amendment gave America the right to intervene in Cuban affairs to protect American lives and property. It put limits on Cuba's right to borrow from foreign powers, and it allowed America to establish two naval stations in Cuba. Many Latin-American nations looked on U.S. expansion into the Caribbean with alarm. They feared that the United States had imperialist ambitions that would threaten their independence.

The Treaty of Paris between America and Spain also provided that Spain cede to America other Spanish insular possessions in the West Indies. Upon payment of $20 million by America, Spain was to relinquish the Philippines to the victor. Hence, Guam, in the Pacific, and Puerto Rico and other areas in the Caribbean gradually became a part of America's growing empire, one that was composed almost wholly of so-called un-developed peoples.

The areas gained by America abounded in resources that would supply the needs of its highly industrialized economic system and in human beings who were potential consumers of commodities provided by America's industries. In Cuba there were more than six hundred thousand blacks and persons of African descent, many of whom were mestizos. Puerto Rico had more than three hundred thousand such persons.[7] Even in Hawaii and the Philippines there were some blacks, with the majority of the population in both places composed primarily of darker peoples.

As time passed, America enlarged its empire through its influence over independent nations of darker peoples. In Santo Domingo (now the Dominican Republic), for example, the control that America exercised in the twentieth century was so extensive as to constitute almost complete domination.[8] After its separation from Haiti in 1844, Santo Domingo, composed largely of blacks and mestizos, succumbed to American "dollar diplomacy," which subsequently brought one Latin-American nation after another within the sphere of influence of the United States.

In 1907, an American citizen was named the general receiver of customs with authority to deposit one hundred thousand dollars each month toward the interest and sinking fund that was held in trust for all national creditors. In May 1916, America landed marines in Santo Domingo to preserve order, and within a few months, civil government had disappeared altogether.[9] Despite the vigorous protests of the Dominican minister in Washington, the marines remained there until 1924. By that time, peace and order had been restored, and the commercial relationship between America and the black republic had become so intimate as to guarantee the domination of its economic life for an indefinite period.

Records show that WILPF's white membership condemned American economic imperialism in Latin America. However, the same records are silent on how the black peace activists in the organization felt. This silence can be attributed to either the lack of an international consciousness beyond the African continent or indifference due to domestic issues. Nevertheless, critics of the U.S. government's policy in these areas urged that it grant independence to the Philippines and Samoa, end its military occupation and financial supervision of Nicaragua, and lend money to Latin-American countries only for "constructive projects that [would] contribute to the prosperity and well being of the people."[10]

Conversely, U.S. involvement on the African continent in the 1920s and 1930s did cause concern among both black and white WILPFers. They were particularly interested in America's economic and political imperialism in Haiti, Liberia, and Ethiopia. Developments in these countries were some of the main issues that dominated WILPF's agenda in the decades between World War I and World War II. The peace organization wanted to end American involvement in these countries, and its black members were some of the most vocal critics of America's foreign policy in Haiti, Liberia, and Ethiopia.

America's involvement in Haiti was similar to that in the Dominican Republic. Within a year after the beginning of World War I, America and Haiti ratified a treaty that permitted the United States to exercise control over Haiti's finances and police force for a period of ten years.[11] This power gave America a justification to dominate every phase of life in the second oldest republic in the New World. In 1917, America placed the country under complete military rule and forced extension of the treaty of 1915 for another ten years. The nature of the intervention was clearly demonstrated in a telegram that an American sent to the secretary of the navy: "Next Thursday . . . unless otherwise directed, I will permit Congress to elect a president."[12] Almost from the beginning, the Haitians resented American occupation of their country, and it was necessary for the marines to kill more than two thousand inhabitants to restore peace and order.[13]

Haitians elicited widespread sympathy, especially from African Americans. Black peace activists watched events in Haiti with growing concern. They were among the first and most energetic critics of America's presence there. But they were not alone in their fight against American policies. They joined with several prominent white peace activists to rid the small country of America's influence. Hunton, Charlotte Atwood, Mary Waring, and others began by persuading WILPF's national leaders to take a stand on America's involvement in Haiti.[14]

In 1920 national WILPF leader Emily Greene Balch, responding to pressure from Hunton, Atwood, and others, suggested to her colleagues on the executive board that they appoint a commission to investigate the situation there. It took the board six years to agree to her request. In 1926 the team leader, Balch, African Americans Addie Hunton and Charlotte Atwood, and three others, including one man, were appointed to an unofficial investigatory commission that proved to be one of the most effective undertakings of WILPF.

The group spent three weeks in the country. Balch was struck most strongly, she wrote, by the "complete hiatus between the sense of what [was] important in life in the eyes of the Haitians" and what Americans thought was significant for the Haitians. The Americans emphasized the good they had done by overseeing the building of roads, bridges, and health care facilities; the Haitians emphasized that American occupation had broken down self-government and left a whole generation to grow up without any sense of political responsibility or experience of it. Even worse, in the view of the Haitians, was that the American occupation had created "a situation between the races powerfully influenced by that which had developed in the former slave states of the United States" and produced within the Haitians a sense of "racial self-consciousness" from which they had before been free.[15]

Balch later clarified these remarks with examples of racism and condescension she had witnessed. "Among American officials in Haiti, even those who pass for the most friendly," she noted, "there is a good deal of joking about Haitians having just stopped living in trees, and that sort of thing."[16] Balch believed that it was impossible for Americans to hide their contempt for the Haitians, and this failure doomed any attempts at mutual cooperation: "If black men, however cultivated, strike our men in Haiti as sort of nigger minstrels masquerading in Paris clothes and aping real men like ourselves, there can never be effective cooperation."[17]

The commission published its findings in a book, *Occupied Haiti*. Although Balch edited and largely wrote the book, Atwood and Hunton wrote two of the book's chapters. They concluded that there was little justification for the continued occupation of Haiti; that self-government should be restored; that American officials should be replaced as far as possible by Haitians and the administration should be demilitarized; that preventive detention should be ended and freedom of the press restored. They also urged the U.S. government to send an official commission of investigation to Haiti to make a firsthand report, which in fact was done.[18]

Meanwhile, Dorothy Detzer, the U.S. section's secretary, and Emily Greene Balch began to put political pressure on the secretary of Latin affairs in the State Department in Washington, D.C. Their goal was to persuade the secretary to withdraw all U.S. troops from Haiti. Balch even visited President Coolidge and provided him with a copy of her group's findings in Haiti. She later submitted that same report to Coolidge's successor, Herbert Hoover. After reviewing the report, Hoover formed an official committee to investigate the situation in Haiti. Once the investigation was over, Hoover issued a report with his administration's findings. Interestingly, Hoover's report echoed many of the recommendations in *Occupied Haiti*, proposals that were implemented in 1934 when American troops were finally withdrawn from the island.[19] Despite the withdrawal, however, Haiti remained a part of America's empire of darker people.

Unlike the situation in Haiti, the Liberian crisis dominated WILPF's international agenda for most of the years leading to World War II. Needless to say, African American peace activists played a role in trying to resolve the Liberian question. From the outset, concerned black peace activists believed that America's involvement in Liberia in the 1920s and 1930s, like its intervention in Haiti, was motivated by racism. Why did African Americans in general and black peace activists in particular become involved in Liberia's affairs? What did the Liberian crisis have to do with WILPF's twin goals of peace and freedom? The answers lie in Liberia's political and economic development.

The Americo-Liberian elite was crudely exploiting native Liberian workers, ironically creating a system akin to American slavery. Black peace activists sensed that the U.S. State Department and certain private business owners sanctioned such behavior because it confirmed their long-held beliefs that blacks were incapable of self-government without proper supervision by whites. The activists disagreed with these same critics who noted that Liberia had failed egregiously since its founding. Consequently, many black peace activists joined their white peace activist colleagues as well as blacks in the larger community in a full-scale attack against imperialists and advocates of forced labor in Liberia. They did so primarily through their affiliation with various all-black or predominantly black organizations interested in the Liberian situation.

Despite their beliefs and subsequent activism, African American pacifists had less of an impact on America's foreign policy in Liberia than they had in Haiti. This difference was due in large part to the nature of America's historical relationship with each of these countries and the timing of the Liberian crisis.

America's direct involvement with Liberia began in the early nineteenth century with the colonization movement. Some Americans envisioned the resettlement of blacks to West Africa for many reasons. For some, resettlement was an excellent way to remove the troublesome free black population from America. For example, the Rev. Dr. Robert Finley, one of the initiators of the American colonization effort, wrote in 1815, "On this subject the state of the free blacks has very much occupied my mind. Their number increases greatly, and their wretchedness . . . [e]verything connected with their condition, including their color, is against them. Nor is there much prospect that their state can ever be greatly ameliorated while they shall continue among us."[20] Southern slave owners articulated different concerns about the growing free black population. They considered free blacks as "an unstable element liable to incite and rouse other blacks," thus endangering the slave regime on which the southern economy and society were founded. Other proponents of resettlement had different motives. Hermanus Bleeker of New York, for example, believed that the African American population was increasing much faster than the white population, and that an increase in crime, murder, and robberies perpetrated by blacks could result in reprisals by whites aimed at annihilating them.[21] Moved by these apprehensions, the legislature in Virginia decided in December 1816 that Congress should act "for the purpose of obtaining territory on the coast of Africa, or at some other place, not within any of the States, or territorial government of the United States, to serve for an asylum of such persons of colour as are now free, and may desire the same, and for those who may hereafter be emancipated within the commonwealth."[22]

Advocates of the 1816 resolution reached the conclusion that African Americans should by some means be removed from America and resettled on the coast of West Africa. In conjunction with the resolution that was passed in the Virginia legislature, the American Colonization Society was designed to send African Americans to a colony, Cape Mesurado, which the Society stumbled upon in West Africa. Cape Mesurado later became known as Liberia.

Liberia encountered many problems. It had laws but could not enforce them. Foreign traders did not want to pay custom duties to Liberia, arguing that it was not a political entity and thus had no right to impose them. Finally, to resolve these problems, on July 23, 1847, the American Colonization Society leaders decided to have the commonwealth proclaimed an independent republic.[23]

America's influence in Liberia was quite evident. Liberia's new constitution was modeled after that of the United States. The American flag, with a slight alteration, was chosen as the national emblem. Unlike the American flag, the Liberian flag had only one star, signifying its status as the only black republic on the African continent that year.[24] The black settlers, original inhabitants of the United States, became known as Americo-Liberians. They assumed all the duties and obligations inherent in the running of an independent state.

Liberia's first president, Joseph Jenkins, tried to do his best with the available resources. European imperialist nations, however, refused to acknowledge Liberia's independence. Since most of Africa was colonized, many leaders of European countries believed Liberia should be as well. Therefore various European countries would do what was necessary to bring Liberia under colonial rule.

Meanwhile, Liberian officials asked America for assistance and protection from European imperialists. America did not want to become involved. After all, American officials did not recognize Liberia's independence either. Some scholars writing on the subject maintain that the unwillingness of American officials to become involved in the Liberian situation was due mainly to the fact that "Southern interest was strong in Washington, and the thought of having a Negro ambassador in the nation's capital was considered politically and socially embarrassing."[25] In 1865, America, along with all nations of the world, finally endorsed Liberia's independence. Despite this recognition, Liberia's sovereignty was constantly being threatened by European powers, namely France and Great Britain.

Concomitant with the threat to its stability from external aggression were the social and economic contradictions that undermined the fragile foundation of the young black republic. When free blacks settled in Liberia, they carried with them many of the characteristics of the American Old South. Their dress and mannerisms reflected the plantation aristocracy. They were determined not only to mimic their former selves in terms of values and preferences but also to create a society structured after that from which they had fled.

The social structure set up in Liberia by the settlers was determined mainly by skin pigmentation. The light-skinned settlers, mainly mulattoes and invariably products of miscegenation on the plantations in the American South, formed the aristocracy. Following them were the dark-skinned settlers, some of whom had come from America and others from the West African coast. At the bottom of the social scale were native Africans who had migrated into the area. The three groups could not intermarry, among other things.[26]

While pigmentation differences hurt the progress of Liberia, they were not the republic's only problem. The Americo-Liberians did not understand how to survive in the African settlement, nor did they make efforts to understand.[27] Furthermore, the Americo-Liberians refused to establish an amicable relationship with the native Africans, whom they believed to be inferior. Native Africans refused to accept the degraded status to which the Americo-Liberians had relegated them and subsequently sought assistance from France and Great Britain to engage in warfare with the Americo-Liberians.[28]

Over the next few decades, both Britain and France spent countless hours trying to establish a strong economic presence in Liberia. Their goal, in the midst of African colonialism by European imperialists, was to take full control of Liberia as well. However, each time Britain and France attempted to do so, America intervened. For example, in the mid-1860s, Liberia profited from the exportation of coffee, sugar, palm kernels, palm oil, and ivory to countries worldwide. Of these products, coffee became Liberia's main cash crop. Before long, a surplus of coffee on the world market hurt Liberia financially. The price of Liberia's coffee dropped by 65 percent.[29] Consequently, Liberia had to cut back on cultivation. By 1870 Liberia's trade and commerce had declined significantly. Britain and Germany immediately began to take over declining Liberian trading houses.[30]

The decline in trade adversely affected government operations, as revenue decreased significantly. Liberia turned to international bankers to meet its commitments. In 1871 the Liberian government negotiated a loan of five hundred thousand dollars in Britain. Liberia pledged as security her custom revenues. Of the original sum, only $135,000 reached Liberia.[31] The Liberian government had been the victim of fraudulent behavior by international bankers in Britain. Furthermore, Liberia, reeling under the economic strains of a failed economy, decided to borrow again to meet its obligations under the loan agreement with Britain. The black republic's president, Edward Roye, negotiated another one-half-million-dollar loan with Britain in 1906. But like the first loan, Liberia received only $150,000 of the original sum. The Americo-Liberians refused to be swindled a second time and decided to rescind the pledge. Refusing to release their hold on Liberia, British officials made certain demands that the Americo-Liberians in charge of the nation's affairs could not meet. Disillusioned and disappointed, the Liberians believed themselves to be hopelessly indebted to British banks and subsequently accepted Britain's demands. By 1908 Liberia was a de facto colony of Britain.

Liberians, realizing the danger posed to their sovereignty by British economic domination, turned to America for economic assistance later that same year. The Liberian government, in exchange for America's assistance, agreed to allow the U.S. State Department to advise Liberia on matters pertaining to international relations, to allow America to establish a bank in Liberia and encourage firms to develop the country's resources, and to allow the United States to use its influence to stop the designs on Liberian territory by the European colonial powers.[32] American officials accepted Liberia's offer and added a few recommendations of their own.

The U.S. government wanted to reorganize Liberia's border patrol and place it under the command of black officers from the U.S. Navy. They then lent $1.7 million at 5 percent interest to Liberia in 1912. The bankers would be both American and European. Liberians also agreed to allow the American president to nominate a financial adviser who would be approved by Liberia's president. This series of actions placed America in a position to supplant Britain as the dominant power in Liberia. The Americo-Liberians welcomed American presence in their country but not that of the British. They had no clue that American officials believed he indigenous peoples to be incapable of taking care of the country, both politically and economically.

Before long, all of the countries were involved in World War I, which forced Britain to demand the repayment of its loans from Liberia. Unable to repay the loan, Liberia requested a moratorium on payments of the 1912 loan but was turned down. Liberia then turned to America for a $5-million loan to liquidate the principal and accumulated interest on the British loan. In 1917 President Wilson authorized the loan, but before processing could be completed, the U.S. Senate, which had to approve all loans, rejected it on the grounds that the black republic was not creditworthy.[33]

A year later, World War I ended. Eight days after the armistice on November 11, 1918, the U.S. State Department informed Britain that the 1912 loan had proven "unworkable and that the U.S. had decided to take full control over the financial affairs of the black republic."[34] The European powers agreed to leave Liberia. By January 30, 1919, Liberia was totally under the economic guidance of America.

Once the Europeans left, American officials advised the Liberian government to seek a loan from private American sources. Thus began the biggest and most public "black scandal" in the history of both Liberia and America. This event aroused the consciousness of African Americans to the point of organized movements to end European and American presence in one of the last black nations on the African continent. Black peace activists became vocal critics of America's questionable involvement in Liberia. They did so as members both of WILPF and of African American organizations. What led to this black public outcry?

Despite being under the guidance and "protection" of the American government, Liberians continued to feel pressure on their border with the French Ivory Coast. They were convinced that France, Britain, and even Germany would do whatever was necessary to end self-rule in Liberia. They had already taken control of the remainder of the African continent. Liberia was one of only two African nations that had not been colonized by European imperialists. Realizing this, Liberians decided that their survival depended on involving America more deeply in the country's affairs. Therefore they took the advice of American officials in the U.S. State Department and signed an agreement with the Firestone Rubber Company of Akron, Ohio.[35] Why an agreement with Firestone?

For years America had imported its natural rubber from the British East Indies. After World War I ended, America became more dependent on the British East Indies for its natural rubber.[36] The price of rubber dropped in 1921, forcing Britain to reduce rubber production in an effort to keep prices stable. This action by Britain hurt America's automobile industry, which produced 80 percent of the world's cars. The cutback in rubber production led to an unusual rise in the price of the product.[37] America, in its denunciation of the British monopoly over natural rubber, decided to take steps to end the practice. Congress appropriated five hundred thousand dollars for an investigatory committee to search for alternate sources of rubber.[38]

For a little more than five years, Firestone Rubber Company had been negotiating with Liberian officials for a contract to plant rubber in the republic. However, Harvey Firestone, the owner of the company, had not been successful in reaching an agreement with the Liberian government. When he learned that America was searching for an alternate rubber source, Firestone informed the U.S. State Department of his intentions in Liberia and subsequently asked for its help. The State Department agreed to do so, since both had similar goals and, in achieving them, would help each other out financially.

While sources do not state whether the U.S. State Department and Firestone Rubber Company conspired to force Liberia into a contract with Harvey Firestone, the events that followed give legitimacy to that claim. Harvey Firestone approached the Liberian secretary of state and offered to grant the republic a loan of $5 million to be "used for liqui-dating the debt incurred from the 1912 loan" that Liberia had obtained from American and European bankers. As security, Mr. Firestone wanted the entire Liberian revenues "to be assigned for repayment, and for the Liberian government to accept a Receiver General, who would be ap-pointed by the president of the United States and would have the power to veto over the expenditures of the government."[39]

The Liberian government refused to accept the terms of the loan for fear that they would give a private company absolute control of its rev-enues.[40] The U.S. State Department then intervened in the negotiations between Liberian officials and Harvey Firestone. The State Department told the Liberian government that Washington "awaits with sympathetic interest the conclusion of the Firestone contracts and believes the suc-cessful establishment of the rubber industry in Liberia will tend to pro-mote the country's welfare by contributing to the development of its resources."[41] Given the historical relationship between Liberia and America, it was virtually impossible for Liberian officials to refuse Harvey Firestone's earlier offer. Perhaps historian Fahnbulleh best summed up Liberia's thoughts after the State Department's intervention. He alleges, "[F]earing that its intransigence over the Firestone loan would weaken the U.S. resolve to defend it from British and French encroachments, the [Liberian] government modified its objection, stating that it would only accept the $5 million if it came from a private source other than the Firestone Rubber Company."[42] This arrangement was acceptable to both Harvey Firestone and the U.S. State Department. Since Liberian officials did not specify which American private company was to lend the money, Harvey Firestone set up a subsidiary—the Finance Corporation of America—to handle the loan to Liberia.[43]

Additional provisions of the contract between Liberia and Firestone Rubber Company made Liberia a virtual American colony. On October 2, 1926, Firestone was granted a ninety-nine-year lease for one million acres of land for the production of rubber. In return, the Finance Corporation of America granted the Liberian government the loan of $5 million at 7 percent interest. Moreover, the company agreed to pay the government a rental fee of six cents for each acre of land and 1 percent of the gross value of rubber and other products it exported from Liberia.[44] The Finance Corporation of America was also to appoint a financial adviser to the Liberian government with the responsibility to review the government's annual budget and advise it on governmental expenditures. An auditor was also appointed by the corporation to countersign all vouchers used by the government. A supervisor of customs, who was to be an American, would be appointed and all financial reports to the Liberian government were to be sent to the U.S. State Department. Finally, the Liberian government could not contract new loans without the written approval of the Finance Corporation of America.[45] After the agreement was signed, America provided Liberia with technical advisers to help its border patrol, which Liberia gladly accepted because it had become tired of trying to protect itself from French and British invasion.

Before the ink was dry on the contract between the Finance Corporation of America and Liberia, Firestone began to move into Liberia and develop its rubber industry. Before long, a thriving natural rubber industry, operated by Firestone and sanctioned by the U.S. State Department and the Finance Corporation of America, was fully functioning in Liberia. Harvey Firestone had finally gotten what he wanted from Liberia. The United States had found an alternate source for natural rubber and could now meet the needs of its expanding automobile industry. While all parties involved seemed to have been satisfied with the arrangement, none could have predicted or foreseen how that arrangement would eventually cause thousands of individuals in organizations like WILPF to call for an end to a corrupt pact. The genesis of the disagreement lies in the labor practices of all groups involved in the agreement.

Liberia was responsible for supplying laborers for the Firestone industry. Consequently, Americo-Liberia continued a practice of procuring laborers that it had used since 1914—recruitment of native Africans. The Liberian government had forced its native African population to work on the Spanish Island of Ferdinand Po for more than ten years. For the governing elite—the Americo-Liberians—forced labor had become a lucrative practice. Therefore, when Harvey Firestone asked for workers, top government officials, who began to hold key positions in the rubber industry, forcefully took more native Liberians from the villages to provide a cheap source of labor for the new rubber industry.[46] As a worldwide depression set in, reducing the demand for, and thus the price of, rubber, the Americo-Liberian aristocracy increased the pillage of Liberia's human and natural resources in an effort to increase its own financial gains. For instance, more members of the aristocracy than ever before began to export native Africans to Ferdinand Po as cheap laborers to compensate for the "dwindling returns from their huge rubber plantations" during the depression. According to historian Fahnbulleh, the logic was simple: "If they could not exploit labor themselves, then they would sell laborers in order to satisfy their avarice."[47] Thus began what Ibrahim K. Sundiata appropriately calls the "black scandal."

Ironically, it was American scholar R. L. Buell who first revealed the trafficking in native Africans for cheap labor. Buell noted that Liberia had signed the Slavery Convention of 1926, and the indulgence of traffic to Ferdinand Po was a violation of the convention. Then, in 1927, immediately after a presidential election in Liberia, the defeated presidential candidate, Thomas Faulkner, traveled to America where he gave interviews to American newspapers, describing the traffic in native Africans and the repressive conditions under the incumbent administration.[48] Faulkner was trying to convince Americans that the regime in Liberia was "corrupt and unscrupulous."[49] The U.S. government was concerned that such allegations would be used by France and Great Britain to embarrass America for its protection of a country that ignored human rights. America's fears were not unfounded. France and Great Britain did criticize America, condemning it for refusing to publicly denounce Liberia's policy of trafficking native Africans. Giving in to pressure, the U.S. State Department wrote to the Liberian government, avowing, "[E]vidence indicate[d] that existing conditions incident to the so-called 'export' of labor from Liberia to Ferdinand Po [had] resulted in the development of a system which seem[ed] hardly distinguishable from organized slave trade . . . and the service and influence of certain high Government officials [were] constantly and systematically used."[50]

The Liberian government denied the charges but agreed to an investigation by a commission from the League of Nations. The League subsequently appointed three persons, one each from the League of Nations, America, and Liberia, to determine whether Liberia was indeed practicing forced labor. African American professor Charles Johnson of Fisk University in Tennessee was the American representative.

The group, which became known as the Christy Commission, began its investigation into whether Liberia practiced forced labor and slavery on April 7, 1930. They found that "slavery in the classic sense of slave markets and slave traders did not exist in Liberia, but that domestic slavery—which was an attribute of traditional society—existed and the system had been excessively abused by some individuals." The commission added that "the blind eagerness for private profit [had] carried the traffic to a point scarcely distinguishable from slavery, and that only by help of the instruments and officers of Government could the traffic have reached such effectiveness."[51] The commission therefore recommended that Liberia accept assistance from the League of Nations in the handling of its fiscal and legal affairs, and that these two areas of operations, including the administration of Liberia, be placed under an international supervisor appointed by the League.[52] The Liberian government agreed to the Christy Commission's recommendation as long as the supervisor was someone from a country without interests in Africa. Liberia was obviously afraid of losing its hard-fought independence to European imperialists who had repeatedly but unsuccessfully tried to colonize the black republic.

African Americans in general and black peace activists in particular shared Liberia's fears. They were not willing to see a European mandate over Liberia. They were also angry that America had refused to intervene to protect Liberia from European imperialist threats when the League withdrew its plan in opposition to Liberia's counteroffer. The U.S. State Department claimed that it would be suicidal for it to become involved in the Liberian crisis. One cannot help but ask whether America chose not to become involved because such a commitment was not in its economic interest. It was well known that Firestone had deliberately cut back on production of natural rubber and its reliance on forced cheap labor, two reasons for America's interest in Liberia.

African Americans believed that racism influenced America's lack of interest in Liberia or unwillingness to protect the country's independence. The State Department denied such allegations, but the reality is that "racism permeating American life had a very definite effect on these relations." According to Ibrahim K. Sundiata, "to most American officials, Liberia was a 'demigovernment' run by a race considered lacking in the requisite skills and capacities for a national self-government."[53] He noted,

"In the mid-1920s, an American official in Liberia could express the opinion that all Liberians sense their inferiority vis-à-vis white men."[54]

Allegations made by African Americans were further confirmed when Professor Johnson of the Christy Commission implied that at least one of his colleagues was influenced by racial considerations. He referred to Cuthbert Christy, who, Johnson claimed, "felt Africans were standing still and [were] 100 years behind England . . . and France . . . , that U.S. Negroes were 100 years behind whites."[55] Johnson said that Christy wanted an administration by white men, while Johnson believed that black self-rule should remain, even if African Americans could assume a more significant role in Liberia.

As time passed, African Americans increasingly voiced their fears about the Liberian situation. By 1933, it appeared to most concerned African Americans that Liberia would lose its independence to European powers, just as most other African nations already had. As African American women and men stepped up their opposition to the League's position, as well as that of the U.S. State Department, more individuals and groups became involved in the debate and battle lines were drawn, even within the black community. On one hand, conservative African Americans, like writer George Schuyler of the *Pittsburgh Courier* and Dr. Charles Moulton, the president of Tuskegee Institute, supported the U.S. State Department and the League of Nations. On the other hand, more aggressive African Americans like W. E. B. DuBois joined forces with black organizations like the NAACP, as well as with white anti-imperialist organizations such as WILPF and the Foreign Policy Association.

The NAACP and WILPF, who shared some of the same female members, were two of the main supporters of Liberian independence. In their criticism, members of both groups often linked America's race problem to Liberia's race problem. African American peace activists, in particular, linked the economic and political exploitation of Liberia by imperialist nations to the twin goals of peace and freedom for which WILPF was fighting. Many black peace activists likened America's handling of the situation in Liberia to its involvement in Haiti a few years before.

On July 31, 1933, a group of prominent African Americans, representing various black organizations and WILPF, met Undersecretary of State William Phillips to discuss the Liberian situation. The group included, among others, Flemmie Kittrell, Addie Hunton, and Dorothy Detzer of WILPF; W. E. B. DuBois of the NAACP; President Mordecai Johnson of Howard University; Rayford Logan of the Association for the Study of

Negro Life and History; Charles Wesley of Howard University's history department; Emmett Scott, the secretary of Howard University; Addie Dickerson, a member of WILPF and the president of the International Council of Women of the Darker Races (to which black peace activists Mary Church Terrell, Addie Hunton, Lucy Diggs Slowe, Mary Talbert, and Mary Waring also belonged); Mrs. Daniel Partridge Jr., the secretary of the Washington branch of WILPF; and Charles Hamilton Houston of the National Bar Association. Dorothy Detzer was the lone white member of the delegation.

The group convened before their meeting with the State Department to draft a statement about Liberia. They called for a supervisory commission to include both a Liberian and an American black, rejected the notion that education in Liberia be turned over completely to missionary societies, and emphasized that African Americans were solidly behind the maintenance of Liberian sovereignty.[56]

Once the delegation met with Undersecretary of State Phillips, they couched their criticism of America's policy toward Liberia in terms of racial solidarity. W. E. B. DuBois, speaking on behalf of the delegation, read a statement in which he maintained that "the darker world had become convinced that it [was] being used and exploited by Europe and America for the benefit and power and luxury of white folk and at the expense of poverty, and slavery for yellow, brown, and black."[57] DuBois further criticized Washington, claiming that it was not interested in a "New Deal" of black states and compared Haiti to Liberia. He then asked that the League of Nation's plan of assistance not be forced on Liberians and urged that the proposed Liberian budget under the plan be amended to include funds for education: "We have too often seen missionary enterprises as the hand-maiden of capitalistic and imperialistic designs and we are sure that the Christian people of America will not wish to supplant Government education by Church education in Liberia any more than in the United States."[58] DuBois also asked that America support the appointment of a chief adviser acceptable to Liberia, that no ultimatum regarding Liberia's acceptance of the plan be sent, and that America officially recognize the Barclay regime.[59]

African Americans supported the Barclay administration, which had only denounced forced labor trafficking of native Africans. The administration also had rejected a recommendation by diplomatic representatives from America, Great Britain, and Germany to impose international governmental control on Liberia to "enable it to crystallize the recommendations and suggestions of the International Commission."[60] This action by the Barclay administration had caused the League of Nations to withdraw its offer in April 1930, since it had suggested some type of international government control of the black republic.

The delegation also expressed their concern with President Herbert Hoover's appointment of Major General Blanton Winship as special commissioner to Liberia.[61] Winship did not like African Americans, and the deal he negotiated between Liberia and Firestone reflected his lackadaisical attitude toward people of African descent.

At first glance, it might appear that Winship had negotiated a plan that benefited Liberia. The African country's loan from Firestone would receive a 2-percent interest rate reduction as long as the country's annual income was less than five hundred thousand dollars a year. But this generosity cost Liberians a great deal. For example, Liberians were forbidden to grant any concessions to another foreign power without the consent of the chief administrator, whose authority would be strengthened. Furthermore, the chief administrator, who was given almost dictatorial powers, had to be an American. Liberians could not use any funds for education, as this function was the responsibility of missionaries.[62] When Detzer first learned of the plan, she noted that it "would in reality have permitted an American corporation to hold Liberia in bondage for a century; in economic bondage through the loan; through prohibition of Liberia's own educational institutions, in cultural bondage; and, through the appointment of an American government administrator, in political bondage."[63]

Shortly after DuBois shared the delegation's position on Liberia with Phillips, the State Department told the press: "Mr. Phillips states . . . that he would be glad to give careful consideration to the views of so large a group of friends of Liberia and that he would transmit them to Major General Blanton Winship, the present American representative on the League Committee, for his consideration and such suggestions to the Committee for alterations as might seem feasible."[64] In the end, both parties had accomplished little.

WILPF and the NAACP, as well as various all-black organizations, continued to lobby the State Department. They believed that the first step for the government was to appoint a black adviser to Liberia and remove the Firestone Rubber Company from the area. Members of both groups also believed that they would have to press the U.S. State Department harder for a black adviser if they were to be successful. Dorothy Detzer, acting on this belief, stepped up WILPF's lobbying efforts in Washington and called on black peace activists in particular to solicit support from members of the black community. Addie Hunton was the first to respond to Detzer's request. In a letter to Detzer, Hunton wrote, "I have read with considerable concern the report on the matter of the Liberian advisor. If you desire further protest from colored groups I would advise use of sororities and fraternities, and the conference of youth. For the sororities and fraternities, a list is to be found in the *Negro Year Book,* College Women's Association, Miss Vivian Cook, President, Colored High School, Baltimore."[65]

Before the Liberian crisis ended, many of these groups had organized in protest of the government's position. By late 1933, the U.S. State Department had changed its position on an adviser and asked members of both WILPF and the NAACP for recommendations. Detzer recommended W. E. B. DuBois "or some other outstanding Negro in the United States," suggesting that such a person would not be "easily swayed by either the State Department or Firestone officials."[66] Meanwhile, Hunton wrote a separate letter to Walter White about the same issue and recommended W. E. B. DuBois.[67] White agreed and then wrote Detzer a letter in which he endorsed DuBois as chief adviser. Detzer then made the recommendation to the State Department, which was subsequently approved.[68]

After much debate and many tense exchanges, both sides finally reached an agreement. On January 1, 1935, the Liberian government and the Finance Corporation of America signed an agreement that resolved the matter of the rubber industry in Liberia and its potential to sanction a form of serfdom. In March of that year, the two sides signed another agreement that addressed the land issue, and in May America extended diplomatic recognition.

Many scholars, especially those writing about the role of peace activists, speciously maintain that while the Liberian crisis dominated the agendas of WILPF and numerous black organizations in the late 1920s and early 1930s, African Americans had little influence on shaping American foreign policy toward Liberia. African American peace activists, such as Addie Hunton, Addie Dickerson, Mary Talbert, Mary Waring, Flemmie Kittrell, and Lucy Diggs Slowe, joined countless other African Americans in condemning America's handling of the crisis in Liberia. Realizing this opposition, the State Department eventually decided that it would not inform African Americans of its position on Liberia until after its officials had made the decision and acted on it. Ellis Briggs of the State Department said that since he was "inclined to believe American Negroes [would] oppose any monkeying with Liberia on the grounds that [the State Department was] helping foreign imperialists to smother that scorbutic nation for whose birth [the State Department was], alas, responsible, . . . little could be gained by taking [African Americans] into [the Department's] confidence in advance." He believed that the government could take its own course of action and then "let [blacks] yell."[69]

Despite Briggs's claims, the State Department did care about what African Americans thought. For instance, in 1933, President Hoover believed that the government would have to resort to military force in Liberia to protect Firestone's, as well as the U.S. State Department's, interests. Secretary of State Henry Stimson, however, opposed the idea. Stimson had already received warning from the NAACP that "if the Department [did not] change its attitude on a question of vital importance [i.e., the Liberian crisis] to colored voters in the United States[, black Americans] would attribute [the State Department's] position to the hostility of the Hoover administration to the Negro race." Stimson advised Hoover not to use military force in Liberia because, according to Stimson's colleague J. P. Moffat, he could "see, probably more clearly than the President, the howl this would produce in Europe and among . . . blacks in this country."[70] When Harvey Firestone later approached Stimson and asked him to reconsider armed intervention in Liberia, Stimson told him that it would probably have "severe repercussions among American blacks," noting that it would definitely receive much press coverage in "Negro newspapers."[71]

Moreover, African Americans realized that they could use the black vote as leverage to influence the government's policies in Liberia. For example, when the NAACP raised strong opposition to a "dictatorial" chief adviser in Liberia, the State Department felt that if they published their position, it would "raise the devil with the colored people, and lose the support of the Hoover administration among blacks."[72]

Hence historian Ibrahim K. Sundiata notes that those who have studied the influence, or lack thereof, of black organizations and "their friends" on American policy toward Africa generally and Liberia in particular conclude that such influence was negligible at best. Sundiata, on the other hand, believes that African Americans and their friends undoubtedly "delimited policy on Liberia."[73] The role blacks played in the crisis between Liberia and Firestone, as well as the U.S. State Department, confirms Sundiata's claim. Because it was mostly behind the scenes, that role is not as evident.

Black peace activists not only protested America's controversial involvement in Haiti and Liberia in the 1920s and 1930s but were equally critical of how top American officials chose to address events in Ethiopia. Their efforts were not masked, however, by the leadership in WILPF or in other organizations that took a public position on events unfolding in Ethiopia.

When Italy invaded Ethiopia, black Americans protested with all the means at their command. African Americans saw Ethiopia as a black nation, the last of the African countries to survive imperialism and colonialism. Its destruction would symbolize the final victory of whites over blacks.

While larger cities set up elaborate organizations, many communities and organizations, such as the United Aid to Ethiopia (later the Ethiopia World Federation), raised funds for the defense of the African kingdom. The *Pittsburgh Courier* sent its historian–news analyst, J. A. Rogers, to cover the war. Upon his return, Rogers issued a booklet, *The Real Facts about Ethiopia,* and lectured to many black and white groups. African Americans urged whites to join them in opposition to the Italo-Ethiopian War. Blacks in interracial organizations encouraged their colleagues to support programs to end Italy's presence in Ethiopia. WILPF was one interracial organization blacks called on for support.

WILPF's initial reaction to events in Ethiopia shocked many black peace activists. Although many understood the then pacifist-controlled WILPF's initial position to avoid war at any cost, black women believed that an exception should be made in this particular case. They maintained that the situation in Ethiopia required immediate action if they were to save the country. WILPF had disappointed its black members, who felt that the organization should have been more involved.

By 1935 the peace efforts of the previous decade were giving way to efforts to prevent another world war. There was indeed reason for concern. By the summer of 1934, the Disarmament Conference had for all practical purposes dissolved in failure. The Hitler terror continued in Europe, and in December 1934 the first clash occurred between Italy and Ethiopia. Japan continued its aggression in the Far East, and Germany withdrew from the League of Nations. Although Benito Mussolini agreed to arbitration in January 1935, it was soon apparent that he merely stalled for time.

It was in this hostile European atmosphere that President Roosevelt asked Congress in early 1935 for its support on neutrality measures. Senators Gerald P. Nye of North Dakota and Bennett Champ Clark of Missouri introduced neutrality bills on April 9, 1935. The first would give the president the power to forbid U.S. citizens from traveling on belligerent ships or in war zones, and the second banned loans and credits to nations for the purpose of purchasing war materials. At the same time, Maury Maverick of Texas and Frank Kloeb of Ohio introduced similar measures in the House. A few weeks later, Nye and Clark introduced a third measure, an embargo on the shipment of arms to all belligerents with the stipulation that shipments of other contraband goods to belligerents would be at the risk of the shipper.[74] While the State Department wavered, peace groups mobilized in support of these measures.

It seemed wisest "to make strategic retreat—or rather, deliberately and frankly to be peace opportunists" by supporting a policy of U.S. neutrality. But WILPF declared, "This does not mean that the WILPF repudiates its efforts for an internationally organized world . . . and we do feel that the neutrality legislation is inconsistent with this policy. Nevertheless we do have the opportunity . . . to secure strong domestic peace legislation." The women were under no illusion that such legislation would provide a "water-tight guarantee against the United States being drawn into another war," but they viewed such laws as an important step in that direction. And if war did break out, affirmed WILPF, "probably the greatest contribution that the United States can make is to remain out . . . and refuse in any way to help or support it."[75] The group decided at its annual meeting in May 1935 to concentrate on obtaining passage of the strongest neutrality legislation possible. Delegates used this occasion to garner publicity for the cause.

In the following months, Senators Nye and Clark and Representative Maverick delivered poignant speeches before Congress and secured a hearing before the House Foreign Affairs Committee to obtain support of neutrality legislation. However, their efforts were in vain. Even the State Department had stalled on the issue.

WILPF, fearing time was running out, immediately took action. In June and July of 1935, "telegrams and letters began arriving in Washington from local branches of the Women's International League . . . refer[ring] to the policy of neutral rights that led to American entry into World War I and appeal[ing] for a new program before war came again in Europe." Several letters commented on the tense Ethiopian situation, warning that it was the "prelude to a great war."[76] Despite the letter-writing campaign, the State Department, Roosevelt, and Congress did not produce neutrality measures. WILPF and other peace groups became increasingly impatient with the constant delays. Mildred Scott Olmsted cautioned members of the need for immediate action to avoid war when she noted,

> [A]ll this legislation is being held up, either by the President or the State Department. Whether the Navy Department or the munitions interests, or both, are behind this . . . hedging, we do not know but the time has come to divert all our energies to demanding neutrality legislation . . . at this session, before it is too late. . . . Unless our neutrality policy is revised before the first loan is made to Italy or Ethiopia, the stopping of such loans . . . could be considered as a hostile act.[77]

In October 1935, Italy, without formally declaring war, launched a full-scale attack on Ethiopia. FDR immediately invoked the recently passed arms embargo, warned Americans against traveling on belligerent ships, and proclaimed to U.S. businessmen that whoever traded with belligerents did so at his own risk. WILPF sent a letter praising Roosevelt for his prompt action.

Immediately after FDR's action, the League of Nations condemned Italy for its aggression against Ethiopia. Accordingly, Italy was penalized with an economic sanction when the League placed an embargo on the shipment of arms to the country and urged all countries that were members of the League to freeze the import of Italian goods.

WILPF also seriously considered the issue of sanctions, which quickly became inextricably bound with its view on neutrality. At its board meeting that occurred the same month Italy invaded Ethiopia, WILPF resolved to continue to oppose arm shipments and loans to all belligerents. Of those casting dissenting votes, Hunton and McNeill were the two African Americans who could not accept such a resolution. They believed the economic sanctions should apply only to Italy[78] and were concerned about the adverse effect that such an embargo would have on Ethiopia.

Board members who supported sanctions against both belligerents felt their support was necessary, since the present law was not neutrality legislation but rather embargo legislation. Therefore, if the law were invoked against the aggressive nation only, it would in all probability force America to become involved in an international war. The proponents of economic sanctions against all belligerents wanted a law that was so rigid Americans could not be drawn into any conflict. As peace historian Carrie Foster asserts, "Although they [supporters of economic sanctions for all belligerents] believed that economic sanctions led to military sanctions, and military sanctions meant war, they [felt] their position [was] the best approach in this particular case." Foster also maintains that these women also viewed the Italo-Ethiopian conflict as "only a curtain-raiser for what may come when Germany [broke] loose, or when Japan [went] too far in the Far East."[79]

Divided internally over the meaning of the Neutrality Act of 1935 and its implications for Italy and Ethiopia, WILPF and other peace groups worked until the latter part of that year to come up with an acceptable replacement law. In December, a bill was introduced that recommended "the continuation of the arms embargo, a ban on loans to belligerents, and a discriminatory embargo on raw materials whereby the President could prohibit the export of strategic items which he considered essential to any war in progress. The embargoes were to apply to all belligerents, but if the President found that any nation went to war in violation of the Kellogg-Briand Pact, with the consent of Congress he could lift all embargoes on the countries that had been attacked."[80]

Most WILPFers heartily opposed the last provision. They thought that the priority should be to keep the United States out of war, which their critics claimed was an isolationist stance. However, they explained that their position was not isolationist "in the accepted sense of the word" but that of "an internationally organized world divorced from any military obligations."[81]

Congress continued to consider neutrality legislation and embargo issues even after the Neutrality Act was expanded in 1936. In 1937 an amendment to the original act allowed belligerents to trade with America on a cash-and-carry basis only. Nations that needed war supplies had to bring their own ships to pick up the material and had to pay cash on delivery of the goods.

Even after its amendment in 1937, the neutrality law was not as rigid as some in the peace community, especially black peace activists, had hoped it would be. As time passed, congressional support for stronger resolutions wavered as leaders of the business community opposed trade restrictions. Also, congressional members began to feel the pressure from members of the Italian American community, which thought that the bills discriminated against Italy.[82]

The national leaders in WILPF divided into two camps over the contentious neutrality issue. An intense debate ensued after the passage of the first Neutrality Act in 1935 and continued until America entered World War II. One camp, led by Dorothy Detzer and Hannah Clothier Hull, argued that neutrality was the only logical choice for America.

Detzer cautioned America against taking sides in the "old imperialistic struggle for control of Europe by trade agreements with other nations, and by helping in every way possible to deal with the basic factors making the world chaos."[83] She and others in her camp felt that America should remain unequivocally neutral.

Black peace activists, such as Bertha McNeill, Addie Hunton, Vera Chandler Foster, and Thelma Marshall, who disagreed joined the other camp, led by Emily Greene Balch and Mildred Scott Olmsted. They believed that America should employ nonviolent methods to resist the expansion of Fascism and aggression. They also felt that the Neutrality Acts gave the president too much authority.[84] No person, regardless of his position, should have the power to prevent the shipment of humanitarian aid, they reasoned. Black peace activists especially held this view because they regarded Fascism as a form of racism. They also did not trust the president, who was subject to political pressure, to make the right decision.

Furthermore, African American peace activists were feeling pressure from the black masses, who increasingly favored an interventionist policy on the Ethiopian question. But many of these blacks realized that if they were to have any effect on America's policy on Ethiopia, "they would have to form alliances with sympathetic white associations."[85] Black peace activists initially thought WILPF was such an organization. Later they were disappointed to learn that WILPF's membership was divided over the issue. Somehow, however, they had to persuade the opponents of an interventionist policy in Ethiopia to change their minds. For African Americans, every son and daughter of African descent needed to stand up and provide concrete assistance to their blood relatives in Ethiopia. They believed that they could not "desert their Race in Africa."[86] It was this belief that continually guided African American peace activists' policy on Ethiopia.

Another major issue that divided WILPF's national leadership into the same two camps was economic sanctions. They could not agree on whether such action could be used as a substitute for war or whether it actually fostered war. This hotly contested issue often divided WILPFers along racial and ethnic lines. In the process, it forced peace activists to reexamine their own consciences.

In 1941 Emily Greene Balch questioned the commitment to racial and human justice of some of the organization's members. In a personal letter to her colleague Dr. Alice Hamilton, whom she was trying to convince to change her position on the subject, Balch pointed out that "it is not enough to sweep before your own door, not to cultivate your own garden, nor to put out the fire when your own house is burning and 'disinterest yourself,' as the diplomat says, when the frame house next door is in flames and the children calling from its nursery windows to be taken out."[87]

As the discussions became more tense, WILPF leaders, both black and white, agreed that gaining consensus was necessary if the organization were to remain intact. Even though McNeill, Hunton, Foster, Marshall, Balch, and Olmsted feared the growth of Fascism, they were more frightened that WILPF would be destroyed as an organization over the issue. Therefore they decided to accept neutrality, with the hope that Roosevelt would act as mediator. Furthermore they made it clear that they did not support American military presence in Italy as a way to halt the spread of Fascism. Besides, Balch, McNeill, and the other women had engaged in this debate with Olmsted and others for years. They realized, perhaps better than anyone, that these women would not waver in their commitment to keeping America out of war. For Balch, Hunton, and others who shared their views, this goal seemed more important than any other issue.

Many African Americans, who realized that they had to balance the desire to help Ethiopia with the need to promote domestic causes, began to shift their position on Ethiopia. An increasing number of African Americans warned "that [they] had a war on [their] own hands—a war that had been going on for generations. It," they maintained," was a war against discrimination, segregation, disfranchisement, illiteracy, ignorance, shiftlessness, peonage, exploitation, bad housing and bad health."[88] For many African American peace activists, their main concern changed as they initiated an NAACP-sponsored antilynching bill. They began to divide their attention between the war in Ethiopia and the antilynching crusade in America.

The national board's final position did not completely please some of its branch members. For instance, according to peace historian Harriet Alonso, the New York branches, whose Jewish, African American, and working-class members were more intimately affected by events in Europe, lost many members. The loss was so great that the New York City branches consolidated, becoming the Greater New York branch.[89] This reorganization occurred all over the country where existing WILPF branches were adversely affected by the Italo-Ethiopian conflict.

Although McNeill, Hunton, and other black peace activists finally agreed with national leaders on the issue of neutrality, many of the black members of local WILPF branches refused to accept that agreement.

Hunton failed to convince African American members of the Greater New York branch, of which she was a member and which contained the largest group of black members in the nation, to support neutrality. They continued to embrace internationalism and intervention, and remained convinced "of the need to unite in protest against Italy."[90] As some peace historians have noted, for WILPF the price of neutrality proved high, for as war drew closer and womanpower more necessary, membership declined.

Black peace activists continued to focus on events in Ethiopia until World War II began. However, they joined various black-led organizations like the NAACP to protest, sometimes doggedly, the Ethiopian situation. They were among the black Americans who continued to believe that Italy's assault on Ethiopia was racially motivated.

Once Germany invaded Poland, all Americans turned their attention to the war in Europe, with most peace activists concerned with whether America would be drawn into the war. Once America declared war on Japan in 1941, peace activists engaged in intense debates over how to address America's failure to remain neutral. They were divided along both ideological and racial lines.

The global nature of the war and its demands on the resources of the belligerents implied from the beginning that its successful prosecution involved the utilization of every resource. For America, the waging of total war presented innumerable problems. Total warfare could not be achieved without the erection of some controls that reduced the freedom of an individual, a move that was strenuously resisted by a considerable portion of the population. Nor could total warfare be achieved unless the country made substantial concessions to its minority groups so that they could contribute to the defeat of the Axis powers. There was also considerable opposition among groups determined to carry on the fight abroad without upsetting the existing pattern of race relations at home. Many Americans had come to believe that for the purpose of increasing efficiency, America would have to deal more justly with its entire people.

On numerous occasions, African Americans at various levels of social and economic life pointed to the tremendous waste of people's effort in their struggle for the right to work and fight for victory. To some Americans, it was indeed embarrassing to try to determine what Berlin or Paris would say about America's racial injustices. African Americans also pointed to the hypocrisy of the slogan "fighting to make the world safe for democracy." As black peace activist Bertha McNeill so astutely pointed out in her criticism of the Austin-Wadsworth conscription bill at the time, too many Americans were still determined to maintain discriminatory practices based on race, creed, and national origin.

Within WILPF, some white national leaders felt compelled to examine their own prejudices. Yet far too many white peace activists, especially in local branches, continued to show biases against certain groups. While some of them attempted to reach out to minority groups, others continued to look the other way. This problem was illuminated in 1938, for example, when some WILPFers protested government actions in Latin America and subsequently tried to extend an olive branch to women concerned about world peace and freedom. American peace activist leaders who opposed the government action tried to organize branches of WILPF throughout Latin America. They were not successful, however, because the majority of WILPFers were not interested in opening their door to Latin American women.[91] Nor were they ready to reach out to the women of Haiti, Liberia, and Ethiopia. The Committee on the Americas and the Committee on Minorities and Race Relations did not make efforts to organize branches in these countries until the late 1960s.

Between 1915 and 1945, black peace activists and some of their white colleagues realized that race had a great deal to do with peace and freedom. They believed that only when all people were treated fairly would peace exist. As historian Linda Schott affirmed, "For these women [black peace activists], work to eradicate injustices committed because of racial and ethnic discrimination was just as essential as work for disarmament or international organization."[92] The peace activism of black women before World War II can certainly be characterized as work for racial justice and peace. Their goal would not change in the postwar era.

African American activists in WILPF continued to believe that peace and freedom were inextricably interwoven, that one could not have peace without freedom in any society, nor would they experience true freedom without peace. In Cold War America, black peace activists would establish this link repeatedly as they fought for peace and freedom in countries where these goals seemed virtually unattainable.

African American peace activist Mary Church Terrell in her early days, before joining
WILPF. Courtesy of the Moorland-Spingarn Research Center, Howard University, Washington, D.C.

American delegation to a meeting of the International Committee of Women for Permanent Peace held in Zurich, Switzerland, in 1919. Mary Church Terrell is standing in the back row *(sixth from left)*. Courtesy of the WILPF National Office, Philadelphia, Pennsylvania.

Peace activist Flemmie Kittrell.
Courtesy of the Moorland-Spingarn Research Center, Howard University, Washington, D.C.

Flemmie Kittrell *(right)* continuing to fight for peace and freedom as a WILPF member in 1962, shown with Adelaide Baker *(center)* and a new member from Indonesia *(left)*. Courtesy of the WILPF National Office, Philadelphia, Pennsylvania. Photo by Leo Rosenthal.

Peace activist Marian Anderson giving a concert at the Lincoln Memorial.
Courtesy of the Moorland-Spingarn Research Center, Howard University, Washington, D.C.

Peace activist Vera Chandler Foster *(far right)* greeting guests at one of her many community activities. Courtesy of the Tuskegee University Archives, Tuskegee, Alabama.

Vera Chandler Foster *(second from left)* years later at a community function.
Courtesy of the Tuskegee University Archives, Tuskegee, Alabama.

Vera Chandler Foster *(third from right)* continuing the fight for peace and freedom in the Tuskegee, Alabama, community. Courtesy of the Tuskegee University Archives, Tuskegee, Alabama.

Peace activist Bertha McNeill *(far right)* with other WILPF officers in the early 1940s.
Courtesy of the Records of the Women's International League for Peace and Freedom, Swarthmore College Peace Collection, Swarthmore, Pennsylvania.

Peace activist Bertha McNeill *(third from right)* at a U.S. State Department meeting on Africa in 1958. Courtesy of the Records of the Women's International League for Peace and Freedom, Swarthmore College Peace Collection, Swarthmore, Pennsylvania.

Peace activist Mayme Williams *(second from left)* in the White House office of Midge Costanza *(far left)* in September 1977. Williams had been involved in WILPF for several years when this photo was taken. Courtesy of the WILPF National Office, Philadelphia, Pennsylvania.

Peace activist Thelma Marshall *(fourth from left)* at the WILPF-USSR seminar in Moscow in 1974. Courtesy of the WILPF National Office, Philadelphia, Pennsylvania.

Peace activist Erna P. Harris *(right)* meeting Mrs. Nikita Khrushchev *(left)* while in Moscow in 1964. Courtesy of the WILPF National Office, Philadelphia, Pennsylvania.

Peace activist Erna P. Harris *(wearing beret)* with other WILPFers at the Kremlin in 1964.
Courtesy of the WILPF National Office, Philadelphia, Pennsylvania.

Peace activist Coretta Scott King *(right)* speaking at a WILPF Congress.

Peace activist Vera Chandler Foster *(fourth from left, standing)* and attorney Sadie Alexander *(fifth from left, seated)* at the American-Soviet women's meeting held at Bryn Mawr College in 1961.

Two of the several delegates at a WILPF Congress.
Courtesy of the WILPF National Office, Philadelphia, Pennsylvania.

Peace activist Thelma Marshall *(sixth from left)* in Moscow in 1974.
Courtesy of the WILPF National Office, Philadelphia, Pennsylvania.

Part Two

1945–1975

A New Generation of Peace Activists

Waging Different Battles in Unpredictable Times

1945–1960 When Japan finally surrendered to the Allies on August 14, 1945, Bertha McNeill breathed a long sigh of relief. She knew many people whose lives the war had devastated. For a large number of them, the wounds were deep, leaving potentially lifelong scars. She hoped they could begin the healing process.

McNeill thought especially about how World War II affected American citizens. Teary-eyed, she recalled the disturbing images of weary mothers embracing sons and husbands who had returned from war-torn Europe. She remembered thinking how the war had taken its toll on the former soldiers both physically and emotionally, leaving most of them looking older than their years.

Furthermore, McNeill realized that the war had changed America's social landscape. She vividly recalled, for instance, the mass migration of Americans, almost nomadic in their continual quest for social, economic, and political opportunities. African Americans, Mexican Americans, European Americans, and women of all races migrated to the North and West in search of jobs in the war-production industries.

Then her thoughts shifted momentarily to African Americans. McNeill smiled briefly when she thought about how the war had created new economic and political opportunities for her people. Consequently, many of them, like her, refused to accept anything less than their rightful place at America's table of opportunity. McNeill's smile turned to sadness, however, as she recalled the racial violence that often accompanied the Negro's relentless search for equal rights. With this unpleasant thought, McNeill realized there was much more work to do in the areas of civil rights and racial justice.[1]

Although World War II had slightly opened some doors of opportunity for African Americans, McNeill probably felt that it was only the beginning. Therefore she might have wanted to make certain that recent gains were not lost in the post–World War II period.[2] Her struggle and those of countless other concerned blacks to hold on to their rights while working to secure additional ones began in America. Their first vigorous demands for human rights in the Cold War period, as well as their anticolonial stance, were best seen in the context of the organization and actual functioning of the United Nations. Like many African Americans, black peace activists tried to influence the shape and character of the United Nations and use it to gain advantage with the American government.

When the United Nations founding conference opened in San Francisco on April 25, 1945, four of WILPF's pre–World War II African American members in key leadership positions remained. They were Bertha McNeill, Vera Chandler Foster, Flemmie Kittrell, and Thelma Marshall. Many of their black peace colleagues had died or had become either inactive or less active. A number of others had left WILPF during World War II because of pressure from war proponents, anti-Communist forces, and powerful government agencies such as the Central Intelligence Agency, the Federal Bureau of Investigation, and the House Un-American Activities Committee.[3] Yet McNeill, Foster, Kittrell, and Marshall were determined to continue the fight for peace and freedom within WILPF.

The slightly built fifty-year-old McNeill, the oldest of the four black women, was the lone black member of the national executive board. She had moved up in the ranks since joining the District of Columbia branch of WILPF in the late 1920s. McNeill was serving her last term as chair of the Committee on Minorities and Race Relations and was preparing to assume leadership of the Committee on the Special Problems of Branches. This change in positions indicated that WILPF was progressing internally as black women began to work on committees other than those pertaining to race.

The three other women, Foster, Kittrell, and Marshall, who had been active in their respective WILPF branches, assumed responsibilities that made them more visible to white national leaders during the war. Thirty-three-year-old Vera Chandler Foster, for instance, was known for her work as an active member of the Tuskegee, Alabama, branch of WILPF. During World War II, she was one of a small number of women who made certain that the branch did not close its doors despite a decline in membership. In addition to supporting peace causes during the war, Foster also led vigils and demonstrations and spoke at meetings in which she expressed her opposition to the war whenever possible.[4]

Flemmie Kittrell, a forty-year-old professor of home economics at Howard University and an active member of the local District of Columbia branch of WILPF, continued the peace work she had started before World War II. Combining her professional training with peace work, Dr. Kittrell focused primarily on the problem of malnutrition faced by the indigenous peoples of West Africa. However, during the postwar period, she expanded her interests to include Asians as well. Kittrell was soon internationally recognized for her work in both Africa and Asia.[5]

Forty-two-year-old Thelma Marshall was committed to peace and freedom in Gary, Indiana. Although the Gary branch temporarily closed its doors during World War II because of a lack of members, its few committed pacifists continued to oppose the war and fight for world peace without benefit of an organized group.

As soon as the war ended, Marshall and several white pacifists met to examine ways to revive the Gary branch of WILPF. Less than three months after Japan surrendered to the Allies, ending World War II, this small group of committed peace activists reopened its WILPF branch and began to explore ways in which it could become more actively involved in the events unfolding in San Francisco.

While African American women tried to stake out a position at the peace table in San Francisco, they also actively recruited other black women for peace work. Both tasks proved to be difficult. Members of the national WILPF executive board, Bertha McNeill, Emily Greene Balch, Jane Addams, Dorothy Detzer, and Carrie Chapman Catt, decided that the organization needed to intensify its recruitment of women of color, especially African American women, to increase its membership. The national board and a few local branches, such as those in New York, Philadelphia, San Francisco, the District of Columbia, and Chapel Hill–Durham, North Carolina, approached all-black organizations and set up recruiting booths at universities and colleges. They also attended meetings held by various black-controlled and interracial organizations and participated in civil rights demonstrations. Moreover, they patronized political functions and black churches to increase their black membership. Between 1945 and 1975, more than fifty African American women joined WILPF.

The new group of black peace activists shared certain characteristics with their foremothers. They were, for the most part, middle-class professionals with college educations. However, they were also quite different. Some of them, of which a few were national politicians, had studied abroad in non-African countries, were either Communists or had Communist ties, and were employed in positions other than education and social work. They also pressed more vigorously within WILPF for full equality and racial justice. Furthermore, these women linked racial oppression in America more forcefully and broadly to human oppression than any of their white colleagues in WILPF.

African American women who joined WILPF during this period include Sadie Sawyer Hughley, Marian Anderson, Virginia Collins, Pearl McNeill, Shirley Chisholm, Diane Nash, Eartha Kitt, Coretta Scott King, Bessie McLaurin, Bess Walcott, Angela Davis, Erna Prather Harris, Bettina Aptheker, Enola Maxwell, and Inez Jackson. In the early 1950s, WILPF's national executive board agreed to open its membership to men. Civil rights activist Rev. Dr. Martin Luther King Jr., economist Rev. Dr. J. Neal Hughley, longtime NAACP chairperson Walter White, and activist W. E. B. DuBois, all of whom had been involved in peace work on some level, became members.

The newcomers did not begin joining WILPF until 1946. Meanwhile, veterans McNeill, Foster, Kittrell, and Marshall were busy. They began addressing their concerns with participants at the UN founding conference, the most important arena in which to wage such a fight after World War II. Issues decided on at the conference would shape human relations and human rights for at least the next century. Blacks wanted to voice their concerns and help decide some of the critical issues that undoubtedly would affect their lives. They also wanted to be active participants at the UN conference. This collaboration did not happen. Initially, the U.S. government had no African Americans present at the United Nations' founding conference.

McNeill and her three black colleagues had at first decided that they would be more successful in helping to shape foreign and domestic policy at the UN conference if they worked with some of the black organizations of which they were active members. They believed, as did many of their black colleagues in these various organizations and as contemporary polls suggested, that they could present a list of black America's concerns at the conference. A *Negro Digest* survey taken in 1944, a year before the conference, for instance, indicated, "91 percent of northern and 85 percent of southern blacks wanted Afro-Americans to participate in the process." Some African American leaders, like Mary McLeod Bethune and A. Philip Randolph, had already begun organizing blacks to "agitate for global racial equality."[6]

Therefore, as United Nations conference participants prepared for the journey to San Francisco, interested black peace activists debated among themselves what issues were important to them. In doing so, a discernible shift became evident in their activism as they moved from black diasporic internationalism to Cold War globalism. Black peace activists began to confront issues that "though not race specific, affected them as a racially specific community."[7] Metz T. P. Lochard, editor in chief of the *Chicago Defender*, declared that "the World Security Conference in San Francisco had but one meaning to the Negro people—that is, how far democratic principles should be stretched to embrace the rights of [their] brothers in the colonies and to what extent the American Negro's own security [should] be guaranteed."[8]

To achieve this objective, various African American groups from around America sent letters and made telephone calls, in which they delivered their requests, to the State Department. Others prepared for representation at the UN conference. Although American government officials knew that blacks wanted to assume an active role in the proceedings in San Francisco, they refused to appoint any African American to the official delegation. State Department officials realized that blacks wanted to address America's racial problems but did not believe that the conference was the proper forum. Furthermore, some officials alleged, it was "un-American." Like all other citizens, African Americans were expected to "be patriotic." State Department officials further maintained that "the minority situation in the U.S. was a purely domestic issue" that should be "shielded from international debate. It," the Government reasoned, "remained outside a language that would link it to more broadly comprehended issues."[9]

It appeared that African Americans would have to find another forum in which to address race concerns, but they refused to accept the State

Department's position on this important issue. Instead they demanded that they be heard. After more pressure from the black community, the Department agreed to open certain sessions of the conference to the public and to certain members of the influential NAACP. The State Department appointed Walter White, secretary of the NAACP, W. E. B. DuBois, the NAACP director of special research, and Mary McLeod Bethune, NAACP vice president, as consultant-*observers* at the San Francisco sessions. These NAACP officers joined representatives of other influential American organizations, such as WILPF, the League of Women Voters, the Lions Club, the National Association of Manufacturers, and the National Education Association.[10]

Many blacks were not pleased with the appointments of Bethune, White, and DuBois. To them, the NAACP did not truly represent the black masses. Consequently, several African American activists went to San Francisco to monitor the activity of the three observers. In an effort to gain their support, DuBois, White, and Bethune decided to "receive counsel from groups as varied as the National Negro Insurance Association, the Knights of Pythias, and the National Association of Colored Graduate Nurses." They also corresponded with mainstream organizations, such as WILPF. White and the other two NAACP observers subsequently "planned to lobby for an international bill of rights, an end to the color bar at home and abroad, and colonial reform." DuBois called for a world bill of rights that "would hold nations accountable for how they treated people."[11] However, the major participants at the San Francisco conference had little concern for these issues.

As time passed, several black organizations kept in touch with the three official black representatives, advocated self-determination for the world's peoples, and called for a universal bill of rights. The organizations included the National Council of Negro Women, the Hampton Institute, the African Orthodox Church, and the Independent Order of St. Luke, all of whom sent delegates to San Francisco even though they could not attend the sessions of the UN founding conference. Their purpose was to keep abreast of developments through their own appointed observers. McNeill, Foster, Marshall, and Edwards were among the members of these various organizations.

Many of these all-black organizations, without official consultative status at the UN conference, believed more needed to be done to include African Americans. Just being there was not enough. While they reluctantly accepted the three official black observers' leadership, they wanted to help define African Americans' positions on the issues and therefore felt that blacks should have a voice. Thus a meeting was held at the Third Baptist Church in San Francisco to establish the coalition National Negro Organizations of America for World Security and Equality. This ad hoc organization included not only black political and social activists but also peace activists like Kittrell and Foster. Its members decided to wire their congressional representatives and demand, among other things, that the UN charter protect minority rights. Furthermore, they agreed to monitor Bethune, DuBois, and White to make certain that the three observers remained focused on black demands.[12]

Bethune, White, and DuBois did not disappoint members of their race. The three black observers rejected their status as mere onlookers and their ostensible inability to influence domestic and foreign policy. They refused to allow the white delegates, who composed 90 percent of the conference participants, to represent the concerns of the rest of the world's people, two-thirds of whom were nonwhite.[13] They did as much as they possibly could on behalf of blacks at the conference. To empower themselves, for instance, the three NAACP observers reached out to delegates of Ethiopia, Liberia, and Haiti by promoting a decolonization and racial equality agenda. They thought that they would be more effective if they could demonstrate that other people of color shared their concerns. Yet, in many ways, the delegates from those countries were like blacks in both America and colonized Africa—on the outside looking in as whites decided both their future and their place in the world.

Bethune, White, and DuBois were flabbergasted to learn that the three independent black states did not support decolonization and equality measures. The black Americans whom DuBois and the other two delegates represented were even more amazed.

Peace activist Flemmie Kittrell, who had worked with the Liberians for years, was especially astounded by the delegates' position on decolonization and racial equality. Although she understood Liberian delegates' concern that the hostile colonial powers around them might attack if they supported a human rights measure, Kittrell did not agree that their position and fear should be the sole basis for turning their backs on those suffering from colonization. She thought the Liberians would have understood better than any of the independent black states how important it was to adopt an anticolonial policy. For many years, Liberia had been a victim of American economic imperialism, and Kittrell had been one of the American government's ardent critics of such a policy in the African nation. Despite what the Liberian delegates claimed, Kittrell, who had traveled throughout Liberia and the neighboring countries of Nigeria and the Gold Coast, often as a WILPF delegate, knew that "there was a deep yearning for independence and self-government in those areas where colonialism was present."[14] Furthermore, Kittrell and Vera Chandler Foster, another peace activist who had done considerable peace work in various parts of Africa, as well as many other African Americans, would not believe one Ethiopian delegate's assertion that "a racial equality clause inserted in the United Nations Charter would do neither good nor harm."[15]

Meanwhile, the three NAACP observers refused to give up. Each decided that since they had worked with various leaders of the three independent states over the years, they might be more effective with the delegates if they approached them on an individual basis. And they did. In the end, Haitian delegates issued a statement that endorsed racial equality and human rights, but Ethiopia remained silent. Liberia did not change its position.

While meeting with delegates from Liberia, Haiti, and Ethiopia, the three observers learned that the American delegation had repeatedly refused to "place a human rights clause in the UN Charter or make specific proposals about racial equality."[16] Yet, despite their position, ministers representing the Big Four—America, China, Britain, and the Soviet Union—approved insertion of a human rights clause in the charter. They asked nations to "develop friendly relations among nations based on respect for the principle of equal rights and self-determination of peoples."[17]

Although this moment was historic for many of the conference's participants, it did not please African Americans in general and the NAACP observers in particular. They were grateful that the principle of human rights had been included in an international legal document. They were even feeling a little invincible, since the Big Four had acquiesced to popular demands to make equality a part of the UN charter. However, the African American community and the NAACP observers were concerned the lack of an endorsement of racial equality from the American delegation, and the charter itself did not provide a practical procedure for implementing actions on human rights violations. What did these omissions mean? For most African Americans, it was a message that racial injustice and the deliberate violation of one's human rights could, and would, continue in Cold War America. The American delegates devalued racial equality. What seemed even more ominous to black peace activists was the American delegates' lack of concern for a warless world.

Surely, they reasoned, these delegates understood that there could be no peace without freedom and no freedom without peace.

Mary McLeod Bethune, concerned about a possible postwar world full of turmoil and conflict, was equally concerned about the role of women. Although Bethune and the members of the National Council of Negro Women, whom she represented, wanted peace and justice for all persons, they also wanted the same rights and privileges as every other citizen. They were not alone for long in their demand for gender equality. Women's organizations in many countries eventually sent letters and petitions to delegates at the UN conference, urging it to adopt gender equality statutes.

Once again, the American delegation rejected all demands for a gender equality measure. Foreign policy historian Gayle Plummer maintains that the "U.S. delegation and its advisers knew that the [America national] Senate would not ratify the UN treaty if it considered it as infringing on domestic powers." She found this particularly true among those senators who had repeatedly opposed current civil rights legislation. Plummer added that some of the political leaders feared that an American commitment to gender and racial equality measures would ultimately lead to the "UN investigating or prosecuting America because of internal racial disputes."[18] It also meant that some Americans had no intention of adopting or implementing civil rights legislation.

African Americans clearly understood the actions of the American delegates and understood more than ever that they needed a voice in the proceedings in San Francisco. Many realized that if they ever were going to have a chance to influence foreign policy, they needed to be a part of an influential organization. Thus they began to seek support from either all-white or interracial organizations that had consultative status at the UN conference. One such organization was WILPF. During the last three months of the UN founding conference, the four veteran black members of WILPF pressured the peace group's representatives to ensure the American delegates remained focused on issues pertaining to colonialism and human oppression. During this time, they virtually left the NAACP and the other organizations to which they belonged.

As time passed, black peace activists were even more convinced that they needed WILPF's support and influence if they were to deal effectively with human rights issues in the future. Moreover, those black women who had considered peace work but had not committed themselves now felt that joining WILPF would prove to be in their best interest as members of an oppressed people. Therefore several African Americans joined over the next few years.

A year after World War II ended, WILPF's black membership had increased twofold. Although African American peace activists were unsuccessful in persuading American delegates to support a gender and racial equality clause in the UN charter, they were determined to be victorious in ensuring that the organization, and even the American government, enforced the UN charter's human rights clause. They felt somewhat hopeful when President Truman issued the Truman Doctrine on March 12, 1947. It asked Americans to accept the "great responsibilities in the struggle against Communism and the national mission to protect free institutions, representative government, free elections, guarantees of individual liberty, freedom of speech and religion, and freedom from political oppression throughout the world."[19] To those outside WILPF, it seemed like a contradiction in principles when black WILPFers supported the Truman Doctrine but also allowed known Communists to join WILPF. For the black WILPFers, however, it was not an inconsistency. For black peace activists, the protection of one's freedoms, which might include the right to espouse any political ideology as long as it did not jeopardize someone else's freedoms, was more important. Known Communists in WILPF had not given black peace activists or anyone else, for that reason, cause to believe that they were trying to either subvert the organization's peace efforts or impose their beliefs on peace activists. At this time, being a peace activist who supported Communism was not a major issue for African Americans in WILPF. None of them had met Communists in WILPF, especially black Communists.

Some peace activists were pleased to learn that the Truman Doctrine was widely supported by Americans. Despite America's response to the historic doctrine, black pacifists believed it was important that they keep their eyes on any developments that suggested a lack of consideration for underprivileged peoples. For example, when they learned that the black people of South Africa were protesting governmental mistreatment, African American peace activists immediately asked WILPF delegates to urge the UN to look into the matter.[20] Despite repeated pleas, the American-dominated United Nations would not involve themselves. Even though the UN refused to address the issue, black peace activists vowed to fight for the oppressed people of South Africa. They were pleased to have called attention to the situation in South Africa and forced the major powers, especially America, to take a public stand on human rights.

However, the American delegates at the UN did not like being forced into taking a public position on human rights, especially one that made them appear insensitive to the conditions of a colonized people. After all, the delegates considered themselves proud members of a model state, one that supported a democratic society for all people. A year later, the American delegates were viewed more favorably when Indians confronted them about discrimination in South Africa.

In 1948, at the third annual meeting of the United Nations General Assembly, India complained that East Indian nationals and their descendants in South Africa were being unjustly treated. The delegates decided to deal with this complaint differently. They adopted a resolution requiring South Africa not only to refrain from such discriminatory behavior but also to report at the next meeting on the steps it had taken to rectify the situation. The resolution was passed by a two-thirds majority, which signaled for some black peace activists a victory for domestic minorities. They felt that African Americans would benefit from the general tendency to consider underprivileged peoples elsewhere in the world. Their satisfaction, however, was dampened somewhat by the fact that America was one of several nations that voted against the resolution.

America's position on race and international politics, as well as that of Britain and several other nations, was further clarified in the late 1940s in South Africa. African American peace activists were appalled at America's actions in the area. The white Afrikaner-based Nationalist Party came to power in 1948 and began erecting apartheid, an elaborate system of racial separation and systematic, legally sanctioned discrimination against nonwhites, who comprised more than 80 percent of the South African population. America's desire to open South Africa to growing American trade and investment and to maintain access to South Africa's copious store of strategic raw materials took precedence, influencing America's position on apartheid in the UN. Moreover, the South African government garnered American support by portraying black aspirations as Communist-inspired and casting its own minority rulers as stalwart defenders of capitalism in Africa.[21] In addition, strong criticism of South Africa seemed difficult in light of America's own racially segregated society. Furthermore, America's burgeoning economic presence in South Africa after 1948, due to the cheap labor supply that apartheid ensured, provided the basis for a growing alliance between America and the white South African government.

Black peace activists meanwhile wondered whether America was prepared to lead the world toward a saner approach to human relations. To ensure that America was indeed prepared, black peace activists decided that it was crucial for them to become more involved in the UN and began to press for such an opportunity. They aimed to influence America's policy in Africa and other parts of the world where people were exploited.

Black peace activists finally received an opportunity to voice their concerns about the situation in South Africa at the first full meeting of the UN General Assembly in 1948. The Council on African Affairs, the Pan African Congress, the African National Congress, and the South African Indian Congress joined the peace activists. Through their combined efforts, discrimination and colonial representation issues, especially in South Africa, became the key agenda items at the first full session of the United Nations. Penny Von Eschen asserts, "Despite the protests of Prime Minister Jan C. Smuts of the Union of South Africa, the fears of the U.S. delegates, and the opposition of the British, the color and colonial issues [hung] like a specter over the entire proceedings of the United Nations General Assembly. . . . Matters concerning India, South Africa, Negro Americans and other oppressed minorities [had] entered the United Nations to stay."[22]

Over the next few years, several African American peace activists served in the United Nations either as WILPF delegates or as members of the American delegation; and each continued to link race issues with peace and freedom issues. For instance, in June 1958 President Dwight Eisenhower appointed peace activist Marian Anderson as a member of the American delegation to the United Nations for its thirteenth session.

Anderson, a nationally known opera singer, was one of the most notable peace activists to join WILPF after 1946. A native of Philadelphia, Anderson had been interested in peace work for some time. She became involved with WILPF just as the initial UN founding conference closed its final sessions and was indeed honored to be given such an appointment. In fact, she found it as exciting and challenging as her experiences as an internationally acclaimed opera singer. Anderson entered her UN office for the first time on September 19, 1946, and said simply, "I like it here."[23]

Anderson chose to serve on the Trustee Committee, which was concerned with the lands, mostly in Africa, that the UN supervised as trustee. Her special responsibility was to study the Cameroons and Togoland and to report to the committee on what she found. She also joined in the discussions and decisions about a wide range of issues and problems.

Anderson was an active delegate whose work and personal intervention helped speed up the granting of independence to the British and

French Cameroons and Togoland. As a UN delegate, Anderson spoke her mind when she felt the need. Once she had to announce that America opposed a special session of the UN General Assembly to take up the problems of the Cameroons. On that occasion, she raised diplomatic eyebrows by making it clear that she personally disagreed with the official American position. However, Anderson, as well as other black peace activists in WILPF, had met and decided that the UN needed to address the problems of the indigenous peoples of the Cameroons.[24]

Other members of the American delegation were impressed with Anderson's candor and hard work. Henry Cabot Lodge, who was the American ambassador to the UN and head of the delegation, had high praise for her: "Peace activist Marian Anderson was the most effective member of the U.S. delegation. She handled all topics assigned her with great skill, and, on the personal plane, was extremely well liked and respected by all."[25] Another member of the delegation said that he knew of no other woman, with the possible exception of Eleanor Roosevelt, who had earned the respect, esteem, and affection of so many people.[26] After her assignment with the UN was over in January 1959, Anderson resumed her singing career and continued to work for peace and freedom in other ways.

Other black peace activists served as UN consultants for WILPF or accompanied other WILPFers to lobby various sessions for world attention to the grievances of African Americans. In doing so, they internationalized the problem of racial discrimination and made some individuals not only more sensitive to the needs of the oppressed but also more likely to point to the UN charter's position on human rights whenever confronted with the issue. Such actions indicated that African Americans gained some influence in the powerful and important UN.

As blacks gained ground on the discrimination issue worldwide, WILPFers in America turned their attention in a different direction. They now focused on the Red Scare whose origin could be traced to the end of World War II.

Immediately after the declaration of peace in 1945, the Cold War between America and the Soviet Union began. American and Soviet domination in the post–World War II world meant that neither atomic weapons nor a peacetime military would be abandoned. Because peace activists were not aware of their government's plans, they continued into 1946 and beyond to press for abolition of both. They struggled to establish a permanent Fair Employment Practices Commission and to create real social, political, and economic equality for women, minorities, and refugees, and called for amnesty for conscientious objectors. They opposed the formation of the North Atlantic Treaty Organization, supported only part of the Truman Doctrine, and deplored the upsurge of anti-Soviet propaganda by the government and media.

Yet WILPF's goal of creating a peaceful, nonviolent, and warless world became increasingly difficult as the 1950s approached. The atomic bomb issue alone brought WILPF face to face with a completely new international trauma. By the late 1940s, development of atomic weapons had undoubtedly become one of WILPF's central concerns. In a chain-reaction response, the newly generated nuclear arms race led to the domestic horror of the McCarthy era, when the Communist threat became a national pastime and being a pacifist turned into a greater liability than ever before.

Peace activists realized, as early as 1945, the possibility of another Red Scare in America, as the controversial atomic bomb issue sparked the nuclear arms race.[27] However, they initially felt that there was no cause for alarm. As American-Soviet tensions increased during the postwar era, peace activists learned that the Soviets had become more interested in expediting their own research and, in August 1949, tested their first atomic bomb. Pacifists were somewhat bewildered when the American government claimed that the Communist nation could not have accomplished such a task without the use of spies. They became alarmed when, a year later, English authorities arrested Klaus Fuchs, a scientist from the Los Alamos research center where the atomic bomb had been assembled, after he confessed to giving secrets to Soviet agents. The arrests of Ethel and Julius Rosenberg, for allegedly recruiting and supervising a spy at Los Alamos, followed that of Fuchs. The Rosenbergs were later convicted of espionage and in 1953 were executed in the electric chair at Sing Sing prison.

Charges of disloyalty, treason, and un-Americanism, however, did not result entirely from the development of the bomb. The American government had a history of harassing dissenters that went back at least as far as World War I. After that war, Americans became increasingly afraid that the Communists would take over the American government. They believed this takeover would begin at the local level and work its way up. This unfounded fear continued over the years and turned to paranoia when the Soviets and the Americans emerged from World War II as the two world superpowers.

Paranoia about a Communist takeover was first fueled by Canadian claims that a Soviet spy ring was operating from within its borders. As a result, in 1947 President Harry Truman ordered investigations into the loyalty of well over three million America government employees. Three years later, employers fired anyone labeled a security risk. There were no avenues of recourse, and many careers were ruined. Soon men and women were being discharged simply because of guilt by association. No one was safe. By 1949, with the continuing development of Communist governments in Eastern Europe, anti-Communist sentiment in America reached an all-time high. In 1950, when Senator Joseph McCarthy claimed to have a list of more than two hundred names of State Department employees who were Communists, the hysteria entered a new stage. Now labeled "McCarthyism," the Red Scare evolved into a series of non-stop hearings before the House Committee on Un-American Activities (HUAC). Individuals, organizations, labor unions, members of the motion picture community, and countless others were ordered to appear before the committee.

The McCarthy era proved extremely trying for WILPF. Its members believed they were under suspicion for their antiwar activities, and they actually were. Several were called before the HUAC to explain their questionable activities. Moreover, during the 1950s, WILPF's membership decreased, many leaving to avoid harassment by the HUAC and other offices of the American government. National membership remained around 4,336 in January 1955.[28] Of this small number, the African American membership made up substantially less than 1 percent. Bertha McNeill was one of the few African American leaders of WILPF during the 1950s.[29] In fact, she was one of the few women of color anywhere in the organization in the late 1940s and 1950s. For many black women, peace activism had been labeled "un-American," a label most black pacifists did not want or need when fighting for racial justice.

The handful of black peace activists who remained in WILPF during these trying years actively engaged in peace work. They acted as though the paranoia rampant in larger society had nothing to do with them, even when it occurred within their respective WILPF branches. For example, in early 1954, the Denver branch was almost torn apart by unfounded accusations that some of its members were Communists. The rumors began as early as 1952, when some members questioned the loyalty of one of its most active members, Eunice Dolan, whose husband, Graham "Cozey" Dolan, had been the publisher of a Communist newspaper, *Challenge,* in the 1940s. Of course, Eunice Dolan's participation in her husband's political work and her guilt by association became a branch issue. Fearful that Communists were trying to take over the branch and that, when discovered, their loyalty would be questioned by the HUAC, several branch members resigned. Some members decided to stay and ignore the accusations, causing division within the branch. Such members often protested the accusations, reiterating that WILPF's avowed policy was "not to inquire into the politics or past activities of any prospective members" as long as they worked "WITHIN THE FRAMEWORK OF THE WIL"—which is what Eunice Dolan did.[30]

After WILPF released its position on Communism, the issue became less important. However, this feeling was short-lived. Less than two years later, William Fogarty, a Denver branch member, raised the issue again. In an article in the *Denver Post*, he accused Eunice Dolan of being an active WILPF member with "Communist sympathies."[31]

Local board members later decided that Fogarty had "acted in bad faith" by copying and distributing the *Post* article about Dolan. Reaction to Fogarty's claim was mixed. While some responded by resigning, others remained members and were publicly critical of Dolan. For instance, one woman, with a doctorate and a long career in the public schools, was distressed by the whole affair and resigned, taking with her another member who claimed, "I can't afford to stay in. . . . I have a job to consider—and my place in the community life."[32] On the other hand, another woman, a devout Christian Scientist, said she was "much more worried about Catholic dangers to the U.S." and could not find time to worry about Communist threats.[33]

The decision in Denver became worse. In early March, the Denver branch appealed to the national WILPF for help. Bertha McNeill, chair of the Committee on the Special Problems of Branches, began to examine the details of the affair to save the branch from complete disintegration. She was asked to resolve one of the most sensitive issues ever faced by either the national organization or its local branches.

After learning more about Fogarty and his intentions, McNeill took action. The traditional WILPF policy, however, was to allow branches complete autonomy. In this way, although some guidelines were mandated, the local membership could be as diverse and independent as possible. The national board realized that in this situation, it could not retain its hands-off policy. In mid-March 1954, the Committee on the Special Problems of Branches called an emergency meeting. Although McNeill and her assistants wanted the Denver women to solve their own problems, they took three decisive steps. First, McNeill offered recom-

mendations regarding the upcoming branch elections. On behalf of the committee, she urged the branch not to run a member for office who was "under suspicion" of being a Communist or any person who had joined the branch within the last year. The suggestion was designed to prevent William Fogarty from running for office. McNeill believed the branch's situation demanded a new slate of officers who would be "above question" in the community.[34] While McNeill had stayed with tradition and not dismissed members suspected to be Communists, she had introduced a new policy. Known Communists, or even those suspected of being Communists, could not hold any office within WILPF.

Second, McNeill sent one of the committee's members, Kitty Arnett, to Denver to offer practical advice and assistance. Third, McNeill wrote a letter to Fogarty, deploring his actions as "non-pacifist and unrepresentative of the methods of the Women's International League for Peace and Freedom." She lambasted Fogarty for not first bringing the problems to the attention of the national board so that much of the bad publicity could be avoided. She also commented that his method was "such a striking example" of what WILPF was not that the committee could not help but feel that the branch's complaints about him were warranted.[35] Arnett's visit to Denver did not produce the results the national board desired. She disagreed with committee member Mildred Scott Olmsted's suggestion that the election of new officers would solve the branch's problems, and told her so. Eunice Dolan resigned, and much of the publicity surrounding her membership subsided. Nonetheless, the leftist influence in the branch was still visible.

The Denver branch, like many of WILPF's other branches, continued to deal with red-baiting problems for the remainder of the 1950s. Moreover, Communism remained the dominant domestic and international peace issue at all levels of WILPF. African Americans, however, were more concerned about peace issues than Communism during the McCarthy era. Some, like Erna Prather Harris, publicly articulated their opposition to both McCarthyism and the House Un-American Activities Committee.[36] Most African American peace activists continued their peace work, seemingly unaffected by the pervasive fear around them. Even Erna Harris, an outspoken critic of Communism, continued her peace activism. For example, from July 23 to July 27, 1956, Harris served as a national delegate of the U.S. section of WILPF at the XIII Triennial Congress in Birmingham, England.[37] Women from Asia, Africa, and Europe, as well as Great Britain and the Americas, attended the Triennial Congress. Later

that year, from August 30 to September 2, Harris attended the World Constituent Assembly at the Peace Tower in Cardiff, Wales.[38] Women from all over the world interested in world citizenship joined Harris.

For many African American peace activists, however, 1950s red-baiting proved a double-edged sword: it prevented them from fully engaging in the struggle for world peace and freedom and deterred them from waging an international struggle for racial justice for America's Negro and any other of the world's oppressed peoples. Red-baiting was the unexpected peril of the decade and a half following World War II that had held so many promises for African Americans and other oppressed peoples in the world.

African American women who managed to continue their fight for freedom and justice during this era did so abroad. Flemmie Kittrell, who served as chair of WILPF's Committee on African Affairs, continued her peace work on both the North American and African continents. In 1955 she visited parts of India and expressed concern about the health, nutrition, and sanitation of the country's citizens. Dr. Kittrell decided to organize a home economics college at the University of Baroda in that country. Using a Fulbright grant, she worked as a professor at the university from August 1955 to September 1956. In addition to the home economics program, Kittrell established a research program for food nutrition at the school. She even taught a course in human nutrition.[39]

To Kittrell, the key to world peace lay in better understanding among peoples and nations. She felt that it was "up to the women of the world to bring this about through enlarged teacher exchange programs and higher education for women."[40] Dr. Kittrell believed she had a responsibility to improve understanding among American, African, and Asian women as part of her peace work. Furthermore, she felt that Americans bickering among themselves about unsubstantiated Communist infiltration in the American government and even in WILPF was not nearly as important as the obvious needs of the various groups living in either India or one of the African countries who were trying to recover from colonialism.

Another problem on the home front that soon occupied the attention of black peace activists was school desegregation. It was in this area that African Americans experienced major legal victories beginning in the 1950s. For instance, the American federal court system "reenacted the tension between domestic sovereignty and international demands for justice" in 1954 when attorneys for plaintiffs in *Brown v. Board of Education* began citing the United Nations charter as part of their arguments.

One legal scholar maintained that "the erosion of the legal dam to racial equality continued with international human rights laws serving as a present but uncredited force."[41]

Although African American peace activists were ecstatic to witness favorable court rulings against racial injustices, they could not become complacent. Too many white Americans were still opposed to equal opportunities for all citizens. Some black peace activists were surprised to learn that even some of their colleagues in WILPF shared such sentiments. This paradox first became evident after the May 17, 1954, *Brown v. Board of Education* ruling.

In *Brown*, all nine Supreme Court justices agreed that legally sanctioned segregation of public schools violated the equal-protection clause of the Fourteenth Amendment. In a simple, straightforward opinion, Chief Justice Earl Warren argued that separate schools were "inherently unequal" and deprived black children of equal educational opportunities. However, one court decision by itself could not produce a revolution in race relations. Bowing to political pressures and the practical problems of education, the Supreme Court later ruled that school desegregation need not be immediate; it should proceed "with all deliberate speed." Ten years after the *Brown* decision, only about 1 percent of African children in the South attended desegregated schools.[42]

Resistance to desegregation hardened after the *Brown* case. Most white southerners protested this "invasion of states' rights"; some denounced the ruling as part of a Communist plot to destroy "the white race"; many pledged massive resistance to school integration. The Ku Klux Klan was revived, and a new organization, the White Citizens Council, became a powerful force in many areas. Not all members of the Klan and Citizens Council endorsed violent resistance, but some did use force against blacks who "didn't know their place."[43] In 1955, for instance, a crowd of whites lynched a young black man, Emmett Till, for allegedly whistling at a white woman.

Southerners also used legal and political stratagems to delay changes in race relations. In 1957, 101 members of Congress signed the Southern Manifesto, a protest against "federal usurpation" of states' rights, and southern senators employed the filibuster to block civil rights legislation. A segregationist image was essential to political survival in many southern states; after a moderate young lawyer, George C. Wallace, lost badly to a segregationist, he announced that he would never be "out-niggraed again."[44]

The most spectacular example of official resistance came in 1957 when Arkansas governor Orval Faubus defied a federal court order to desegregate Little Rock High School and used his national guard to keep African American children out of the building. With national authority openly challenged, the Eisenhower administration could not avoid the issue. Although never a firm supporter of school desegregation, Eisenhower placed the Arkansas National Guard under federal control, augmented it with regular army troops, and enforced the court order. The following year, Arkansas officials tried to block desegregation through the courts. Meeting in an emergency session, the Supreme Court rejected Arkansas' claim that the state need not obey national court orders and buried once again the states' rights argument. After the Little Rock incident, the Supreme Court declared unconstitutional the evasive tactics of closing down public schools and gerrymandering school districts, and it pressed southern school districts for realistic desegregation plans.

Desegregation of public schools in the South gained the support of a number of influential people and organizations. As soon as the Supreme Court made its ruling in *Brown*, for example, the Civil Rights Committee of WILPF asked the peace group to help enforce the decision reached in the case. Black peace activists Bertha McNeill, Bessie McLaurin, and Erna Prather Harris, who led the committee, believed that WILPF should act immediately because to hesitate was "to show contempt for the Supreme Court ruling."[45] In many ways, they were not wrong; however, it was not easy for them to persuade WILPF leaders to support such a controversial issue. A few black peace activists were amazed that WILPF's national board had reservations about endorsing and supporting the enforcement of the landmark *Brown v. Board* ruling.

Finally, after much prodding from McNeill, McLaurin, and Harris, WILPF's national board agreed to endorse the Civil Rights Committee's position to help enforce the *Brown* ruling. WILPF officials finally agreed to "oppose the use of the more subtle but equally violent means of discrimination against the minority peoples" of their "own country." They also pledged to use all their ability in nonviolent means of desegregation, knowing that in the process their youth would "be freed for fuller living" and their growth would "be more abundant."[46]

Soon after adopting this position, the national board's officers, as well as those of the various national committees and interested local branches, began to take steps to ensure integration of public schools in the South. Some WILPFers spent the remainder of the 1950s participating in ral-

lies and demonstrations as they confronted this and other domestic racial injustices.

Meanwhile, other WILPFers continued their involvement on the international scene. In June 1959, Dr. Kittrell was one of three women to
represent WILPF at the Nongovernmental Organizations Conference on
the Eradication of Prejudice and Discrimination held in Geneva. This
conference undoubtedly was welcomed by many in the peace community who had begun to see what lay ahead for people all over the world.
While at the conference, Kittrell served on the Education Commission.[47]
There she was given the opportunity to suggest ways for nations to work
together more harmoniously.

One month later, Kittrell attended the XIV Triennial Congress of
WILPF in Stockholm. The congress adopted as its theme "Alternatives
to Violence." It was realized that new and better policies must be formu-
lated before real progress could come.

Flemmie Kittrell and 249 other delegates from sixteen countries gath-
ered in the Parliament House. Many visitors, observers, and fraternal delegates were present, among them one representative each from the League
of Polish Women and the East German Frauenrat; and from the Soviet
Women's Committee, Maria Ovajanikova, editor of *Soviet Woman*.[48]
Since the last congress, death had taken a heavy toll of the League's oldest members, but younger women were coming forward to revivify the
movement. Three new members, for example, were elected to the Executive Committee that year, one being Dr. Kittrell.

The congress was divided into three commissions for detailed discussions of policy; they were concerned with human rights, Poland settle-
ments, and world disarmament and development. Dr. Dorothy Hutchin-
son, an American on the political commission, expressed the broad aims
of the congress: "WILPF sets its sights far higher than the mere preven-
tion of World War III. Our concern is for positive human well-being and
for a peace, which are not simply the absence of war but the presence of
justice, freedom and a richer life for all men. We envisage political settle-
ments, not only as relieving the present intolerable tensions and dangers
but also as setting free the material resources of the world and the minds
of men to serve the physical and spiritual needs of mankind."[49]

The human rights commission, on which Dr. Kittrell chose to serve,
maintained that human rights must constantly be renewed and emphasized the importance of dissent. Kittrell's views could be seen very clearly
in the commission's aims: "The tyranny of the majority must not be

permitted to stifle new ideas, even when these raise fundamental questions as to the established order. If change does not come by peaceful means through the interchange of ideas in the marketplace of world opinion, it will eventually come by violence, to which we in the Women's International League for Peace and Freedom are unalterably opposed."[50]

Dr. Kittrell was quite pleased with the goals established at the Stockholm Congress. She felt that they characterized solutions sought in the spirit of goodwill. Hence Kittrell's efforts, as well as those of her interested colleagues, had been fruitful during one of America's most critical eras. The period from 1945 to 1960 undoubtedly offered as much ambiguity as clarity for African American peace activists. As the nation moved beyond the 1950s, the perils of the postwar years appeared to have passed; the promise of the American Dream once again seemed in view for most African Americans. Certainly there were lingering problems: McCarthyism at home and the explosive issue of race relations. Social and political critics, however, seemed to accentuate the positive. The national security establishment and the United Nations finally seemed, to many, capable of safeguarding the nation's global interests. Congress seemed determined to bring about racial justice, passing several pieces of civil rights legislation. Moreover, the Supreme Court made numerous rulings favorable to African Americans.

Beneath the surface, however, the unresolved postwar tensions remained, only to become major issues of contention in the 1960s. African American peace activists continually pointed to some of these tensions as they linked race with peace and freedom. New to the peace movement and to WILPF, this group of peace activists, unlike many of their foremothers, were much more cantankerous and quicker to challenge the status quo. They brought to the organization different historical experiences that influenced their peace activism. Like their foremothers, these women continued to link race to peace and freedom as they addressed domestic issues. Their international activism, however, differed from that of their foremothers. They no longer focused exclusively on Africa and the black diaspora in their quest for universal peace and freedom.

Redefining Racial Justice

Here, There, and Everywhere

7

1960-1975

In 1967, African American peace activist Enola Maxwell, minister of the Olivet Presbyterian Church in San Francisco, never thought that her willingness to serve as a spiritual adviser to the controversial Black Panthers would create such a stir within pacifist circles. While WILPF had always supported peace and freedom, its members could not endorse a group as radical as the Panthers. Despite the feelings of WILPF and other peace groups about the Black Panthers, Maxwell chose to remain with them. She believed that those who did not know the Black Panthers for Self-Defense as she did would never understand her reasons for working with them on any level.

Maxwell definitely did not condone the violence sometimes attributed to the Black Panthers. Nor did she agree with their public display of weapons and their militant and confrontational rhetoric, both of which often made people uncomfortable. However, Maxwell did agree with their antiwar position. The group's leader, Bobby Seale, had argued forcefully against the Vietnam War, thereby setting the tone and voicing the wider concerns of the group.

When Maxwell was asked by her church body to resign, she proudly stood before members of Olivet Presbyterian Church and said, "I am a

spiritual adviser to the Black Panthers for Self-Defense and I will not resign from that position."[1] She later stated in an interview with peace historian Judith Adams, "Everybody, of course, was scared of the Black Panthers. I was going to their meetings, and I was encouraging them to use nonviolence. . . . I was a Martin Luther King person."[2] Maxwell did not perceive the Black Panthers the same way most of her contemporaries did. She saw them as another group seeking freedom and justice for everyone. She once said, "If the day comes when I can't speak for freedom and justice, I've lived long enough. That's all there is to it. I have nothing else that's more important than speaking for peace, justice and equality."[3] Hence Maxwell, like so many other African Americans, whether peace activists or not, believed that they had to use whatever resources were available to achieve freedom and justice. Their life experiences required that they sometimes establish questionable relationships to reach those two lofty goals.

The 1960s was a trying decade for African Americans in general and black peace activists in particular. Wartime economic gains produced a desire among black Americans for broader attacks on discrimination. Even the climate of the Cold War seemed to call for measures to improve race relations at home.

The civil rights issue, however, provided only another example of the gap between promise and performance. There was a good deal of popular opposition even to limited moves toward equality. Throughout the nation, racists violently opposed the drive for integration. The upsurge in white violence was one more impediment to the pace of national action against racial discrimination.

For many African Americans and liberals, advances in the commitment to legal equality came too slowly. As the United States proclaimed that it, not the Soviet Union, offered the proper model for other nations to follow, continued legal discrimination against nonwhites in America itself proved difficult to explain.

Black peace activists realized this contradiction and used America's own 1960s foreign policy to expose its hypocrisy. In doing so, they helped WILPF build its international links to various countries. As the organization's numbers increased, and as it continued to attract more African American women interested in peace work, its influence could be seen and felt in the construction of its 1960s peace agenda.

For the first time in its history, WILPF could boast of a sizeable black membership. The peace group had at least forty black activists on its

membership rolls by then. The women who joined WILPF in this decade included, among others, Sadie Sawyer Hughley, Coretta Scott King, Erna Prather Harris, Fannie Lou Hamer, Angela Davis, Bessie McLaurin, Eartha Kitt, and Diane Nash. They were indeed a diverse group of peace activists who were engaged in, among other things, a wide range of professional activities and represented practically every geographical region in America. Each peace activist in her own way proved to be an asset to WILPF.

Sadie Sawyer Hughley and her husband, J. Neal Hughley, for example, an economist and a clergyman, settled in Durham, North Carolina, in the early 1950s. Both were employees at the North Carolina College for Negroes (now North Carolina Central University). Sadie Sawyer Hughley was a part-time librarian. Both Hughleys clearly were middle-class African Americans from a family of activists and pacifists.

Before attending Columbia University, Sadie Sawyer lived in Texarkana, Arkansas, where she enjoyed the comforts of a well-to-do household. Her parents were community activists who instilled in their six children the ideas of peace and freedom for all humankind.[4]

Sadie Hughley's husband, J. Neal, understood and respected her work as a peace activist. He too was a devout pacifist who supported the goals espoused by WILPF. In 1961 Mr. Hughley joined the Chapel Hill–Durham branch of WILPF, where his wife was an active member. As peace activists, the Hughleys often worked side by side on peace issues.

Like many of their foremothers in WILPF, both Mr. and Mrs. Hughley linked peace and freedom with domestic race issues. This bond was quite evident during the civil rights movement in the 1960s. Mrs. Hughley pointed out more than once the hypocrisy in America's society, and even in WILPF, as the leadership tried to deal with issues of racial injustice and human oppression everywhere except in America. The Hughleys did not believe that America could address racial injustices anywhere until its society was free of racism.[5]

Another peace activist couple, Coretta Scott King and Rev. Dr. Martin Luther King Jr., held similar beliefs. However, although both Scott King and her spouse were concerned about world peace, Dr. King became extremely involved in black America's civil rights struggle, thus leaving little time for the peace movement. Focusing primarily on world peace, Scott King eventually joined WILPF because she was convinced that the "women of the world, united without any regard for national or racial divisions, [could] become a most powerful force for international peace and brotherhood."[6] Therefore she became increasingly active in the peace movement in the 1960s, eventually becoming internationally recognized for her efforts.

Peace activist Erna P. Harris also became nationally recognized in the 1960s for her critical attacks on America's social and racial ills. Instead of demonstrating, however, Harris used the pen as her weapon. It had proven in the past to be an extremely effective tool in generating support for racial justice. In the 1940s, for instance, Harris exposed the Red Cross's practice of segregating blood plasma according to whether it was from European American or African American donors. Harris quoted a nurse as saying, "Most of our army officers are Southerners, and they didn't want to tell parents that they were putting Negro blood in their boys' veins."[7] After the story broke, the Red Cross claimed to have stopped the practice.

After World War II ended, Harris continued her fight against racial injustice. Her efforts finally led her to a local WILPF meeting in San Francisco in 1950. Less than a year later, she was convinced that WILPF offered an excellent forum in which she could further her struggle for justice and social reform. Soon after joining the San Francisco branch, however, the fear of Communism nearly closed its doors. Harris then turned her attention to other organizations interested in race work. She did a considerable amount of work with the San Francisco Cooperative Program. Later, like her colleague Maxwell, she served as adviser to the Black Panthers, the militant civil rights group organized in 1966.[8] A year later, the Black Panther Party staged a "Stop the Draft" week at the Oakland Induction Center.[9] Like the majority of African Americans, the Black Panthers opposed the draft because they believed it was racist and an attempt to commit genocide against blacks.

Black peace activists who had ties to the Black Panthers, like Harris and Maxwell, advised them not to fight in "colonial wars of aggression."[10] Furthermore, the militant organization's advisers made certain that Panther members did not violate the party's bylaws. For example, rule 6 of the Black Panther Party's bylaws stated that "no party member [could] join any army or force other than the Black Liberation Army."[11] Many African American peace activists were intrigued by the party's willingness to fight for the right to avoid war. In some ways, one of America's most radical organizations adopted a peace goal.

After the Red Scare tapered off, Harris returned to WILPF and peace work. Her assertiveness and aggressiveness, as well as leadership skills, enabled her to move quickly upward in WILPF's ranks. By the early 1960s, she had become an active and important member of the national board, serving two terms as vice president of its southwestern region. Harris helped to build a stronger alliance between the national board in Philadelphia and various branch offices in the western part of America.

WILPF also attracted several African Americans from the South in the 1960s. This step was an important one for the organization. Of all the women who joined southern branches of WILPF, the most prominent was Fannie Lou Hamer. WILPF's national leaders believed that securing Hamer was a major coup for the peace group.

Hamer had repeatedly demonstrated a commitment to a society free of racial injustice. WILPF's national leadership was especially impressed by Hamer's vigor and ability to organize, almost single-handedly, a political machine that would forever change the direction of politics in Mississippi. They were equally amazed that Hamer did so without benefit of a formal education.

A sharecropper's wife, Hamer brought fellow Mississippians face to face with their intolerance, racism, bigotry, hatred, and hypocrisy in the late 1950s and early 1960s. She often asked, "Is this America?" The question referred to the climate of hysteria that permeated the very fiber of Mississippi, and America, as African Americans battled to achieve justice and equality. "Is this America?" acknowledged that a vital segment of American society was being continually oppressed. Hamer was determined to change things, especially in Mississippi. In her quest for social justice, Hamer never lost the indomitable spirit of a woman with a mission.

In 1961 she and a few other Mississippians set the wheels in motion for the Mississippi Freedom Democratic Party (MFDP). As the civil rights movement gained momentum, white Mississippians heightened their efforts to keep blacks from becoming registered voters. Locked out of the Mississippi Democratic Party, Hamer and a few others formed the MFDP in 1964. The goal of the party was to expose the segregation principles of the Mississippi Democratic Party. The MFDP favored the liberal principles of the national party and rejected the "old politics" of the state Democratic Party by attempting to replace it with a system based on participatory democracy.[12] As one of the party's cofounders, Hamer was eventually appointed cochair. In that position, she spoke on behalf of the organization in various forums.

Under Hamer's leadership, the MFDP continually fought against the legitimacy of the lily-white faction. The party, however, had little national support. Furthermore, countless efforts were made to discredit the MFDP. Consequently, it began a slow descent into obscurity but left its mark on politics in Mississippi, as well as national Democratic Party politics. More important, it catapulted to fame a woman who sought to expose America's hypocrisy and dispel the image of America as being the land of the free and home of the brave. Through the MFDP, Hamer brought America one step closer to dismantling the barriers that kept African Americans on the periphery of political involvement. She was undoubtedly committed to the eradication of racial injustice and the attainment of peace, freedom, and equality for everyone.

WILPF was eager to recruit Hamer for other reasons. The MFDP's activism received a great deal of media exposure, and so did Fannie Lou Hamer. WILPF had anxiously waited to bring her on board as it sought to increase and diversify its membership in the 1960s. If Hamer joined WILPF, she would be the group's second African American member who was also involved in state and national politics. The first was Shirley Chisholm, a New York congresswoman who later ran for president of the United States and whose work is surveyed later in this study.

Members of the national WILPF first approached Hamer at the March 7, 1965, Selma to Montgomery March. Both Bessie McLaurin and Sadie Sawyer Hughley were asked by the national executive board to encourage Hamer to join the peace group. McLaurin, who chaired the Civil Rights Committee of WILPF at the time, and Hughley, an officer of the Chapel Hill–Durham branch of the organization, met with Hamer at a WILPF-sponsored peace vigil immediately after the march. Hughley recalled that "it didn't take much arm twisting to get Fannie Lou to join. She had already heard of the organization and had attended several of its peace rallies in Mississippi. She knew what WILPF stood for and, therefore, seemed eager to join."[13]

Hamer brought the same spunk and courage into WILPF that she was known for as a civil rights activist. She waged a critical attack on the Vietnam War that was as caustic as any she waged about the racial injustices in Mississippi and elsewhere in America. Hamer was indeed a refreshing change for WILPF, which had become known for its middle-aged, middle-class elitist women. She brought a new kind of vitality to the group.

Hamer's acceptance by national WILPF members also indicated that the organization's leadership was beginning to understand that if it truly wanted to increase its African American leadership, it would have to reach out to women who had been traditionally excluded. Other African American women who joined in the 1960s were an affirmation of this gradual change in attitude toward those who might not have fit the organization's carefully designed description of the ideal peace activist. Their acceptance is also symbolic of a changing American society. For instance, both Diane Nash, a young civil rights activist, and Angela Davis, a well-known Communist, joined WILPF in the 1960s.

Nash was first courted by WILPF leaders and asked to join after her graduation from college. Nash had grown up in Chicago and spent a year at Howard University in Washington, D.C., before transferring to Fisk University in Nashville, Tennessee, in 1959. Experiencing the jim crow system there for the first time, Nash felt "stifled and boxed in since so many areas of living were restricted." Raised as a Catholic, she viewed the desegregation movement as "applied region" [sic] designed to "bring about a climate in which there [was] appreciation of the dignity of man and in which each individual [was] free to grow and produce to his fullest capacity." She saw the effects of southern barriers to black advancement in the South's "slow progress in industrial, political and other areas" and in the "weakening of American influence abroad as a result of race hatred."[14]

Nash had developed a nonviolent consciousness before joining WILPF. She had also begun to link racial oppression in America with peace and freedom issues, as well as with human oppression in other parts of the world. In other words, Nash had already begun to think about peace and freedom domestically and globally before joining the peace group.[15]

Angela Davis also developed a political consciousness early in life, one that later influenced her peace ideology. A brilliant graduate student in philosophy at the University of California at San Diego, Davis developed a powerful interest in the issues of race and class inequality. In 1963 and 1964, she was an exchange student in France. As a Brandeis University junior, she had the opportunity to meet North and South Vietnamese students opposed to the government in Saigon and began to understand the nature of their opposition to the American military presence in South Vietnam. Davis had taken part in increasingly militant demonstrations against American imperialism as a graduate student in philosophy at the University of Frankfurt from 1965 to 1967.[16]

By the time Davis returned to America in 1967, she had embraced socialism. She had also become committed to applying Marxist-Leninist thought to the struggle of oppressed people for liberation. She was a member of the ChenLumumba Club, an all-black division in the Los Angeles chapter of the Communist Party. While actively working with the ChenLumumba Club, Davis met some members of WILPF in Los Angeles and later decided to join the peace group.

WILPF had always straddled the fence on the issue of Communism. The national board had tried to present WILPF as non-Communist, but it was still, as one peace historian claims, "anti-anti-Communist."[17] As such, WILPF supported the right of Communist Party members to free speech even though its leaders disagreed with the Communist Party's politics. This position by WILPF's leadership attracted propeace Communists like Angela Davis. She was equally fascinated with the organization's antiwar activities. Davis vehemently opposed the Vietnam War and often linked aggression in the war with racism and repression at home. WILPF provided her with a forum in which to wage a battle against the Vietnam War and the subsequent oppression of Vietnam's people.

Davis's membership, however, was a mixed blessing for WILPF. On one hand, she could provide the organization with the kind of commitment to world peace and freedom that it so desperately needed from its members. However, on the other hand, her mere association with the organization could cause the HUAC and other government organizations to monitor closely the activities of the organization and engage in red-baiting tactics against the members.[18]

Several of WILPF's members, including Bertha McNeill, Vera Chandler Foster, Thelma Marshall, and Mildred Scott Olmsted, could not forget how trying the McCarthy era had been for the organization. These women remembered all too well how the strong arm of McCarthyism was felt from the national board down to its local branches. During those years, membership did not expand, and meeting places were sometimes hard to find. Although McNeill, Foster, and other veteran members had not forgotten the McCarthy scare, they refused to allow red-baiting to interfere with their more important cause of peace work anymore than they had permitted it to present problems a decade earlier. Hence Davis's commitment to world peace and freedom was much more important to WILPFers than her political affiliation.

Therefore Davis was one of many black peace activists to wage a critical attack on the world's social and political ills in the 1960s. In doing so, she, like the others, internationalized America's racial problems and brought attention to the civil rights movement. Whenever possible, 1960s peace activists linked civil rights issues with certain global issues, namely the continuous conflict between the Soviets and America, South African apartheid, the unexpected Cuban missile crisis, and the controversial Vietnam War. It was during the 1960s that African American peace activists confronted issues that, though not always race-specific, affected them as a racially specific community.

In 1961 the national WILPF organization sponsored its first seminar intended to establish a network with Soviet women. This meeting, at Bryn Mawr College in Pennsylvania, opened the door to many other interchanges held in both America and the Soviet Union. Some of these conferences proved fruitful for all parties represented. For example, in 1964, in particular, Vera Chandler Foster accompanied eight other WILPF women across the European continent to Moscow for a second conference with Soviet women. She was quite concerned about the impending exploitation of weaker nations by stronger ones if the arms race was not prohibited. The focus of the Soviet Congress was to allow Soviet and American women to determine ways to ease the arms race and to begin talks between the two superpowers. WILPF hoped that the American delegation would also exert pressure on Soviet disarmament policy while in the USSR.

The atmosphere at the conference was described as one of "growing hopefulness," as Foster and others agreed to the following: a general reduction of tensions due to the Test Ban Treaty; the agreement not to put vehicles carrying nuclear weapons in outer space; and the direct, "hot-link" communication between Washington and Moscow. These women wanted "general and complete disarmament." Foster and the other American delegates emphasized that peaceful coexistence was not enough. They maintained there must be peaceful cooperation between countries with differing systems.[19]

Erna P. Harris, another black peace activist and delegate to the conference, perceived it as a series of grassroots discussions about problems confronting the USSR and America in their mutual relationship. She also saw it as an attempt to find solutions palatable to the respective governments and to the people. Harris maintained that they "did reach accord on many things" in their "search for common grounds because both sides could speak frankly with each other" due to their "unofficial status."[20] She was quite impressed with the Soviet delegates.

Moreover, Harris believed the peace conference was successful. American and Russian delegates agreed on the need for the "achievement of a comprehensive test ban treaty; conclusion of a non-aggression pact between NATO and Warsaw treaty member states; the establishing of nuclear-free zones; noninterference in each nation's internal affairs, coupled with respect for national sovereignty; exchanges in fields of science, culture and broad economic trade between Russia and the United States"; and as previously mentioned, "universal and total disarmament under international control." The only dissonant note in the peace conference was the "vague feeling some American delegates received that the Soviet women were reluctant to speak in any way but generalities about their government's actions toward peace." However, instead of trying to convert Soviets to their way of thinking, the American peace delegates "tried to understand them."[21]

Harris was equally impressed with the Soviet's treatment and perception of African Americans and believed that America could learn something about race relations from them. For instance, on civil rights, Harris said, "The delegation's host refrained from using the U.S.'s troubles as a means of embarrassment and seemed genuinely concerned about the Negroes' lot. You know," she added, "the Soviet Union—and each member state—have laws much more far-reaching than the pending civil rights legislation here, forbidding discrimination," although discrimination still existed despite the laws. That discrimination, she maintained, "[was] directed at Jewish citizens and [was] similar to anti-Semitism per se in addition to being politically motivated." Harris further noted that the "Jewish culture [did] not conform with this kind of government and so there [was] always a raw edge evident between the country and the Jewish people."[22] She then linked her peace work in Moscow with civil rights issues in America when she maintained,

> At the Moscow Conference, we discussed disarmament ways to strengthen cooperation in the United Nations, and the German problem. But after a school was burned in Alabama, we talked about how the racial turmoil in the United States affects international tension. The Soviet delegation was particularly concerned about the violence involved. I don't think they want our country to fall apart, but they realize that unless we can correct our international image, we won't be leading anyone much longer.[23]

Harris's last comments were surprising to both black and white Americans. Some could not believe that Harris suggested that America might learn something about race relations from the Soviets. From all that they had heard and witnessed, the Soviet government's leadership was composed of a group of Communists who found pleasure in torturing their masses. Furthermore, many Americans reasoned, the Soviets had one of the worst human rights records of any developed nation. Hence they saw the Soviets as a threat and any contact with them treasonous.[24]

The reaction of Americans to Harris's comments did not surprise her. She had felt the same way about the Soviets until she had the opportunity to engage in dialogue with them. "Perhaps," she thought, "Americans were reacting out of ignorance. If they had met the Soviets and talked with them," as she had done, "maybe they would have a different perception. They would understand that there were some Soviets, especially women, who wanted the same thing that [Americans] wanted."[25]

Another international peace link that activists built in the 1960s was with Latin America, a region of great concern to WILPF. In much of the world, Latin America had long been seen as part of America's domain. The terms of the Monroe Doctrine of 1823 stated that foreign nations outside the hemisphere were unwelcome in the area, and in 1904, the Roosevelt Corollary to the Doctrine provided for American military intervention if those nations south of the U.S. border seemed unsettled or in danger of foreign interference. These two policies gave America the unilateral power to make decisions and take actions that determined the fate of Central and South Americans and all the peoples of the Caribbean. WILPF spoke out against American military presence in the area and especially against American colonization of Puerto Rico. To WILPF women, the 1954 invasion of Guatemala, the 1965 invasion of the Dominican Republic, and American troop placement in Puerto Rico, Cuba, and Central America seemed ominous.

The greatest insult to peace in the Americas during this period was the Bay of Pigs invasion in 1961. American government leaders were concerned that the Cuban Revolution of January 1959 had been successful. Fidel Castro, the leader of the new government, established the first Communist nation in the Americas. With the Monroe Doctrine as justification, first President Eisenhower and then President Kennedy planned secret invasions of the island, claiming that Castro was being controlled by Moscow and therefore Cuba was under foreign control. Eisenhower, and later Kennedy, authorized the CIA to train a volunteer force of Cuban exiles to return to Cuba to overthrow the new government. Much to their surprise when the American troops arrived at Playa Giron (the Bay of Pigs), they met with organized resistance and total failure.

Immediately after the failure of the Bay of Pigs invasion, the national board of WILPF issued a statement demanding that Cuban exiles not be encouraged to continue in their vendetta with Castro and that under no circumstances should they be given weapons or trained for the military. WILPFers also wanted America to end its economic boycott of Cuba, stressing that friendly relations with the country were desirable and historically natural and that to continue the present policy would only encourage the island's reliance on trade and support from the Soviet Union. A year later, they were proven correct when Cuba's request for placement of Soviet-made missiles to deter further American aggression initiated the Cuban missile crisis. Although people all over the world were frightened by how close the confrontation came to nuclear war, when it was over, America continued its economic boycott and political harassment of Cuba and the Soviet Union. WILPF members continued to protest.

It was not surprising that African American peace activist Erna Prather Harris helped lead the movement by WILPF against America's treatment of Cuba. This time her position was consistent with the organization's stand against American intervention in Latin America. It also reflected their point of view that Communist nations should be integrated into the "democratic" world so that they might benefit from its openness.

Harris was so adamantly opposed to America's intervention in Cuban and Soviet affairs that she wrote to Hubert Humphrey, a U.S. senator on the Foreign Relations Committee. She maintained that America had acted too hastily and without respect for the indigenous peoples of Cuba and the Soviet Union. Harris was also extremely critical of Humphrey for his views on Cuba. Humphrey replied that he emphasized in the Senate that the president "[had] made it unmistakably clear" that any attempt by Cuba "to become an offensive military base of significant capacity for the Soviet Union" would be met with the requisite degree of force by America. He added that America, threatened by the massive buildup of offensive weapons in Cuba and continuing Soviet deceit, acted courageously and with full justification in the quarantine of Cuba. Humphrey justified American action against Cuba and the Soviet Union by maintaining that it was a preventive action. When Harris expressed concern that America's actions would not lead to a peaceful resolution, Humphrey insisted that the president had "chosen a course which allow[ed] the maximum time for a peaceful settlement if the Soviet government [was] willing to dismantle its nuclear weapons . . . stationed in Cuba."[26] Despite Humphrey's explanations, Harris did not change her views about America's involvement in Cuba. She also remained greatly concerned about American relations with Latin America and did not hesitate to let American officials know how she personally felt about their involvement in the region.

Meanwhile, Harris also led the fight by WILPF in the 1960s against apartheid in South Africa. For the second time in two decades, black peace activists attempted to link WILPF with South Africa and apartheid. In this case, Harris connected the civil rights struggle waged by African Americans for political, economic, and social equality with the struggle by South Africans against political and economic disempowerment, as they unsuccessfully tried to end apartheid on their own. Harris noted that the unresolved racial inequalities in South Africa would have devastating effects on the entire continent as well as on people of African descent all over the world. This trickle-down effect, so to speak, would ultimately harm the "relationship of white and nonwhite members of the human race." Harris expressed concern that, if left unresolved, the problem of apartheid in South Africa could lead to a race war. The only hope for peace, she insisted, was for other countries to take a stand against apartheid. Such "cooperation between that continent and the rest of the world" would undoubtedly bring about world peace.[27]

Harris asked fellow members of WILPF to support, either as part of the peace organization or as individual workers, total economic sanctions against South Africa. And she insisted that WILPF not stop there. Instead she wanted the peace organization to take practical steps to assist in positive peacemaking within South African society. Harris wanted her peace activist colleagues to influence public opinion through education and information, and to press cultural and athletic visitors to South Africa to refuse invitations unless they could perform before mixed audiences or compete with nonsegregated teams. Furthermore, she asked them to apply the "shopping-basket" boycott as a form of demonstration and to arouse public opinion.[28]

Harris's plea to WILPF did not go unheeded. The peace group did not hesitate to endorse a policy on South African apartheid that had been drafted mainly by its black members. WILPF consistently spoke out against apartheid in South Africa, *making it one of the first American organizations to do so publicly.*[29]

The women lobbied American leaders, who sanctioned extensive trade with the minority-controlled white South African government, to exert pressure on South Africa to abolish apartheid, just as America was attempting to eliminate racial oppression at home. In 1965, for example, WILPFers organized a boycott of products and investments in Mississippi. Among the companies targeted were Armstrong Tire, International Paper, International Telephone and Telegraph, Kraft Foods, Proctor and Gamble, Pet Milk, Borden, Swift Dairy Products, and Hunt's Foods. In this effort, the organizers pressed for American economic sanctions against South Africa until apartheid ended.[30] The women also stressed the allocation of American aid to help all the developing African nations. In such an effort, the women preferred that the money be dispersed through such UN organizations as UNICEF, UNESCO, and the World Health Organization. WILPF thought it would be great if America shared its good fortune with the international community.

By the mid-1960s, the concerns of black peace activists in general and the national leaders of WILPF in particular had shifted from the Cuban missile crisis, apartheid in South Africa, better relations between America and the Soviet Union, and civil rights to American involvement in Vietnam. America became embroiled in South Vietnam after the French were defeated in 1954. The use of troops there did not become a concern until President Johnson increased America's military presence in 1965. The Vietnam War ripped America apart. As time passed, more antiwar organizations emerged to protest the conflict.

As early as 1962, when President John Kennedy deployed military advisers to South Vietnam, WILPF leader Annalee Stewart acknowledged that America was carrying on "an undeclared war there."[31] By the late sixties, much of WILPF's time and effort centered on the Vietnam War, including cosponsorship of and participation in almost every national antiwar demonstration, from Washington, D.C., New York, and San Francisco to hundreds of other cities and towns. WILPF members worked ceaselessly to end the war, for the sake of both American personnel and the countless Vietnamese being terrorized, maimed, or killed.

African American women played a major role in the various WILPF-sponsored activities. Just as they had argued in previous international causes since World War II, black peace activists perceived the racial conflict in America and the war in Southeast Asia as directly related and essentially linked. Coretta Scott King best summed up the views of other black pacifists when she proclaimed, "Freedom and destiny in America are bound together with freedom and justice in Vietnam."[32]

Several black women who were actively involved in various vigils, demonstrations, and protests against the war in Vietnam also engaged in verbal criticism, on behalf of WILPF, against the controversial conflict. Some of them equated the organized opposition to the government's position on the Vietnam war and the war itself as part of a general Third World struggle, a universal world movement by all people of color. Therefore, whether they placed their opposition to the war in the context of maternal pacifism (or as some historians have more accurately coined it, political femininity), anti-imperialism, or revolutionary solidarity, African American activists all opposed the war for essentially the same reason. They believed that America's involvement in the war was being driven by racist motives. The American government lacked respect for the Vietnamese, another people of color, and subsequently disregarded what the indigenous people wanted. Instead America was merely concerned about lining its own pockets.

For these reasons, African American peace activists, like most blacks, could identify with the Vietnamese. In doing so, they used "color" as a means of identification to speak of Vietnam. A Student Nonviolent Coordinating Committee college peace activist, Diane Nash used this type of identification when she said, "You know I just saw one of those Vietcong guerillas on TV. He was dark-skinned, ragged, poor and angry. I swear, he looked just like one of us."[33]

Even Martin Luther King's rhetoric broadened in 1968 to include all oppressed people of the world. Peace activist Coretta Scott King contends that her husband once likened Vietnam to the struggle for the rights of the oppressed. Hence, Scott King noted, her spouse stressed "the common cause of all the disinherited. . . . He spoke out sharply for all the poor in all their hues, for he knew if color made them different, misery and oppression made them the same."[34] King added, "[W]hat [was generally] happening in the United States . . . [was] a significant part of a world development."[35] He encouraged blacks to end the exploitation of their races and lands. His final views on the subject explain why black peace activists opposed America's involvement in Vietnam. King concluded that as a black man, he could relate to the situation in Vietnam because "the determination of Negro Americans to win freedom from any form of oppression springs from the same profound longing for freedom that motivates oppressed peoples all over the world."[36] African American peace activists unequivocally internationalized the civil rights struggle in America.

This move to internationalize the black struggle was also articulated by Coretta Scott King in comments she delivered at a March 1968 press conference held by WILPF officers. Believing that the oppression in America could not be separated from the oppression in Vietnam, Scott King stated, "As long as we kill men, women and children in Vietnam, millions of poor people face an unnecessary death and suffering in America. As long as we lay waste to the beautiful countryside and communities of Vietnam, we shall see destruction and chaos in the ugly ghettos of America.

As long as we are poisoned by hatred of a freedom-seeking people in Asia, the sickness of racism will exploit our own minorities and corrupt the American majority."[37]

Earlier that same year, WILPFer Eartha Kitt had voiced similar sentiments. On January 18, 1968, singer-entertainer Kitt was one of a group of women, black and white, invited to a White House luncheon, hosted by Lady Bird Johnson, to discuss ways of combating juvenile delinquency. When asked to speak, Kitt stated, to the astonishment of those assembled, "You send the best of this country off to be shot and maimed. They rebel in the street. . . . They don't want to go to school because they're going to be snatched off from their mothers to be shot in Vietnam. . . . You have children of your own, Mrs. Johnson—we raise children and send them to war!"[38] Those assembled, however, should not have been surprised by what Kitt stated. She was a well-known peace activist who had shared equally scathing critiques of the war in other forums.

The surrounding uproar had a negative effect on Kitt's career, but she was instantly praised for her courage by opponents of the war, many of whom were her peace colleagues in WILPF. Across the country, African American women rallied to Kitt's defense. In letters to the editors, particularly in black newspapers, support for Kitt was nearly unanimous. Comments made by Kitt's proponents varied. In her Los Angeles hometown, women wrote,

> I thought it was great because she told the truth.
>
> Someone should have done it sooner. . . . Miss Kitt was definitely in her right.
>
> I think she was courageous. She was the first to get the opportunity to say what she had to say to people who are partly responsible for the war.
>
> I think it was appropriate. She was not out of place; she was exercising her freedom of speech.[39]

While Scott King and Kitt defined peace activists' protest activities within the traditional sphere of motherhood or womanhood, other African American female opponents of war more directly rooted their antiwar views in the "male-dominated public sphere of political protest."[40]

Peace activist Fannie Lou Hamer of the Mississippi Freedom Democratic Party, for instance, was among them. When the fighting in South Vietnam escalated, so did Hamer's opposition. She was quite critical of America's presence in Vietnam, publicly demanding that the troops be withdrawn immediately and sent to protect southern blacks battling the injustices associated with racism. Moreover, she was critical of the federal government for not taking stronger measures against the white minority's 1965 usurpation of power in Southern Rhodesia. As Hamer sarcastically claimed at a WILPF-sponsored peace rally, "The Johnson administration wasn't worried about it 'cause it was black folk."[41] Hamer's last statement implied that she believed the American government's involvement in Vietnam was also racially motivated against the Vietnamese, another people of color.

Some African American peace activists went a step further and linked the disenfranchisement of southern rural African Americans with the disempowerment of Vietnamese peasants. For example, peace activist Diane Nash, one of the American women invited to visit North Vietnam in late 1966 as a member of a WILPF delegation, came away from meetings with Ho Chi Minh and other National Liberation Front leaders permanently impressed with the struggle being waged by the North Vietnamese. Nash had once described herself as an opponent of war because "I am against using murder as a solution to human problems." In interviews in black publications after her return from Hanoi, she stated, "Sweethearts, mothers and other relatives of black soldiers fighting in Viet Nam can forget any notions that the Vietnamese people will give in to American aggression. The only way white Americans will defeat the people of Viet Nam is to murder each and everyone of them."[42]

While expressing an anti-imperialist perspective that equated "oppression and exploitation by the white West" to conditions faced by African Americans, Nash was particularly impressed by the resolve and determination of the North Vietnamese women. As a mother, she expressed empathy for those women who buried their children. "The death and destruction I witnessed was far worse than any picture could communicate." Yet in spite of the destruction of their country, Nash maintained, North Vietnamese women had expressed their "unyielding dedication to Vietnamese independence and freedom from foreign domination."[43]

Four years later, as part of a six-member fact-finding team sent to Vietnam by the WILPF in New Delhi, peace activist Sadie Sawyer Hughley witnessed similar experiences by Vietnamese women. Upon reaching Hanoi, Hughley and her companions were greeted by people she found to be "warm, curious, industrious and dedicated to their cause."[44] They spent eight days in the North Vietnamese capital, meeting with various political leaders, study groups, educators, military leaders, and the general public. The objective of Hughley and her companions was to try to understand the way the North Vietnamese lived, "how they thought and what they thought about the war and the United States' involvement in the war."[45]

Kay Camp, one of Hughley's team members, later wrote, "Profoundly moving were other talks with victims of United States' bombardment, defoliation, and search-and-destroy missions. What does one say when, followed by the entire village, one is led to a small thatched hut where a woman lifts her wide trouser to show the stump of her leg? Or to two mothers who had been sprayed with defoliants during their second month of pregnancy and sit patiently waiting to show you their obviously deformed babies?"[46] Hughley, in remembering these particular encounters, felt a sense of sisterhood with the Vietnamese women—women about whom she too could recall such graphic details concerning their suffering as women or, more to the point, as Vietnamese mothers.

These comments by Scott King, Kitt, Hamer, Nash, and Hughley marked what historian Gerald Gill considered as the beginnings of an ideological transformation in the public political critiques of African American peace activist women that would continue to be made for the next few years. But the war was not only seen in the context of anti-imperialism or maternal pacifism. The opposition of a growing number of African American peace activists emerged from some of the revolutionary organizations to which they belonged. Such groups called for the destruction, if not the radical transformation, of the American political, economic, and social order. Members of these organizations were restless, tired of waiting for change. They wanted immediate economic, political, and social equality for blacks and any other oppressed groups in America.

Most of the black peace activists who joined WILPF after the McCarthy era belonged to this group of war critics. While these women were members of the predominantly white-led WILPF, most remained within or aligned with existing black organizations. Some of these predominantly black groups were extremely radical in comparison with the traditional civil rights organizations. They were also involved with the plight of the black masses. For example, well-known WILPF activist Angela Davis was a member of the Black Panther Party, which embraced a revolutionary nationalist ideology. The Black Panthers' members believed that African Americans "should not be forced to fight in the military to defend a racist government that [did not] protect [them]. They also said they would not "fight or kill other people of color in the world who, like black people, [were] being victimized by the white racist government of America."[47] Peace activists involved with the group shared the views publicly expressed by members of the Black Panther Party, like Eldridge Cleaver and Stokely Carmichael.

Angela Davis, inarguably the party's most prominent and most visible African American, believed that the war was "not just a bloody and unjust war but a war by the U.S. to maintain the status quo and refuse people the right to self-determination." She called for African Americans "to look toward Vietnam because they [were] really on the front lines of the battlefield in the fight against repression."[48] Davis was arrested in 1970 for, among other things, her opposition to the American military presence in Vietnam. However, she remained an outspoken opponent of the war. By that time, moreover, Davis had begun placing more emphasis on the role of women in revolutionary movements. The struggle of Vietnamese women was "part and parcel of a total revolution," and its lessons would be "especially critical with respect to the effort to build an effective black liberation movement."[49]

Davis's later statements demonstrate how she and a few other African American peace activists, like Diane Nash, had become more cognizant of and more forthright in demanding general equality in revolutionary movements. By challenging institutional as well as intraracial forms of oppression, these women pacifists were continuing, in the words of sociologist Patricia Hill Collins, the "Black women's activist tradition."[50]

While the voices of African American peace activists became more radical and more revolutionary, other voices of protest in WILPF became prominent. One was that of Representative Shirley Chisholm of Brooklyn, New York. From her initial run for Congress in 1968 through the American defeat in Vietnam, Chisholm became one of the most persistent congressional critics of continued American involvement in southeast Asia. Chisholm repeatedly criticized the billions of dollars spent yearly on an "immoral war." Calling for the massive reordering of the nation's priorities, Chisholm vowed to vote against every bill introduced in Congress to provide funds for the Defense Department. "I could not vote for money for war while funds were being denied to feed, house, and school Americans."[51] As the war dragged on, her exasperation grew. In a speech lamenting government lies and cover-ups about the war, Chisholm angrily charged, "What conceivable gain can be worth all this? Is there no end to this insanity? This grotesque absorption in war and all its offshoots has virtually destroyed the ability of our government to function effectively at home, and to respond to the process of change and revolution which our society is undergoing today."[52]

In a later speech to Congress in 1969, Chisholm attacked the Pentagon for its lavish spending.[53] Two years later, in June 1971, she first sheltered and then aided in the legal defense of two black GIs, Bernard Tucker and Nathaniel Holms, who had fled West Germany after their conviction in court-martial of raping a girl at Bad Kreuznach.[54] Despite Chisholm's criticism and efforts, America's involvement in Vietnam continued. A year later, Nixon openly talked about possible peace.

Chisholm, then seeking the Democratic Party's nomination for president, rejected the Nixon administration's call for peace with honor, claiming, "This vile tragedy continues in Indochina because this Administration is now trapped by its own overweening self-obsession, self-delusion, and its moral and intellectual poverty into an endless, violent and blundering search for a settlement on its own ludicrously unrealistic terms." Chisholm called for Congress to terminate immediately all funding for the war.[55] Her pleas fell on deaf ears.

In 1973 Congresswoman Chisholm announced her support for the sixteen Norfolk sailors accused of participating in the brig riot of November 26, 1972. By then, she had nothing but "total disgust for the Department of [the] Navy" in its handling of the cases and pledged to pursue the matter "to the fullest extent possible." Consequently, Chisholm sent two aides to interview the sailors and called for a "Defense Department or congressional investigation into the cause of the brig riot."[56] In many ways, Chisholm's position on this issue was similar to those of Mary Church Terrell fifty years before when Terrell fought to protect the rights of the wrongfully accused black American troops in Germany.

Unlike Terrell, however, Chisholm was a policymaker—one who was critical of the war but was still willing to work within the existing American political framework. Chisholm's actions and position on Vietnam brought some criticism from WILPF colleagues who thought that her language was too harsh. However, the national board generally supported her, just as they had Terrell a half century before.

From early 1966 until the end of the war, what galvanized most black women to oppose the war was the escalating number of black troops killed in Vietnam. A 1969 *Newsweek* survey showed that almost half of all African Americans in general thought the draft was racially biased and was an attempt to commit genocide against African Americans.[57] Christina McCullough of Chicago, whose army son was killed in 1966 felt that "black boys [were] giving their lives in a war they [didn't] understand and [couldn't] win."[58] Another woman, Juanita Butcher of Queens, New York, stated, "My husband told me before he died that the war is useless."[59] Perhaps Millie Reid of Brooklyn, New York, best expressed how black women felt about the seemingly increasing deaths of African American men. In 1969, expressing her grief at the news of the death of a neighbor's son in the war, she exclaimed, "Now he's dead. In a place we don't know—can't even pronounce the names—and for reasons we don't understand at all."[60] McCullough's, Butcher's, and Reid's anguish was similar to that expressed by others who lost relatives and friends over the course of the war.

Indeed the mounting deaths of black military personnel in South Vietnam firmly and unalterably changed the thinking of many African American women throughout the nation and caused them to vigorously oppose the continued fighting in Vietnam by 1965. While many black women felt that the war was hurting domestic conditions, others were concerned that black men were being called on in disproportionate numbers to fight a war against people who were, in many ways, treated just as they were.

Although some of these war critics were not members of WILPF, their views influenced the position taken by African Americans on the Vietnam War issue. Black peace activists in WILPF believed they represented these people. Responding to African American critics of the war, peace activist Sadie Sawyer Hughley once said, "It was really ludicrous for Americans, especially politicians, to concern themselves with the Vietnamese, whether or not they were going to be taken over by Communism, when we had so many domestic issues with which to deal. So many Americans at that time were in poverty, hungry, in need of clothes and shelter. The last place we needed to be was in Southeast Asia. There were too many problems to tackle here. It just didn't make sense to many of us."[61]

And for most African Americans in general and black WILPFers in particular, the Vietnam War did seem foolish and unnecessary.

Coretta Scott King, Sadie Sawyer Hughley, Angela Davis, Fannie Lou Hamer, Diane Nash, Erna Harris, Eartha Kitt, and many other prominent peace activists often appeared on behalf of WILPF and other peace groups to speak out against the Vietnam War. When doing so, they always took advantage of the opportunity to hurl criticisms at America's acts of racial injustice. While these activists spoke before large audiences at antiwar rallies and demonstrations, many other black women opponents of war were in the audiences. They too expressed their sentiments about the Vietnam War and civil rights in America.

Some of these demonstrators were members of WILPF, while others were high school and college students, working women, and self-described welfare mothers who often participated in all-black contingents.[62] Recalling her participation as a seventeen-year-old in an April 15, 1967, antiwar demonstration, Laura Moorehead remembered, "As far as I could see down any of the streets, there were demonstrators. It was raining and people were standing there. It was Antiwar City that day. I stood right there and saw Martin Luther King speak. That was a big thrill for me because I had waited so long for him to come out against the war and I became so excited when he actually did. That was one of the main reasons I came—because I knew King was going to speak and publicly identify himself with the demonstration, and I hoped that would help win my parents over."[63] Owen Walter also described the reason he and a contingent of African American students came to Washington from Detroit to take part in the march on the Pentagon. He stated their purpose was "to show the country that black people [were] concerned with the international issue of colored peoples all over the world."[64]

Audiences often influenced the critiques of black peace activists. It appears that in the 1960s, at least, black peace activists and their black listening audience were certainly of one accord. Most polls, whether public opinion polls or those conducted by black publications, showed that most black women opposed the war in Vietnam. Although their reasons varied, they all agreed that black men and women had no valid reasons for being in southeast Asia fighting a racially motivated war that was being driven further by economic greed and a desire for power. Instead, African Americans needed to be in America trying to resolve their own problems. In other words, they contended that America's focus in the 1960s should not have been on how to further oppress and bring under its control a group of people thousands of miles away. Rather, it should be on how to resolve its domestic problems pertaining to race relations.

While national WILPF's white leadership opposed American involvement in Vietnam and spent countless hours engaged in antiwar activities, its critiques of the war were neither caustic in tone nor a public indictment of the American government's failure to deal with its own problems of racial injustice. Yet most black women who hurled such criticism were members of WILPF who felt that they represented the views of the organization. Whether this feeling was true or not, the national body faced a dilemma.

If the white leadership distanced itself from black peace activists, then its position on civil rights became questionable. If they chose to remain silent, then the world would assume that the black peace activists' critiques represented their views as well. White pacifists chose to remain silent. One can only assume that they did not want to take on this fight. Consequently, the organization went in a different direction in its critiques and actions waged against the Vietnam War.

WILPF undoubtedly was changing, and much of that change was because of the African American peace activists' courage and commitment to racial justice and human rights. The connection repeatedly made by black peace activists in the 1960s and early 1970s between human rights and civil rights arguably helped the civil rights struggle in America. Furthermore, as black women and their white colleagues traveled all over the world in the name of peace and freedom, they were repeatedly asked about race relations in America. For example, when people in the Congo asked Vera Chandler Foster about the Little Rock, Arkansas, school case, she discussed with them America's problem with racism.[65]

Peace activists like Foster shared these queries with the American government in memos, antiwar demonstrations, congressional hearings, and rallies. Because the world was watching America—the country that had often billed itself as the arsenal of democracy—its citizens knew that they had to work toward a society in which all people were equal if they were to maintain international respect. This expectation, in the end, helped black peace activists in their dual battles of international and domestic peace and freedom. For they knew that without peace, there could be no freedom, and without freedom, there certainly could be no peace. The two goals of WILPF and the peace movement were inextricably intertwined for African American female peace activists.

Conclusion

The words of Mary Church Terrell before an all-white audience at the International Congress of the Woman's Peace Party in 1919 were prophetic. "White people might talk about permanent peace until doomsday," Terrell warned, "but they could never have it till the dark races were treated fair and square."[1] This central theme emerges from the story of African American peace activism. For WILPF to achieve domestic and international peace and freedom, black peace activists reasoned, its members had to be ready to eradicate all vestiges of racial injustices at home as well as all human oppression abroad.

For black peace activists, the limitations and obligations of being both African American and female shaped their participation in the movement. Their sense of responsibility to the Negro race and experiences as black women helped determine their goals, motivations, and activities.

Peace and freedom, therefore, had a different meaning for black women in WILPF. To them the twin goals of WILPF meant not only world disarmament, an end to colonialism, and a peaceful resolution of international conflicts but also an end to racial and human oppression and the beginning of racial liberation. This viewpoint shaped black female activism and determined their priorities in the peace movement.

Because they could not always depend on their white colleagues in WILPF for support on race-related issues between 1915 and 1975, African American women also joined organizations charged with improving the lives of blacks. The organizations in which they became involved between 1915 and 1945 provided intensive training not in African American culture, which was implicitly judged inadequate, but in the mainstream white American culture of the period. After 1945, black women joined organizations whose goals were to fight for social, political, and economic equality for African Americans. Hence black peace activists did not compartmentalize their lives in a way that would permit others to assess them in relation to WILPF activities alone.

The views of African American women about peace and freedom caused them to change WILPF from the moment they joined the organization, perhaps more than even they realized. When WILPF was formed, everything about it was designed to differentiate it from the male-led and male-controlled peace organizations. However, its charter members never gave any serious thought as to how the organization's original goals would change if, and when, black women became active participants.

On the basis of accounts given in various peace studies, white women in WILPF sometimes had a relatively difficult relationship with each other. Once black women joined WILPF, relationships between peace activists became even more problematic. Racism pervaded the organization, especially in local branches, and often prevented full and equal cooperation between the two races. It was well known that not all peace activists advocated racial equality, and even those who did sometimes exhibited patronizing attitudes toward their black colleagues. Some local branches tried to keep blacks out altogether. Nevertheless, once black women joined WILPF, they developed rhetoric of their own, employing concepts not traditionally used by white peace activists. Whether they spoke about wars, colonialism, economic imperialism, or oppression, African American women's language embodied a "womanist consciousness." They interpreted world peace through the eyes of African Americans, in the images of African Americans, and with African Americans' needs in mind. This interpretation is why the black peace activist's vision is appealing. It roots peace soundly in race, making racial justice the very essence of a warless world. African American women believed that war is inevitable without freedom; freedom cannot exist without war.

Racial justice is the one continuous theme of black peace activism, especially for those women in WILPF. Successive generations of African

American women peace activists have established a link between race and peace. The tendency of black peace activists to make this connection led to discussions among them about whether peace activists were capable of doing more than merely talking about racial justice or could even be sensitive to injustices. Although black women have taken the lead in linking race with peace, their message too often has been reluctantly embraced by many of WILPF's white members.

The racial justice theme, however, though continuous, has not guaranteed a larger black membership in WILPF. Perhaps one reason WILPF has not been able to attract more black women is because very few either understood or could make the linkages between peace and race that were necessary to warrant their involvement in peace work. In fact, WILPF could maintain a large African American membership only when its black members could more easily make the connection. That is why WILPF did not experience an unusually high level of black peace activism until the 1960s. During the turbulent decade characterized by the civil rights movement and the Vietnam War, African American women in WILPF could understand how peace coalesced with their own conditions in America. However, most blacks could not make that leap. Consequently, the majority of African American women decided not to become members of the peace organization.

The refusal of most African American women to commit to WILPF has been a constant problem for the organization. WILPF's white national leadership tried to attract black women between 1915 and 1975. Despite the many methods employed to bring black women into the organization, WILPF's white leadership never enjoyed a high success rate. While many women could not connect peace with race issues, an even larger number did not feel comfortable in the organization. Most in the black community who had heard of WILPF perceived its participants as members of the elite who had been born with silver spoons in their mouths. Blacks who held such beliefs did not feel that they had anything in common with members of the predominantly white WILPF. African Americans also believed that WILPF was just another interracial organization that extended an invitation to people of color but denied them positions of responsibility after they joined. Many blacks were even more convinced of this when WILPF's own membership struggled with the divisive and controversial Interracial Committee.

African Americans failed to realize, however, that black peace activists, though few in number, were able to exercise considerable influence because of their positions of power. This situation held true both during and after World War II. Prior to the war, Mary Church Terrell, for instance, was one of the first black peace activists in a position of responsibility and power. In addition to serving on WILPF's first executive board, she also accompanied several white pacifists to the founding meeting of the peace group in Zurich in 1919. At that time, while giving a speech on behalf of the American delegation, Terrell commented openly on the fact that she was the only African American woman there. While Terrell served on WILPF's executive board, Helen Curtis and Sadie Daniels St. Clair chaired the New York City and Washington, D.C., branches, respectively. Vera Chandler Foster and Thelma Marshall also were elected as chairs of their respective WILPF branches. Addie Hunton, a key participant in the Interracial Committee effort, was at one time active in the New York branch. In the 1950s, Bertha McNeill became most important as chair of the Committee on Special Problems of Branches, which dealt with several McCarthy-era accusations.

Moreover, several black peace activists represented WILPF at international conferences. For example, in 1937, Bertha McNeill was a WILPF U.S. delegate to the Stockholm World Congress, where she exposed racial injustice in America's famous Scottsboro case. Dr. Flemmie Kittrell was one of three women to represent WILPF at the Nongovernmental Organizations Conference on the Eradication of Prejudice and Discrimination, in Geneva. Each time that black peace activists traveled abroad for WILPF, they assumed major responsibilities, sometimes chairing committees and at other times leading conference sessions. This pattern of activism continued for black peace activists for most of the period of this study. They were least active during both world wars and the 1920s Red Scare.

After World War II, WILPF's leadership continued to recruit African American women. The women who subsequently joined held positions of leadership and responsibility within WILPF. On the local levels, Erna Prather Harris, Thelma Marshall, Inez Jackson, Sadie Sawyer Hughley, Enola Maxwell, and veteran Vera Chandler Foster were elected as chairs of their respective WILPF branches. Hughley later served as vice president of the southeastern region of WILPF, while Erna Prather Harris served two terms as vice president of the southwestern region. Both Hughley and Harris filled these positions on WILPF's national board, which allowed them to have some authority in influencing the peace group's national agenda. Also, in these positions, Hughley and Harris were responsible for several branches within their respective regions.

Black peace activists were actually involved in peace work even on the international level. Both Foster and Harris attended the Second Conference between the United States and the Soviet Union in 1964. Six years later, Hughley joined a six-member fact-finding team to Vietnam. Just as they had done prior to 1945, black women who traveled for WILPF during the Cold War also chaired committees and presided over conferences as Harris once did.

After the 1970s, fewer blacks served on WILPF's national board or in positions of leadership in the various local branches. According to peace historian Harriet Alonso, in 1990, there were only two black women on a board of approximately thirty-five members. While the U.S. section of WILPF was successful in electing its first African American chair, Betty Burkes, to a three-year term in 1996, it continues to have difficulty attracting and retaining black women interested in serving in leadership positions. Today, only a handful of African American women remain in the organization, and of those, a small number chair WILPF's various committees. Consequently, WILPF continues to lag behind several other interracial organizations.

Some peace historians maintain that although "racism has shown itself on some occasions in a few WILPF branches, such cases are rare."[2] What these scholars fail to realize is that racism is not as evident when black women are not present. Furthermore, if black women were not marginalized in these studies, the conclusions drawn by these historians about racism within WILPF might be different. I agree with scholars writing on the subject that something certainly had to cause African American women to feel, at times, ill at ease within WILPF. As Harriet Alonso alleged, perhaps WILPF would have been more successful in recruiting African Americans if it had examined its own members' problems with race. However, as she notes, the peace group did not do so until 1988.[3]

Today, many of WILPF's members realize that much work remains in helping each other come to terms with their own prejudices and racial indifferences. At a recent meeting of the organization's XXVIII Triennial Congress in Plainfield, Vermont, many members acknowledged that far too many of their colleagues harbor racist beliefs and exhibit racist behavior about African Americans. However, these same women quickly noted that the organization is committed to eradicating this social ill from among WILPF's ranks as well as society at large. That commitment remains to be seen. Unfortunately, most African American WILPFers at the latest Triennial Congress were members of the organization's Uniting for Racial Justice Campaign Committee, one of four drives adopted by WILPF in 2002. Since WILPF's members chose the campaign with which they wanted to become involved, the absence of white women from the campaign for racial justice could indicate that white women were not interested. On the other hand, the presence of the organization's black members on the Uniting for Racial Justice Campaign Committee could suggest that African American peace activists continue to root peace soundly in race. Two of WILPF's many goals remain an increase in racial diversity within the organization and the fight against racial injustice wherever it exists—even if that means within the peace organization. Few organizations can make such a noble claim.

Despite few black women having joined WILPF, their presence altered the organization and its goals in many important ways. In addition, white peace activists were compelled to revisit from time to time their own conceptions of peace and freedom. This is not to say that African American women were exclusively concerned with racial issues. It is clear to those studying this subject that black women participated in many of the same activities as white pacifists. However, their role in the movement has been multilayered. For these black women activists, the limitations and obligations of being black people, who happened to be female, shaped their participation in the movement. Economics, family, and their historical experiences as an oppressed people helped to determine their goals, motivations, and activities. Yet, ultimately, individual personalities and perceptions of their roles as peace activists made each woman distinctive in her own right, regardless of external circumstances.

The continued existence of racism both within and outside WILPF and the peace movement did not render black women completely powerless or silent. Rather, the strength of their commitment to bringing about world peace and justice led black women peace activists to form their own patterns of participation, which they carried throughout the twentieth century and perhaps will continue into the twenty-first. In her speech to peace activists in 1919, Terrell accurately predicted the future of black women's activism within the movement. No one believed her; not even her longtime friend Addie Hunton, who questioned Terrell's charges of alleged racism within WILPF in the late 1920s. However, before their peace activism ended, black women well understood that "race-ing peace" was the only way to keep their white peace activist colleagues focused on racial justice issues in an organization that prided itself on such under the exceptionally large banners emblazoned with peace and freedom. Black women activists well understood that there could be no peace without freedom and no freedom without peace. These words guided, and undoubtedly will continue to guide, their peace activism.

Notes
Bibliography
Index

Notes

Introduction

1. Report to executive board of WILPF from Caroline Singer, chair, Intra-American Committee, November 1937, U.S. section of WILPF Papers, manuscript division, Swarthmore College Peace Collection, Swarthmore College (hereafter referred to as SCPC), series B2, box 46.

2. Peter Brock and Nigel Young, *Pacifism in the Twentieth Century* (Syracuse, NY: Syracuse University Press, 1999), 37–38; *Tribunal* 167 (July 14, 1919): 1. Emphasis is in the original.

3. Harriet Alonso, *Peace as a Woman's Issue: A History of the U.S. Movement for World Peace and Women's Rights* (Syracuse, NY: Syracuse University Press, 1993), 51.

4. Alonso, *Peace as a Woman's Issue,* 8.

5. Ibid., 86.

6. Ibid.

7. See Marie Degen, *The History of the Woman's Peace Party* (Baltimore: John Hopkins University Press, 1939), 38; and Carrie Foster, *The Women and the Warriors: The U.S. Section of the Women's International League for Peace and Freedom, 1915–1946* (Syracuse, NY: Syracuse University Press, 1995), 11.

8. Carol Moore, telephone conversation with author, December 18, 1993.

9. See W.I.L. Record on Race Recognition, July 1, 1930, U.S. section of WILPF Papers, SCPC.

10. Annual report of the Minorities Committee, 1940, Bertha McNeill Papers, SCPC.

11. Foster, *Women and the Warriors,* 159.

12. Ibid.

13. Mildred Scott Olmsted to Mercedes Randall, February 1972, SCPC, box 26.

14. Alonso, *Peace as a Women's Issue,* 146.

15. Doing so was not always easy. Black peace activists often had to contend with whites, who sometimes questioned their decisions or suggestions unnecessarily. See letter from Mary Church Terrell to Emily Greene Balch, February 1, 1929, Emily Greene Balch Papers, SCPC. As time passed, African American women found that they received less respect from their white colleagues on the local level. It was easier to become involved in the decision-making process on the national level.

16. See the following works for additional information: Constance Marteena, *The Lengthening Shadow of a Woman* (New York: New York Exposition Press, 1977); Pamela Jones-Burnley, "African-American Women in WILPF," *Peace and Freedom: Journal of the Women's International League for Peace and Freedom* 56 (January–February 1991): 16–18.

17. Jones-Burnley, "African-American Women in WILPF," 16–18.

18. Alonso, *Peace as a Women's Issue,* 8.

19. Ibid., 12. Emphasis on *only* is mine.

20. Foster, *Women and the Warriors,* 9.

21. Linda Schott, *Reconstructing Women's Thoughts: The Women's International League for Peace and Freedom Before World War II* (Palo Alto: Stanford University Press, 1997), 131–49.

22. Gertrude Bussey and Margaret Tims, *Pioneers for Peace: The Women's International League for Peace and Freedom, 1915–1965* (Oxford: Alden Press, 1980); and Catherine Foster, *Women for All Seasons: The Story of the Women's International League for Peace and Freedom* (Athens: University of Georgia Press, 1989).

23. The four benefits mentioned here were originally quoted in Joyce Blackwell-Johnson, "African-American Activists in the Women's International League for Peace and Freedom, 1920s–1950s," *Peace and Change: Journal of Peace Research* 23, no. 4 (October 1998): 467–68.

24. See Hazel Carby, *Reconstructing Womanhood: The Emergence of the Afro-American Woman Novelist* (New York: Oxford University Press, 1987).

25. See Paula Giddings, *When and Where I Enter . . . The Impact of Black Women on Race and Sex in America* (New York: William Morris, 1984).

26. See bell hooks, *Ain't I a Woman?: Black Women and Feminism* (Boston: South End Press, 1981).

27. See Joyce Ladner, *Tomorrow's Tomorrow* (Garden City, NY: Doubleday, 1972).

28. See Gerda Lerner, *Black Women in White America: A Documentary History* (New York: Vintage Books, 1972).

29. See Rosalyn Terborg-Penn, *African-American Women in the Struggle for the Vote, 1850–1920* (Bloomington: Indiana University Press, 1998).

30. See Stephanie Shaw, *What a Woman Ought to Be and to Do: Black Professional Workers During the Jim Crow Era* (Chicago: University of Chicago Press, 1996).

31. See Deborah Gray White, *Too Heavy a Load: Black Women in Defense of Themselves, 1894–1994* (New York: W. W. Norton and Company, 1999).

32. See Tera Hunter, *To 'Joy My Freedom: Southern Black Women's Lives and Labors after the Civil War* (Cambridge: Harvard University Press, 1997).

33. Darlene Clark Hine has written many works. Several that focus on the experiences of women include *A Shining Thread of Hope: The History of Black Women in America* (New York: Broadway Books, 1998; coauthored by Kathleen Thompson); *Hine Sight: Black Women and the Re-Construction of American History* (New York: Carlson Publishing, 1994); and *Black Women in White: Racial Conflict and Cooperation in the Nursing Profession, 1890–1950* (Bloomington: Indiana University Press, 1989). Hine coedited, with David Gaspar, *More Than Chattel: Black Women and Slavery in the Americas* (Bloomington: Indiana University Press, 1996). She also coedited, with Elsa Barkley Brown and Rosalyn Terborg-Penn, a two-volume set, *Black Women in America: An Historical Encyclopedia* (Brooklyn, NY: Carlson Publishing, 1993).

34. Patricia Hill Collins, *Black Feminist Thought: Knowledge, Consciousness, and the Politics of Empowerment* (Boston: Unwin Hyman, 1990), 10–11.

35. Ibid., 11.

36. James Scott, in *Weapons of the Weak: Everyday Forms of Peasant Resistance* (New Haven: Yale University Press, 1985), defines consciousness as the symbols, norms, and ideological forms people create to give meaning to their acts. For Theresa De Lauretis, in *Feminist Studies/Critical Studies: Issues, Terms and Contexts* (Bloomington: Indiana University Press, 1996), consciousness is a process, a "particular configuration of subjectivity . . . produced at the intersection of meaning with experience. . . . [C]onsciousness is grounded in personal history, and self and identity are understood within particular cultural contexts. Consciousness is never fixed, never attained once and for all, because discursive boundaries change with historical conditions" (8).

37. This description of the socioeconomic status of black peace activists holds true for the period of this study. In the early 1960s, however, a few working-class black women began to join the WILPF.

1. Bold Beginnings: The First Ten Years, 1915–1925

1. Carrie Chapman Catt to the *New York Times,* February 6, 1915, Carrie Chapman Catt Papers, SCPC, 1, series C1, box 1.

2. Harriet Alonso, *Peace as a Women's Issue: A History of the U.S. Movement for World Peace and Women's Rights* (Syracuse, NY: Syracuse University Press, 1993), 62; Carrie Chapman Catt to Jane Addams, December 29, 1914, Woman's Peace Party Papers (hereafter referred to as WPP), SCPC, 1, series C1, box 2.

3. Alonso, *Peace as a Women's Issue*, 78.

4. Ibid., 60–61; Robert Marcus and David Burner, *America Firsthand: From Reconstruction to the Present* (New York: St. Martin's Press, 1989), 203–4.

5. Carrie Foster, *The Women and the Warriors: The U.S. Section of the Women's International League for Peace and Freedom, 1915–1946* (Syracuse, NY: Syracuse University Press, 1995), 2–3.

6. For specific and detailed accounts of the various race riots that occurred between 1908 and 1919, consult the following sources: Robert Haynes, *A Night of Violence: the Houston Riot of 1917* (Baton Rouge: Louisiana State University Press, 1976); Kenneth Kusmer, *A Ghetto Takes Shape: Black Cleveland, 1870–1930* (Urbana: University of Illinois Press, 1976); Elliott Rudwick, *Race Riot at East St. Louis, July 2, 1917* (Cleveland: World Publishing, 1966); Roberta Senechel, *The Sociogenesis of a Race Riot: Springfield, Illinois, in 1908* (Urbana: University of Illinois Press, 1990); William Tuttle, *Chicago in the Red Summer of 1919* (New York: Atheneum, 1970); Lee Williams, *Anatomy of Four Race Riots: Racial Conflicts in Knoxville, Elaine (Arkansas), Tulsa, and Chicago, 1919–1921* (Hattiesburg: University and College Press of Mississippi, 1972).

7. Darlene Clark Hine, William Hine, and Stanley Harrold, *The African-American Odyssey* (Upper Saddle River, NJ: Prentice-Hall, 2000), 395.

8. John Inscoe, "The 'Clansman' on Stage and Screen: North Carolina Reacts," *North Carolina Historical Review* 64 (April 1987), 139–61. The retrogression theory is also discussed in the following works: Joel Williamson, *The Crucible of Race: Black-White Race Relations in the American South since Emancipation* (New York: Oxford University Press, 1984), 115–20; John Smith, *An Old Creed for the New South: Proslavery Ideology and Historiography, 1865–1918* (Westport, CT: Greenwood Press, 1985), 48–53; and George Frederickson, *The Black Image in the White Mind: The Debate on Afro-American Character and Destiny, 1817–1914* (New York: Harper and Row, 1977), 236–39.

9. Inscoe, "'Clansman' on Stage and Screen," 142.

10. Thomas Cripps, "The Reaction of the Negro to the Motion Picture 'The Birth of a Nation,'" *Historian* 25 (May 1963): 358–59.

11. Hine, Hine, and Harrold, *African-American Odyssey*, 312.

12. William Sheppard, "How I Put Over the Klan," *Collier's*, July 14, 1928, 34; Maxim Simcovitch, "The Impact of Griffith's 'Birth of a Nation' on the Modern Ku Klux Klan," *Journal of Popular Film* 1 (Winter 1972): 46.

13. Sheppard, "How I Put Over the Klan," 34.

14. Cripps, "Reaction of the Negro," 31.

15. Ibid., 351.

16. Ibid., 352.

17. Hine, Hine, and Harrold, *African-American Odyssey*, 395.

18. Marcus and Burner, *America Firsthand*, 203–4.

19. Nancy Woloch, *Women and the American Experience* (New York: McGraw-Hill, 1994), 269.

20. Ibid.

21. See Alonso, *Peace as a Women's Issue;* Harriet Alonso, *The Women's Peace Union and the Outlawry of War, 1921–1942* (Knoxville: University of Tennessee Press, 1989); David Bennett, *The Party of Fear: From Nativist Movements to the New Right in American History* (Chapel Hill: University of North Carolina Press, 1988); Nancy Cott, *The Grounding of Modern Feminism* (New Haven: Yale University Press, 1987); John Craig, "Redbaiting, Pacifism, and Free Speech: Lucia Ames Meade and Her 1926 Lecture Tour in Atlanta and the Southeast," *Georgia Historical Quarterly* 71 (1987): 601–22; Charles DeBenedetti, *The Peace Reform in American History* (Bloomington: Indiana University Press, 1980); Catherine Foster, *Women of All Seasons: The Story of the Women's International League for Peace and Freedom* (Syracuse, NY: Syracuse University Press, 1995); Joan Jensen, "When Women Worked for Peace: Helen Marston and the California Peace Movement, 1915–1945," *California History* 67 (1988): 118–31, 147–48; Stanley Lemmons, *The Woman Citizen: Social Feminism in the 1920s* (Urbana: University of Illinois Press, 1973); C. Roland Marchand, *The American Peace Movement and Social Reform, 1898–1918* (Princeton: Princeton University Press, 1972); Robert Murray, *Red Scare: a Study in National Hysteria, 1919–1920* (Minneapolis: University of Minnesota Press, 1955); William Preston, *Alien and Dissenters: Federal Suppression of Radicals, 1903–1933* (Urbana: University of Illinois Press, 1994); and Linda Schott, *Reconstructing Women's Thoughts: The Women's International League for Peace and Freedom Before World War II* (Palo Alto: Stanford University Press, 1997).

22. Joan Jensen, "All Pink Sisters: The War Department and the Feminist Movement in the 1920s," in *Decades of Discontent: The Women's Movement, 1920–1940,* ed. Lois Scharf and Joan Jensen, 211 (Westport, CT: Greenwood Press, 1983).

23. The WILPF was not the only peace group to oppose the National Defense Act. So did the Woman's Peace Society, Women's Peace Union, Fellowship of Reconciliation, and Quakers of the American Friends Committee. Some scholars believe that WILPF encountered more criticism because some of its members also belonged to several of the other opposition groups and aggressively campaigned against candidates who were pro-military. Furthermore, they testified in Congress against increased appropriations for the military. For a fuller discussion of this subject, see Foster, *Women and the Warriors,* 45–46.

24. Jensen, "All Pink Sisters," 209.

25. Lucia Ames Mead to John Weeks, April 12, 1923, WILPF Papers, SCPC, microfilm, reel 39.

26. Ibid.

27. Francis Ralston Walsh to Mrs. John L. C. Harvey, March 24, 1924, WILPF Papers, SCPC, series C1, box 1.

28. "News Release," April 1924, WILPF Papers, SCPC, series C1, box 3.

29. Robert Tucker, minister, to WILPF executive officials, May 26, 1924, WILPF Papers, SCPC, series C1, box 3.

30. WILPF, *Peace at Any Old Price* (proceedings of the Annual Conference of the Women's International League for Peace and Freedom, 1923).

31. Ibid.

32. Alonso, *Peace as a Women's Issue*, 111.

33. "Half-Truths and Falsehoods about the Women's Peace League," n.d., WILPF Papers, SCPC, series C1, box 1.

34. John Weeks to Maude Wood Park, chair of the Women's Joint Congressional Committee, n.d., WILPF Papers, SCPC, series C1, box 2. The Women's Joint Congressional Committee was organized in 1920. It was a clearinghouse for seventeen national women's organizations, which had representatives in Washington, D.C., for the purpose of keeping in touch with federal legislation of interest to women. The members brought to it the endorsements of their respective organizations. WILPF was one of those seventeen members.

35. Jensen, "All Pink Sisters," 211.

36. Mrs. Berlin to Caroline Singer, n.d., WILPF Papers, SCPC, series C1, box 1.

37. Schott, *Reconstructing Women's Thoughts*, 10.

38. Foster, *Women and the Warriors*, 49.

39. Ibid., 83; "Lists Americans as Pacifists," January 25, 1919, WILPF Papers, SCPC, series C1, box 2.

40. Addie Hunton, branch letter, June 5, 1924, WILPF National Interracial Committee Papers, SCPC, series E4, box 1.

2. In Search of the Perfect Black Peace Activist, 1915–1945

1. Report on Zurich Conference, 1919, WILPF Papers, SCPC, series C1, box 31.

2. Ibid.

3. Mary Church Terrell, *A Colored Woman in a White World* (New York: G. K. Hall, 1996), 333.

4. Carrie Foster, *The Women and the Warriors: The U.S. Section of the Women's International League for Peace and Freedom, 1915–1946* (Syracuse, NY: Syracuse University Press, 1995), 159.

5. Emily Greene Balch to Mildred Scott Olmsted, January 11, 1929, WILPF Papers, SCPC, series C1, box 6.

6. Terrell, *Colored Woman in a White World*, 328–35; Foster, *Women and the Warriors*, 158.

7. Foster, *Women and the Warriors*, 158–60.

8. Ibid., 157.

9. Nancy Woloch, *Women and the American Experience* (New York: McGraw-Hill, 1999), 254–68; Allen Davis, *American Heroine: The Life and Legend of Jane Addams* (New York: Oxford University Press, 1973); Jane Addams, *Twenty Years at Hull House* (New York: Phillips Publishing and MacMillan, 1910; New York: New American Library, 1930). Citation of the work by Addams is to the New American Library edition.

10. Nancy Cott, *The Grounding of Modern Feminism* (New Haven: Yale University Press, 1987); Carrie Chapman Catt and Nellie Rogers Shuler, *Woman Suffrage and Politics: The Inner Story of the Suffrage Movement* (New York: C. Scribner's Sons, 1923); Harriet Alonso, *Peace as a Women's Issue: A History of the U.S. Movement for World Peace and Women's Rights* (Syracuse, NY: Syracuse University Press, 1993), 102; Rosalyn Terborg-Penn, "Discontented Black Feminists: Prelude and Postscript to the Passage of the Nineteenth Amendment," in *Decades of Discontent: The Women's Movement, 1920–1940*, ed. Lois Scharf and Joan Jensen, 270–71 (Boston: Northeastern University Press, 1987).

11. See Mercedes Randall, *Improper Bostonian: Emily Greene Balch, Nobel Peace Laureate* (New York: Twayne Publishers, 1972).

12. Caroline Singer to Mrs. Hommel, n.d., WILPF Papers, series C1, box 1.

13. Alonso, *Peace as a Women's Issue,* 102; Terborg-Penn, "Discontented Black Feminists," 261–78.

14. Addie Hunton, "Negro Womanhood Defended," *Voice* 1 (1904): 278.

15. Terrell, *Colored Woman in a White World,* 152–53.

16. All quotations in this and the previous two paragraphs, ibid., 154.

17. Kevin Gaines, *Uplifting the Race: Black Leadership, Politics, and Culture in the Twentieth Century* (Chapel Hill: University of North Carolina Press, 1996), 6.

18. Ibid., 3.

19. Samyne Miller, "First Black Millionaire," *Dawn,* October 3, 1925, 4.

20. Terrell, *Colored Woman in a White World,* 1–17; Beverly Washington Jones, *Quest for Equality: The Life and Writings of Mary Eliza Church Terrell, 1863–1954* (New York: Carlson Publishing Company, 1990), 8; Annette Church and Roberta Church, *The Robert R. Churches of Memphis: A Father and Son Who Achieved in Spite of Race* (Memphis: A. E. Church, 1974), 23.

21. For an excellent description of the Church family, see the first nine chapters of Terrell, *Colored Woman in a White World.*

22. Terrell, *Colored Woman in a White World,* 65.

23. Ibid., 260.

24. Ibid., 157.

25. Biographies L–Z, WILPF Papers, SCPC, box 1, folder 2.

26. Ibid.

27. Ibid.

28. Vera Chandler Foster, telephone conversation with author, September 7, 1996.

29. Ibid.

30. Ibid.

31. Biographies A–K, WILPF Papers, SCPC, box 1, folder 1.

32. Inez Jackson, interview by Judith Addams, tape recording, October 22, 1985, Stanford Oral History Collection, Stanford University Press, Palo Alto, CA.

33. Ibid.

34. Ibid.

35. R. W. Francis J. Grimke, "The Logic of Woman Suffrage," *Crisis,* August 1915, 186.

36. Addie Hunton, "Activities of Interracial Department, Women's International League," May–October 1934, WILPF Papers, SCPC, box 2.

37. Memorandum, n.d., Bertha McNeill Papers, SCPC, box 1.

38. Bertha McNeill to Mildred Scott Olmsted, December 28, 1935, Bertha McNeill Papers, SCPC, box 1.

39. Biographies A–K, WILPF Papers, SCPC, box 1, folder 1.

40. Mildred Scott Olmsted to Flemmie Kittrell, July 8, 1948, WILPF, series C, general correspondence, Fellowship of Reconciliation, 1948–1949, microfilm, reel 78.

41. Ibid.

42. Ibid.

43. Grimke, "Logic of Woman Suffrage," 181.

44. Bertha McNeill to Mildred Scott Olmsted, January 13, 1936, WILPF Papers, SCPC, series C1, box 1.

45. Ibid.

46. Caroline Singer, report to New York WILPF branches, n.d., WILPF Papers, SCPC, box 28.

47. Foster, *Women and the Warriors,* 152.

48. Caroline Singer to Mrs. Berlin, n.d., WILPF Papers, SCPC, box 3.

49. Ibid.

50. Theodore Kornweibel Jr., *"Seeing Red": Federal Campaign Against Black Militancy, 1919–1925* (Indianapolis: Indiana University Press, 1998), xii.

51. Ibid., 20.

52. Inez Jackson, interview by Judith Adams, October 22, 1985, tape recording, Stanford Oral History Collection, Stanford University Press, Palo Alto, CA.

53. Caroline Singer to editor, *New York Times,* April 5, 1937, WILPF Papers, SCPC, box 6.

54. Charles Patterson, *Marian Anderson* (New York: Franklin Watts, 1988), 122–25.

55. Inez Jackson, interview by Judith Adams, October 22, 1985, tape recording, Stanford Oral History Collection, Stanford University Press, Palo Alto, CA.

56. Caroline Singer to Lyn Smith and Dorothy Hommel, memorandum, December 29, 1937, WILPF Papers, SCPC, box 12.

57. Bertha McNeill, branch letter, March 31, 1936, Bertha McNeill Papers, SCPC, box 3.

58. Caroline Singer to Mrs. Berlin, n.d., WILPF Papers, SCPC, series C1, box 3.

59. Singer, chair, Intra-American Committee, New York State Boards, report, February 25, 1938, WILPF Papers, SCPC, series A2, box 1.

3. Building a Coalition while Avoiding Confrontation, 1928–1941

1. Caroline Singer, chair, Intra-American Committee, WILPF executive board and branches, report, 1937, WILPF Papers, SCPC, series A2, box 1.

2. Ibid.

3. Singer to Mrs. Hommel, n.d., WILPF papers, SCPC, series C1, box 3.

4. Bertha McNeill, branch letter, March 31, 1936, Bertha McNeill papers, SCPC, box 3.

5. Carrie Foster, *The Women and the Warriors: The U.S. Section of the Women's International League for Peace and Freedom, 1915–1946* (Syracuse, NY: Syracuse University Press, 1995), 160.

6. Addie Hunton to Mildred Scott Olmsted, December 21, 1928, WILPF papers, SCPC, series C1, box 1.

7. Mildred Scott Olmsted to Emily Greene Balch, January 7, 1929, Balch papers, SCPC, series C1, box 3. Terrell was not reelected after she refused to sign a petition generated in March 1921 by the WILPF executive board requesting the removal of black troops from occupied Germany. (This incident is discussed in detail in chapter 4.) The national board therefore was left with no prominent black member, a matter of some concern to WILPF leaders. See also Foster, *Women and the Warriors,* 160; and Linda Schott, *Reconstructing Women's Thoughts: The Women's International League for Peace and Freedom Before World War II* (Palo Alto: Stanford University Press, 1997), 136.

8. Emily Greene Balch to Mildred Scott Olmsted, January 11, 1929, Balch papers, SCPC, series C1, box 2; Schott, *Reconstructing Women's Thoughts,* 136.

9. Emily Greene Balch to Addie Hunton, January 11, 1929, SCPC, WILPF papers, series C1, box 2; Schott, *Reconstructing Women's Thoughts,* 136.

10. Addie Hunton to "Lady Mollie" [Terrell], January 19, 1929, Balch papers, SCPC, series C1, box 2. Ironically, by the mid-1930s, Hunton informed her peace colleagues that she was leaving the organization because it appeared the WILPF was not interested in racial justice either within or outside the organization. This issue is discussed in a later chapter.

11. Emily Greene Balch to Addie Hunton, January 29, 1929, Balch Papers, SCPC, series C1, box 2; Schott, *Reconstructing Women's Thoughts,* 136.

12. Mary Church Terrell to Emily Greene Balch, February 1, 1929, Balch Papers, SCPC, series C1, box 2; Schott, *Reconstructing Women's Thoughts,* 136.

13. Ibid.

14. Mary Church Terrell to Addie Hunton, February 1, 1929, Balch Papers, SCPC, series C1, box 2; Schott, *Reconstructing Women's Thoughts,* 136.

15. Mildred Scott Olmsted to Emily Greene Balch, February 15, 1929, Balch Papers, SCPC, series C1, box 3; Note, February 12, 1929, Balch Papers, SCPC, series C1, box 3; and Schott, *Reconstructing Women's Thoughts,* 136.

16. Schott, *Reconstructing Women's Thought,* 136.

17. Addie Hunton, report of the Inter-Racial Committee, May 1932, WILPF papers, SCPC, series E4, box 1.

18. Addie Hunton, report of the Inter-Racial Committee, May 1933, WILPF Papers, SCPC, series E4, box 1.

19. Addie Hunton to Dorothy Detzer, January 8, 1935, WILPF Papers, SCPC, reel 59.

20. Bertha McNeill, chair, National Interracial Committee, branch letter, March 1936, Bertha McNeill Papers, SCPC, box 5.

21. Addie Hunton, report of the Inter-Racial Committee, May 1934, WILPF Papers, SCPC, series E4, box 2.

22. Martha Helen Elliott to Addie Hunton, March 18, 1936, Bertha McNeill Papers, SCPC, box 2; Addie Hunton to Bertha McNeill, note, March 18, 1936, Bertha McNeill Papers, SCPC, box 2. A similar move was advocated for the New York branch by Caroline Singer. See Caroline Singer to Lyn Smith and Dorothy Hommel, memorandum, December 29, 1937, WILPF Papers, SCPC, series C1, box 4.

23. Doris McElwain to Bertha McNeill, April 15, 1937, Bertha McNeill Papers, SCPC, box 3.

24. Bertha McNeill, branch letter, Inter-Racial Committee, March 31, 1936, Bertha McNeill Papers, SCPC, box 3.

25. Ibid.

26. Caroline Singer, chair, Intra-American Committee, New York State Board, report, WILPF, February 25, 1938, WILPF Papers, SCPC, series A2, box 3.

27. Ibid.

28. Caroline Singer, chair, Intra-American Committee, to Mrs. Sutro, Mrs. J. X. Cohen, Mrs. Bloomgarden, Mrs. Bates, and other Long Island and upstate WILPF division chairs, April 1, 1937, WILPF Papers, SCPC, series C1, box 2.

29. Caroline Singer to Mrs. Frank Goewey, January 8, 1938, WILPF Papers, SCPC, series C1, box 3.

30. Singer to Sutro, Cohen, Bloomgarden, Bates, and other Long Island and upstate WILPF division chairs, April 1, 1937, WILPF Papers, SCPC, series C1, box 2.

31. Ibid.

32. Singer offers proof of this in the following document: Caroline Singer

to Lyn Smith and Dorothy Hommel, memorandum, December 29, 1937, WILPF Papers, SCPC, series C1, box 2.

33. Singer to Eleanor (last name unknown), March 15, 1939, WILPF Papers, SCPC, series C1, box 2.

34. Addie Hunton, annual report, 1939, "Interracial Work of the Women's International League for Peace and Freedom," WILPF Papers, SCPC, box 1.

35. Ibid.

36. Addie Hunton to Dorothy Detzer, June 22, 1934, WILPF Papers, SCPC, series C, box 20, folder 5.

37. Addie Hunton to Dorothy Detzer, 1934, WILPF Papers, SCPC, series C, box 20, folder 5.

38. Hunton to Detzer, June 22, 1934.

39. Ibid.

40. Addie Hunton to Dorothy Detzer, 1934, WILPF Papers, SCPC, series C, box 20, folder 5.

41. Ibid.

42. Addie Hunton, chair, National Interracial Committee, annual report, 1940, "Interracial Work of the Women's International League for Peace and Freedom," series C, box 22, folder 5.

43. Ibid.

44. Ibid.

45. Dorothy Hommel to Katherine A. Arnett, June 5, 1938, WILPF Papers, SCPC, series C1, box 3; Foster, *Women and the Warriors,* 279.

46. Ibid.

47. Foster, *Women and the Warriors,* 231; Hannah Clothier Hull to editor, *Philadelphia Enquirer,* August 19, 1936, Hannah Clothier Hull Papers, SCPC, series C1, box 2.

48. Foster, *Women and the Warriors,* 232; Dorothy Detzer to Emily Cooper Johnson, October 9, 1936, WILPF Papers, SCPC, series C1, box 3.

49. Foster, *Women and the Warriors,* 149.

50. Hine, Hine, and Harrold, *African-American Odyssey,* 474.

51. Ibid.

4. Race-ing Domestic Peace, 1915–1945

1. This scenario, while partly fictional, is a re-creation of the way in which Hunton and many other African American women first became involved in peace work. Their main reason for engaging in the struggle was to further the cause of racial justice. They had to be able to establish a link between race and peace.

2. Ibid.

3. John Hope Franklin and Alfred Moss Jr., *From Slavery to Freedom: A History of African Americans* (New York: Alfred A. Knopf, 2000), 326–32.

4. Ibid., 324–25.

5. Ibid., 326.

6. For example, see Linda Schott, *Reconstructing Women's Thoughts: The Women's International League for Peace and Freedom Before World War II* (Palo Alto: Stanford University Press, 1997), 68–72; and Allen Davis, *American Heroine: The Life and Legend of Jane Addams* (New York: Oxford University Press, 1973), chapter 13.

7. "On War Work," report at executive and state chair meeting, November 19–20, 1915, WPP, SCPC, box 1. This issue is also discussed in Schott, *Reconstructing Women's Thoughts;* Carrie Foster, *The Women and the Warriors: The U.S. Section of the Women's International League for Peace and Freedom, 1915–1946* (Syracuse, NY: Syracuse University Press, 1995); and Gertrude Bussey and Margaret Tims, *Pioneers for Peace: The Women's International League for Peace and Freedom, 1915–1965* (Oxford: Alden Press, 1980).

8. Addie Hunton and Kathryn Johnson, *Two Colored Women with the American Expeditionary Forces* (Brooklyn, NY: Eagle Press, 1920), 8–9.

9. Theodore Kornweibel Jr., *"Seeing Red": Federal Campaign Against Black Militancy, 1919–1925,* (Indianapolis: Indiana University Press, 1998), 56.

10. Hunton and Johnson, *Two Colored Women,* 26.

11. Ibid., 32.

12. Ibid.

13. Ibid., 39.

14. Mary Church Terrell, *Colored Woman in a White World* (New York: G. K. Hall, 1996), 253.

15. Lucia Ames Mead to state chairs, April 6, 1917, WPP, SCPC, box 1.

16. For comments on this last point, see minutes of session 3 of annual meeting, 1916, WPP, SCPC, box 1.

17. Terrell, *Colored Woman in a White World,* 360–64; Foster, *Women and the Warriors,* 160.

18. Bussey and Tims, *Pioneers for Peace.*

19. Franklin and Moss, *From Slavery to Freedom,* 336.

20. Kornweibel, *"Seeing Red,"* 55.

21. Franklin and Moss, *From Slavery to Freedom,* 336–39; Robert Moton, *Finding a Way Out: An Autobiography* (New York: Doubleday, 1920), 263.

22. Terrell, *Colored Woman in a White World,* 360–64; Emily Greene Balch to Mildred Scott Olmsted, January 11, 1929, WILPF Papers, SCPC, box 2.

23. Terrell, *Colored Woman in a White World,* 363–64.

24. Foster, *Women and the Warriors,* 15. See Belle LaFollette to Lucy Biddle Lewis, March 27, 1922, LaFollette Papers, Library of Congress, box 2; Mildred Scott Olmsted to Emily Greene Balch, January 7, 1929; and Emily Greene Balch to Mildred Scott Olmsted, January 11, 1929, Balch Papers, SCPC, box 1.

25. Resolution on Race Prejudice, 1922, WILPF Papers, SCPC, series E4, box 1.

26. Bertha McNeill to board members, March 22, 1930, Bertha McNeill Papers, SCPC, series C1, box 1.

27. Foster, *Women and the Warriors,* 164–65; minutes, board meeting, May 23, 1930, WILPF Papers, SCPC.

28. See Denton Watson, *Lion in the Lobby: Clarence Mitchell, Jr.'s Struggle for Passage of Civil Rights Laws* (New York: Morrow, 1997), 47; James Chadburn, *Lynching and Law* (Chapel Hill: University of North Carolina Press, 1993); Arthur Raper, *The Tragedy of Lynching, 1909–1950* (New York: New American Library, 1969); and Raymond Wolters, *Negroes and the Great Depression: The Problem of Economic Recovery* (Westport, CT: Greenwood Publishing, 1970), 206.

29. Addie Hunton to Dorothy Detzer, 1934, WILPF Papers, SCPC, series C1, box 3.

30. Ibid.

31. Foster, *Women and the Warriors,* 164. For the work of peace activists Mary Talbert, Mary Church Terrell, Marian Anderson, and Thelma Marshall with the NAACP, see the following studies: Langston Hughes, *Fight for Freedom: The Story of the NAACP* (New York: Berkeley Publishing, 1962); Charles Kellogg, *NAACP: A History of the National Association for the Advancement of Colored People, 1909–1920* (Baltimore: John Hopkins University Press, 1967); and Terrell, *Colored Woman in a White World.*

32. The W.I.L. Interracial Record, WIL Records, SCPC; and statement and policies, April 24–27, 1929, SCPC, box 4.

33. "Statement of Policies Accepted at Annual Meeting, April 24–27, 1929," *Pax International* 10 (June 1929), WILPF Records, SCPC, series A, box 2, folder 6.

34. Dorothy Detzer, branch letter 7, January 11 and February 2, 1935, WILPF Papers, SCPC, series C1, box 2.

35. Bertha McNeill, branch letter, Inter-Racial Committee, April 4, 1935, WILPF Papers, SCPC, box 4.

36. Addie Hunton to Dorothy Detzer, June 15, 1933, WILPF Papers, SCPC, series E4, box 1.

37. "Resolutions Adopted by the Annual Meeting . . . , April 30–May 1, 1937," WILPF Papers, SCPC, box 2.

38. Ibid. See also Dorothy Detzer, branch letter 43, April 2, 1937, WILPF Papers, SCPC, box 2.

39. Franklin and Moss, *From Slavery to Freedom,* 435.

40. For example, on October 25, 1940, Col. Benjamin O. Davis became the first black to be promoted to the rank of brigadier general. However, election day was too close to convince all African Americans that the promotion was made without political considerations. William H. Hastie was appointed civil-

ian aide to the secretary of war, and Col. Campbell Johnson became an executive assistant to the director of the Selective Service.

41. Dorothy Detzer, branch letter 114, February 22, 1942, WILPF Papers, SCPC, box 2.

42. Foster, *Women and the Warriors,* 298.

43. Foster, *Women and the Warriors,* 297–98.

44. Dorothy Detzer, branch letter 115, April 1, 1942, WILPF Papers, SCPC, box 2.

45. Mildred Scott Olmsted, organizational letter, December 1, 1942, WILPF Papers, SCPC, box 2.

46. Ibid.

47. Dorothy Detzer, branch letter 124, February 11, 1943, WILPF Papers, SCPC, box 3. Emphasis is original.

48. Mildred Scott Olmsted, organizational letter, March 17, 1943, WILPF Papers, SCPC, box 3.

49. Norman E. Byrd, chair of National Non-Partisan Council on Public Affairs of Alpha Kappa Alpha Sorority, to Mildred Scott Olmsted, March 27, 1943, Mildred Scott Olmsted Papers (hereafter referred to as MSO), SCPC, box 2.

50. Ibid.

51. Testimony of Walter White, secretary of the NAACP, before the Senate Military Affairs Committee, April 1, 1943, MSO, SCPC, box 3.

52. Ibid.

53. Ibid.

54. Byrd, March 27, 1943, MSO, SCPC, box 2.

55. Ibid., testimony of Walter White, secretary of the NAACP, before the Senate Military Affairs Committee, April 1, 1943, MSO, SCPC, box 2.

56. Ibid.

57. Byrd, March 27, 1943, MSO, SCPC, box 2.

58. Dorothy Detzer to Mildred Scott Olmsted, February 11, 1943, Women's Committee to Oppose Conscription Papers, SCPC, box 1.

59. Mildred Scott Olmsted, "Statement on House Resolution 1742, . . . May 1943, with Mildred Scott Olmsted," May 11, 1943, MSO, SCPC, box 2.

60. Bertha McNeill to Walter White, November 3, 1943, Bertha McNeill Papers, MSO, SCPC, box 1.

61. Dorothy Detzer, branch letter 150, August 13, 1945, WILPF Papers, SCPC, box 1; A. J. Muste to Harry Truman, August 17, 1945, Fellowship of Reconciliation Papers, SCPC, box 1.

5. Race-ing International Peace, 1915–1945

1. Biographies A–K, WILPF Papers, SCPC, box 1, folder 1.

2. Ibid.

3. International Council of Women of the Darker Races, Mary Church

Terrell Papers, Moorland-Spingarn Research Center (hereafter referred to as MSRC), Howard University, Washington, D.C., box 102, folder 12.

4. Margaret Murray Washington Papers, Hollis-Burke Frissell Library, Tuskegee University, Tuskegee, Alabama, box 2.

5. Jane Porter Barrett to Margaret Murray Washington, February 12, 1925, Margaret Murray Washington Papers, Hollis-Burke Frissell Library, Tuskegee University, box 2.

6. International Council of Women of the Darker Races, Mary Church Terrell Papers, MSRC, Howard University, box 102, folder 12.

7. John Hope Franklin and Alfred Moss Jr., *From Slavery to Freedom: A History of African Americans* (New York: Alfred A. Knopf, 2000), 303.

8. Ibid.

9. Ibid., 305.

10. See "Statement of Policies," April 24–27, 1927, 2, WILPF Papers, SCPC, box 2; minutes of annual meeting, May 3–5, 1928, WILPF Papers, SCPC, box 1; Dorothy Detzer to chairwomen of state and local branches, June 1, 1928, Emily Greene Balch Papers, SCPC, box 1.

11. Rayford Logan, *The Diplomatic Relations of the United States with Haiti, 1776–1891* (Chapel Hill: University of North Carolina Press, 1941), 48. The relations of the United States and Haiti also receive attention in George W. Brown, "Haiti and the United States," *Journal of Negro History* 8 (April 1923): 48–62.

12. Logan, *Diplomatic Relations,* 48.

13. Franklin and Moss, *From Slavery to Freedom,* 306; Logan, *Diplomatic Relations,* 53.

14. Logan, *Diplomatic Relations,* 53.

15. Emily Greene Balch, "Social Values in Haiti," reprinted in *Beyond Nationalism: The Social Thought of Emily Greene Balch,* ed. Mercedes Randall, 145 (New York: Twayne Publishers, 1972).

16. Emily Greene Balch, "Memorandum on Haiti," repr. in ibid., 150.

17. Gertrude Bussey and Margaret Tims, *Pioneers for Peace: The Women's International League for Peace and Freedom, 1915–1965* (Oxford: Alden Press, 1980), 58.

18. Bussey and Tims, *Pioneers for Peace,* 59; Mercedes Randall, *Improper Bostonian: Emily Greene Balch* (New York: Twayne Publishers, 1964), 304–5.

19. Ibrahim K. Sundiata, *Black Scandal: America and the Liberian Labor Class, 1929–1936* (Philadelphia: Institute for the Study of Human Issues, 1980), 38.

20. Yekutiel Gershoni, *Black Colonialism: The Americo-Liberian Scramble for the Hinterland* (Boulder, CO: Westview Press, 1985), 6; Archibald Alexander, *A History of Colonization on the Western Coast of Africa* (New York: Negro Universities Press, 1969), 78.

21. Werner T. Wickstrom, *The American Colonization Society and Liberia, 1817–1867* (Monrovia, Liberia: College of West Africa, 1960), 35.

22. Alexander, *History of Colonization*, 76–77; Gershoni, *Black Colonialism*, 13.

23. Gershoni, *Black Colonialism*, 13.

24. H. Boima Fahnbulleh Jr., *The Diplomacy of Prejudice: Liberia in International Politics, 1945–1970* (New York: Vantage Press, 1985), 11.

25. Fahnbulleh, *Diplomacy of Prejudice*, 12; Raymond Bixler, *The Foreign Policy of the United States in Liberia* (New York: Pageant Press, 1957), 3.

26. Abayomi Karnga, *History of Liberia* (Liverpool, England: Tyte and Company, 1926), 25.

27. Fahnbulleh, *Diplomacy of Prejudice*, 13.

28. Raymond Leslie Buell, *Liberia: A Century of Survival, 1847–1947* (Philadelphia: University of Pennsylvania Press, 1947), 25.

29. C. L. Simpson, *The Symbol of Liberia* (London: Diplomatic Press and Publishing Company, 1961), 99–100; Fahnbulleh, *Diplomacy of Prejudice*, 15.

30. Fahnbulleh, *Diplomacy of Prejudice*, 15.

31. Ibid., 17.

32. Simpson, *Symbol of Liberia*, 102.

33. For an account of the pros and cons regarding the loan to Liberia and the rejection of the loan plan by the U.S. Senate, see Bixler, *Foreign Policy*, 37–57.

34. Fahnbulleh, *Diplomacy of Prejudice*, 23.

35. George Padmore, *Pan-Africanism or Communism* (New York: Doubleday, 1972), 39.

36. The increased importation of rubber into America was the consequence of the use of balloon tires in the automobile industry. America imported 70 percent of the world's rubber, and Britain controlled 80 percent. See Bixler, *Foreign Policy*, 60–61; and Fahnbulleh, *Diplomacy of Prejudice*, 23.

37. The then American secretary of commerce, Herbert Hoover, reported to the Committee on Interstate and Foreign Commerce of the U.S. House of Representatives that America had paid $430 million for crude rubber in 1925, while the year before, the same quantity had cost only $230 million. See Fahnbulleh, *Diplomacy of Prejudice*, 24; and Benjamin Nnamdi Azikiwe, *Liberia in World Politics* (London: A. W. Stockwell, 1935), 141.

38. Fahnbulleh, *Diplomacy of Prejudice*, 24; and Azikiwe, *Liberia in World Politics*, 141.

39. Fahnbulleh, *Diplomacy of Prejudice*, 24; and Bixler, *Foreign Policy*, 68.

40. On April 28, 1925, the Liberian secretary of state wrote to the American minister in Monrovia concerning Liberia's objection to the Firestone loan: "The fundamental position which the Liberian government takes upon this question is that it is politically inadvisable in their view to place the Republic under financial obligations to any private concern operating in the country under grants from the Government. This is a line of policy from which there can be no departure." Quoted in Buell, *Liberia*, 30–31; Fahnbulleh, *Diplomacy of Prejudice*, 24–25.

41. Quoted in Fahnbulleh, *Diplomacy of Prejudice,* 25.

42. Ibid.

43. Buell, *Liberia,* 31–32.

44. Simpson, *Symbol of Liberia,* 134–46.

45. Fred Van der Kraaij, "Firestone in Liberia," in *Dependence, Underdevelopment and Persistent Conflicts—On the Political Economy of Liberia,* edited by Eckhard Hinzen and Robert Kappel, 31 (Bremen, Germany: Unersee-Museum, 1980).

46. Christopher Clapham argues that the government powers were used to "provide an adequate supply of effectively forced labor to the Firestone Plantation." *Liberia and Sierra Leone: An Essay in Comparative Politics* (Cambridge: Cambridge University Press, 1976), 104.

47. Fahnbulleh, *Diplomacy of Prejudice,* 30.

48. Ibid; Azikiwe, *Liberia in World Politics,* 184–85.

49. Fahnbulleh, *Diplomacy of Prejudice,* 31.

50. Ibid.

51. Ibid., 31–32.

52. J. Gus Liebenow, *Liberia: The Evolution of Privilege* (Ithaca, NY: Cornell University Press, 1969), 69; Fahnbulleh, *Diplomacy of Prejudice,* 33.

53. Sundiata, *Black Scandal,* 83.

54. Ibid.

55. Ibid., 85.

56. Mordecai Johnson to Walter White, July 27, 1933, NAACP Papers, Library of Congress. There was a difference of opinion on some issues. Some members of the delegation wanted an American as chief adviser, while others wanted a European (preferably a Scandinavian).

57. Nancy Forderhase, "The Plans That Failed: The United States and Liberia, 1920–1935" (Ph.D. diss., University of Missouri, 1971).

58. Ibid.

59. Statement of W. E. B. DuBois at State Department, July 31, 1933, NAACP Papers, Library of Congress.

60. Azikiwe, *Liberia in World Politics,* 252.

61. Dorothy Detzer, *Appointment on the Hill* (New York: Henry Holt, 1948), 132.

62. Carrie Foster, *The Women and the Warriors: The U.S. Section of the Women's International League for Peace and Freedom, 1915–1946* (Syracuse, NY: Syracuse University Press, 1995), 175–76.

63. Detzer, *Appointment on the Hill,* 132; Foster, *Women and the Warriors,* 176.

64. State Department press release, July 31, 1933, NAACP Papers, Library of Congress.

65. Addie Hunton to Dorothy Detzer, June 14, 1933, SCPC, microfilm, reel 130.50.

66. Dorothy Detzer to Walter White, October 25, 1933, SCPC, microfilm, reel 130.53; Foster, *Women and the Warriors,* 176.

67. Addie Hunton to Walter White, October 28, 1933, WILPF Papers, SCPC, box 1.

68. Dorothy Detzer to Walter White, October 21, 1933, WILPF Papers, SCPC, microfilm, reel 130.53; Walter White to Dorothy Detzer, October 24, 1933, WILPF Papers, SCPC, microfilm, reel 130.53.

69. Sundiata, *Black Scandal,* 98–99.

70. Ibid., 99.

71. Ibid.

72. Arnold Taylor, "The Involvement of Black Americans in the [Liberian] Forced Labor Controversy, 1929–1935," in *The Proceedings of the Conference of Afro-Americans and Africans: Historical and Political Linkages, June 13–14, 1974,* 73–74 (Washington, DC: Howard University Press, 1975).

73. Foster, *Women and the Warriors,* 138; Sundiata, *Black Scandal,* 47, 98.

74. Foster, *Women and the Warriors,* 226–27.

75. Dorothy Detzer to branch 15, May 15, 1935, WILPF Papers, SCPC, box 1.

76. Mildred Scott Olmsted to branch 19, August 1, 1935, WILPF Papers, SCPC, box 1.

77. Bertha McNeill and Addie Hunton to executive board members, memorandum, October 23, 1935, Bertha McNeill Papers, SCPC, box 3.

78. Dorothy Detzer, "What Neutrality Means," *Nation* 141 (December 4, 1935): 642; Foster, *Women and the Warriors,* 226.

79. Foster, *Women and the Warriors,* 225.

80. Robert Divine, *The Illusion of Neutrality: Franklin D. Roosevelt and the Struggle over the Arms Embargo* (Chicago: University of Chicago Press, 1962), 135–36.

81. Dorothy Detzer, "United States and Neutrality," *Pax International* 11 (January–February 1936), WILPF Papers, University of Colorado Peace Collection, Boulder, CO, box 3.

82. Ibid.

83. Dorothy Destzer, "The Pro-Neutrality Pattern," appended to branch letter 70, February 28, 1939, quoted in Barbara Miller Solomon, "Dilemmas of Pacifist Women, Quakers and Others in World Wars I and II," in *Witnesses for Change: Quaker Women over Three Centuries,* ed. Elisabeth Potts Brown and Susan Mosher Stuard, 123 (New Brunswick, NJ: Rutgers University Press, 1989); Harriet Alonso, *Peace as a Women's Issue: A History of the U.S. Movement for World Peace and Women's Rights* (Syracuse, NY: Syracuse University Press, 1993), 136.

84. "First Interview Between Mildred Scott Olmsted and Mercedes Randall in New York City," February 1972, Mildred Scott Olmsted Papers, SCPC, box 9; Bertha McNeill and Addie Hunton to Dorothy Detzer, May 1938, Bertha McNeill Papers, SCPC, box 2.

85. William Scott, *The Sons of Sheba's Race: African-Americans and the Italo-Ethiopian War, 1935–1941* (Indianapolis: Indiana University Press, 1992), 39.

86. Ibid., 55.

87. Letter from Emily Greene Balch to Alice Hamilton, February 20, 1941, quoted in Solomon, "Dilemmas of Pacifist Women," 153; Alonso, *Peace as a Women's Issue,* 138.

88. Scott, *Sons of Sheba's Race,* 56.

89. Alonso, *Peace as a Women's Issue,* 139.

90. Scott, *Sons of Sheba's Race,* 56.

91. "Report to Tenth International Congress of WILPF," 1946, WILPF Papers, SCPC, box 2.

92. Linda Schott, *Reconstructing Women's Thoughts: The Women's International League for Peace and Freedom Before World War II* (Palo Alto: Stanford University Press, 1997), 149.

6. A New Generation of Peace Activists: Waging Different Battles in Unpredictable Times, 1945–1960

1. This fictional scenario is a reconstruction of how noted peace activist Bertha McNeill might have viewed World War II and its effects on post–World War II America.

2. Ibid.

3. Carrie Foster, *The Women and the Warriors: The Story of the WILPF* (Syracuse, NY: Syracuse University Press, 1995), 329.

4. Biographies A–K, WILPF Papers, SCPC, folder 1, box 1.

5. Ibid.

6. Brenda Gayle Plummer, *Rising Wind: Black Americans and U.S. Foreign Affairs, 1935–1960* (Chapel Hill: University of North Carolina Press, 1996), 125.

7. Ibid., 3–4.

8. Penny M. Von Eschen, *Race Against Empire: Black Americans and Anti-Colonialism, 1937–1957* (Ithaca, NY: Cornell University Press, 1997), 78; Metz T. P. Lochard, "Parley May Skip over Hot Issue of Colonies," *Chicago Defender,* May 5, 1945, 2; Thomas Borstelmann, *Apartheid's Reluctant Uncle: The United States and Southern Africa in the Early Cold War* (New York: Oxford University Press, 1993), 65.

9. Plummer, *Rising Wind,* 23–24.

10. Ibid., 132; emphasis is mine.

11. Plummer, *Rising Wind,* 132.

12. Plummer, *Rising Wind,* 135; Jake Miller, *The Black Presence in American Foreign Affairs* (Washington, DC: University Press of America, 1978), 90.

13. Rayford W. Logan, "The 'Little Man' Just Isn't Here," *Pittsburgh Courier,* May 5, 1945, 3.

14. Biographies A–K, WILPF Papers, SCPC, folder 1, box 1.

15. Plummer, *Rising Wind,* 138–39.

16. Ibid., 140.

17. Ibid.

18. Ibid., 145.

19. Eschen, *Race Against Empire,* 107; Michael Hunt, *Ideology and U.S. Foreign Policy* (New Haven: Yale University Press, 1983), 158. Black peace activists did not support the part of the Truman Doctrine that advocates the use of military force by Americans in situations where persons were being subjugated against their will.

20. Walter White to Dorothy Detzer, WILPF executive board, May 23, 1945, WILPF Papers, SCPC, box 3.

21. For further information about America's position on apartheid in South Africa, see Gabriel Kolko, *Confronting the Third World: United States Foreign Policy, 1945–1980* (New York: Pantheon Books, 1988); and Thomas Noer, *Cold War and Black Liberation: The United States and White Rule in Africa, 1948–1968* (Columbia: University of Missouri Press, 1985).

22. Eschen, *Race Against Empire,* 84–85.

23. Charles Patterson, *Marian Anderson* (New York: Franklin Watts, 1988), 147; Marian Anderson, "My Life in a White World, as Told to Emily Kimbrough," *Ladies' Home Journal,* September 1960, 4.

24. Patterson, *Marian Anderson,* 147.

25. Shirlee P. Newman, *Marian Anderson: Lady from Philadelphia* (Philadelphia: Westminster Press, 1966), 124.

26. Patterson, *Marian Anderson,* 148.

27. For a detailed description of the Manhattan project and the scientists' feelings about the bomb, see Richard Rhodes, *The Making of the Atomic Bomb* (New York: Touchstone, 1986); and Alice Kimball Smith, *A Peril and a Hope: The Scientists' Movement in America, 1945–1947* (Chicago: University of Chicago Press, 1965).

28. Harriet Alonso, *Peace as a Women's Issue: A History of the U.S. Movement for World Peace and Women's Rights* (Syracuse, NY: Syracuse University Press, 1993), 172.

29. Ibid., 175.

30. Ibid., 173–74.

31. *Denver Post,* January 15, 1954, 1.

32. Alonso, *Peace as a Women's Issue,* 175.

33. Ibid.

34. Ibid., 178.

35. Ibid.

36. Erna P. Harris, "Statement," WILPF, Harris and Sissom Papers, SCPC, box 1.

37. "Delegate to Tell of International Meet," November 27, 1956, Harris and Sissom Papers, SCPC, box 1.

38. Ibid.

39. Mary Sissom to Meta Riseman, president of U.S. section of WILPF, April 1956, WILPF Papers, SCPC, box 3.

40. Elinor Lee, "She's Off to the Congo to Organize a College," *Washington Post,* July 30, 1962, 6.

41. Ibid.

42. Plummer, *Rising Wind,* 201.

43. Harvard Sitkoff, *The Struggle for Black Equality, 1954–1992* (New York: Hill and Wang, 1993), 133–216.

44. Ibid., 144; cochairs, Civil Rights Committee, "Statement to the WILPF Branches on the Supreme Court Decisions of May 17, 1954, and May 31, 1955," memorandum, November 1955, Bertha McNeill Papers, SCPC, box 3.

45. Bertha McNeill, Bessie McLaurin, and Erna P. Harris, cochairs, Civil Rights Committee, memorandum, November 1955, Bertha McNeill Papers, SCPC, box 3.

46. Gertrude Bussey and Margaret Tims, *Pioneers for Peace: The Women's International League for Peace and Freedom, 1915–1965* (Oxford: Alden Press, 1980), 227.

47. Ibid.

48. Ibid.

49. Ibid., 224.

50. Ibid., 225.

7. Redefining Racial Justice: Here, There, and Everywhere, 1960–1975

1. Judith Adams, *Peacework: Oral Histories of Women Peace Activists* (Boston: Twayne Publishers, 1991), 110–12.

2. Ibid.

3. Ibid., 114.

4. Sadie Sawyer Hughley, interview by author, tape recording, Durham, North Carolina, March 16, 1993.

5. Ibid.

6. Coretta Scott King, *My Life with Martin Luther King, Jr.* (New York: Holt, Rinehart and Winston, 1969), 209.

7. Larry Doughtery, "Archivist Harris Recalls Her Life Fighting Racism," *Daily Californian,* February 26, 1986, 11; Becky Hart, "Harris Lived an Independent Life," *Wichita State University Alumni News* 3, no. 6 (May–June 1995), 5.

8. Ibid.

9. James Weistheider, *Fighting on Two Fronts: African Americans and the*

Vietnam War (New York: New York University Press, 1997), 32; "Draft Cases Snag U.S. Courts," *Black Panthers,* September 13, 1969, 20.

10. Weistheider, *Fighting on Two Fronts,* 33.

11. Ibid.

12. Juan Williams, *Eyes on the Prize: America's Civil Rights Years, 1954–1965* (New York: Viking–Penguin Press, 1987), 241–42; see also Kay Mills, *This Little Light of Mine: The Life of Fannie Lou Hamer* (New York: Penguin Books, 1993), 136–72; Reese Cleghorn, "Who Speaks for Mississippi?" *Reporter,* August 13, 1964, 31.

13. Sadie Sawyer Hughley, interview by author, tape recording, Durham, North Carolina, March 16, 1993; Bessie McLaurin, "Notes on Selma to Montgomery March," *WILPF Journal* (Chapel Hill–Durham branch), June 1965, 1.

14. Diane Nash, "Inside the Sit-ins and Freedom Rides: Testimony of a Southern Student," in *The New Negro,* ed. Matthew H. Ahmann, 44, 45, 48, 49 (New York: Biblo and Tannen, 1969).

15. For a detailed account of Diane Nash's political activism, see Clayborne Carson, *In Struggle: SNCC and the Black Awakening of the 1960s* (Cambridge: Harvard University Press, 1985), 32–46, 52–54.

16. See Angela Davis, *Angela Davis: An Autobiography* (New York: Random House, 1974), 180–85.

17. Harriet Alonso, *Peace as a Women's Issue: A History of the U.S. Movement for World Peace and Women's Rights* (Syracuse, NY: Syracuse University Press, 1993), 170.

18. Ibid., 159–72.

19. Gertrude Bussey and Margaret Tims, *Pioneers for Peace: The Women's International League for Peace and Freedom, 1915–1965* (Oxford: Alden Press, 1980), 243–44.

20. Henry Bussey, "Peace Worker Finds Small Chink in Russian Public Relations Front," *Portland Reporter,* May 21, 1964, 1, Harris and Sissom Papers, SCPC, box 1.

21. Barbara Coleman Fox, "Philadelphia Woman Meets Mrs. K: Russians Greet Delegates of League for Peace and Freedom," *Women Today,* May 3, 1964, 3, Harris and Sissom Papers, SCPC, box 1.

22. Ibid.

23. Cornelia Weil, "International Peace Delegate Says Irrational Discrimination Must End," *Eugene Register Guard,* May 20, 1964, 3, Harris and Sissom Papers, SCPC, box 1.

24. Alonso, *Peace as a Woman's Issue,* 196.

25. Erna Prather Harris to national board members, memorandum, July 26, 1964, Harris and Sissom Papers, SCPC, box 1.

26. Erna Prather Harris to Hubert Humphrey, September 20, 1962, Harris

and Sissom Papers, SCPC, box 3; Hubert Humphrey to Erna Harris, October 29, 1962, Harris and Sissom Papers, SCPC, box 3.

27. Erna Prather Harris, "South Africa and World Peace," memorandum, n.d., Harris and Sissom Papers, SCPC, box 1.

28. Ibid.

29. Alonso, *Peace as a Women's Issue*, 197, 199; Erna Prather Harris to WILPF executive board, memorandum, June 1965, Harris and Sissom Papers, SCPC, box 3.

30. Annalee Stewart to Beatrice Pearson, December 13, 1962, Orlie Pell Papers, Rutgers University Libraries, Special Collections and Archives, box 2.

31. *New York Times*, November 28, 1965, 4.

32. Octavia Vivian, *Coretta: The Story of Mrs. Martin Luther King, Jr.* (Philadelphia: Fortress Press, 1970), 105–6; Phyl Garland, "Coretta King: In Her Husband's Footsteps," *Ebony*, September 1968, 155.

33. Howard Zinn, *Vietnam: The Logic of Withdrawal* (Boston: Beacon Press, 1967), 19.

34. Martin Luther King Jr., *Where Do We Go from Here?: Chaos or Community* (New York: Harper and Row, 1967), 38.

35. Ibid.

36. Martin Luther King Jr., "Nonviolence and Racial Justice," in *The Burden of Race: A Documentary History of Negro and White Relations in America,* ed. Gilbert Osofsky, 523 (New York: Harper and Row, 1967).

37. *Washington Post*, April 16, 1968; Coretta Scott King, "Statement at WILPF Conference," in *My Country Is the Whole World: An Anthology of Women's Work on Peace and War,* ed. Cambridge Women's Collective, 183–84 (London: Pandora Press, 1984).

38. Eartha Kitt, *Alone with Me: A New Autobiography* (Chicago: Henry Regnery, 1976), 237, 245–46.

39. Kitt, *Alone with Me,* 250–54, 257; editorial, *Muhammad Speaks,* February 2, 1968; *New York Amsterdam News,* January 27, February 3, 10, 24, and March 9, 1968.

40. Rochelle Gatlin, *American Women since 1945* (Jackson: University Press of Mississippi, 1987), 116.

41. Mills, *This Little Light of Mine,* 216–35; Fannie Lou Hamer, "Sick and Tired of Being Sick and Tired," 162, Fannie Lou Hamer Papers, Widener Library, Harvard University, reel 2.

42. Diane Nash Bevel, "Journey to North Vietnam," *Freedomways* 7 (Spring 1967): 119; *Muhammad Speaks,* February 10 and 24, 1967; *Afro-American,* February 4, 1967.

43. *Muhammad Speaks,* February 10 and 24, 1967.

44. Sadie Sawyer Hughley, interview by author, tape recording, Durham, North Carolina, February 15, 1993.

45. Ibid.

46. Kay Camp, "Report of Mission to Vietnam," *Pax et Libertas,* January–June 1971, 2–3.

47. Philip S. Foner, ed., *The Black Panthers Speak* (New York: Da Capo Press, 1995), 2, 46; *Black Panther,* September 14, 1968.

48. Angela Davis, *Autobiography,* 151, 190; Angela Davis, "I Am a Black Revolutionary Woman," in *The Voice of Black America: Major Speeches by Negroes in the United States, 1797–1973,* ed. Philip S. Foner, 1179–80 (New York: Simon and Schuster, 1972); Angela Davis, *If They Come in the Morning: Voices of Resistance* (New York: New American Library, 1971), 190–91.

49. Davis, *Autobiography,* 151, 190; Davis, *If They Come in the Morning,* 190–91.

50. See Patricia Hill Collins, *Black Feminist Thought: Knowledge, Consciousness, and the Politics of Empowerment* (Boston: Unwin Hyman, 1990), 142, 155–56. See also Rosalyn Terborg-Penn, "African Feminism: A Theoretical Approach to the History of Women in the African Diaspora," in *Women in Africa and the African Diaspora,* ed. Rosalyn Terborg-Penn, Sharon Harley, and Andrea Benton Rushing, 45–50 (Washington, DC: Howard University Press, 1987).

51. Shirley Chisholm, *Unbought and Unbossed* (Boston: Houghton-Mifflin, 1970), 94–99; Shirley Chisholm, "All We Are Saying Is—," *Freedomways* 12 (Second Quarter 1972): 118.

52. Chisholm, "All We Are Saying Is—," 118.

53. "Chisholm Blasts Hard at Defense Spending," *Pittsburgh Courier,* April 12, 1969, 2.

54. "Two Black GIs Convicted of Rape Ask Help of Pentagon," *Chicago Tribune,* June 9, 1971; Joel Dreyfuss, "Shirley Aids Black GIs' Fight," *Washington Post,* August 11, 1971, 9.

55. Chisholm, "All We Are Saying Is—," 119.

56. "Free the Camp Allen Brothers," *Winter Soldier* 3 (June 1973), 14, in Vietnam Veterans Against the War/*Winter Soldier* file 7019, box 1.

57. Richard Scammon, "Report from Black America," *Newsweek,* June 30, 1969, 19; Weistheider, *Fighting on Two Fronts,* 33.

58. Heather Brandon, *Casualties: Death in Vietnam; Anguish and Survival in America* (New York: St. Martin's Press, 1984), 93–94, 211, 212.

59. Ibid., 211.

60. Ibid., 212.

61. Sadie Sawyer Hughley, interview by author, tape recording, Durham, North Carolina, March 16, 1993.

62. Jocelyn H. Cohen, Ellen Dwyer, and Jean Robinson, *Women in Social Protest: The U.S. since 1915 (Photographic Postcard)* (Bloomington, IN: Helaine Victoria Press, 1989), picture of demonstration; Fred Halstead, *Out Now!: A*

Participant's Account of the American Movement Against the Vietnam War (New York: Monad Press, 1978), 282; *Chicago Defender,* October 18, 1969.

63. Halstead, *Out Now!,* 282.

64. *New York Times,* October 23, 1967.

65. Vera Chandler Foster, interview by author, telephone, Alexandria, Virginia, February 22, 1997.

Conclusion

1. Report on Zurich Conference, 1919, WILPF Papers, SCPC, box 31.

2. Both Harriet Alonso's *Peace as a Women's Issue: A History of the U.S. Movement for World Peace and Women's Rights* (Syracuse, NY: Syracuse University Press, 1993) and Carrie Foster's *The Women and the Warriors: The Story of the WILPF* (Syracuse, NY: Syracuse University Press, 1995) made this claim.

3. Alonso, *Peace as a Women's Issue,* 231.

Bibliography

Primary Sources

Manuscript Collections

Boulder, Colorado. University of Colorado. Women's International League for Peace and Freedom Papers.

Cambridge, Massachusetts. Harvard University. Widener Library. Fannie Lou Hamer Papers.

Swarthmore, Pennsylvania. Swarthmore College Peace Collection.

Anna Melissa Graves Papers
Bertha McNeill Papers
Carrie Chapman Catt Papers
Dorothy Detzer Papers
Emily Greene Balch Papers
Erna Prather Harris and Mary Sissom Papers
Fellowship of Reconciliation Papers
Hannah Clothier Hull Papers
Jane Addams Papers
Jane Addams Peace Association Papers
LaFollette Family Papers
Mary Church Terrell Papers
Mildred Scott Olmsted Papers
National Council on the Cause and Cure for War Papers
Woman's Peace Party Papers
Women's International League for Peace and Freedom Papers
Women's Committee to Oppose Conscription Papers
Women's Peace Society Papers

Tuskegee, Alabama. Hollis-Burke Frissell Library Archival Collection, Tuskegee
    University.
    Martha Murray Washington Papers
    Monroe Work Papers
    Vera Chandler Foster Papers
Washington, D.C. Howard University Moorland Spingarn Research Center.
    Mary Church Terrell Papers.
Washington, D.C. Library of Congress. NAACP Papers.

Interviews

Foster, Vera Chandler. Interview by author. Telephone. February 22, 1997. Al-
    exandria, Virginia.
Harris, Erna Prather. Interview by Judith Adams. October 2, 1985. Transcript,
    Stanford Oral History Collection, Stanford University, Palo Alto, California.
Hughley, Sadie Sawyer. Interview by author. February 15, 1993, and March 16,
    1993. Durham, North Carolina.
Jackson, Inez. Interview by Judith Adams. September 23, 1985. Transcript,
    Stanford Oral History Collection, Stanford University, Palo Alto, California.
Maxwell, Enola. Interview by Judith Adams. September 23, 1985. Transcript,
    Stanford Oral History Collection, Stanford University, Palo Alto, California.
Moore, Carol. Interview by author. Telephone. December 18, 1993. Philadelphia,
    Pennsylvania.
Okun, Beth, Tan Schwab, Charlotte Adams, and Ann Ivey. Interview by author.
    February 15 and March 16, 1993.

Secondary Sources
Books

Addams, Jane. *Peace and Bread in Time of War.* Boston: G. K. Hall, 1960.
———. *Twenty Years at Hull House.* New York: Phillips Publishing and Mac-
    millan, 1910. Reprint, New York: New American Library, 1930.
———. *The Second Twenty Years at Hull House.* New York: Macmillan, 1935.
Ahmann, Matthew H., ed. *The New Negro.* New York: Biblo and Tannen, 1969.
Alexander, Archibald. *A History of Colonization on the Western Coast of Africa.*
    New York: Negro Universities Press, 1969.
Alonso, Harriet. *Peace as a Women's Issue: A History of the U.S. Movement for World
    Peace and Women's Rights.* Syracuse, NY: Syracuse University Press, 1993.
———. *The Women's Peace Union and the Outlawry of War, 1921–1942.* Knox-
    ville: University of Tennessee Press, 1989.
Azikiwe, Benjamin Nnamdi. *Liberia in World Politics.* London: A. W. Stockwell,
    1935.
Bacon, Margaret Hope. *One Woman's Passion for Peace and Freedom: The Life
    of Mildred Scott Olmsted.* Syracuse, NY: Syracuse University Press, 1992.

Balch, Emily Greene, ed. *Occupied Haiti.* New York: Garland Publishers, 1927.

Bennett, David. *The Party of Fear: From Nativist Movements to the New Right in American History.* Chapel Hill: University of North Carolina Press, 1988.

Bixler, Raymond. *The Foreign Policy of the United States in Liberia.* New York: Pageant Press, 1957.

Blauner, Bob. *Black Lives, White Lives: Three Decades of Race Relations in America.* Berkeley: University of California Press, 1989.

Borstelmann, Thomas. *Apartheid's Reluctant Uncle: The United States and Southern Africa in the Early Cold War.* New York: Oxford University Press, 1993.

Brandon, Heather. *Casualties: Death in Vietnam; Anguish and Survival in America.* New York: St. Martin's Press, 1984.

Brinker-Babler, Gisela. *Women Against War.* Frankfurt, Germany: Fischer Taxchenbuch Verlag, 1980.

Brock, Peter. *Twentieth-Century Pacifism.* New York: Van Nostrand Reinhold Company, 1970.

Brock, Peter, and Nigel Young. *Pacifism in the Twentieth Century.* Syracuse, NY: Syracuse University Press, 1999.

Brown, Elizabeth Potts, and Susan Mosher Stuard, eds. *Witnesses for Change: Quaker Women over Three Centuries.* New Brunswick, NJ: Rutgers University Press, 1989.

Buell, Raymond Leslie. *Liberia: A Century of Survival, 1847–1947.* Philadelphia: University of Pennsylvania Press, 1947.

———. *The Native Problem in Africa.* New York: Macmillan, 1928.

Bussey, Gertrude, and Margaret Tims. *Pioneers for Peace: The Women's International League for Peace and Freedom, 1915–1965.* Oxford: Alden Press, 1980.

Carby, Hazel. *Reconstructing Womanhood: The Emergence of the Afro-American Woman Novelist.* New York: Oxford University Press, 1987.

Carr, Robert. *The House Committee on Un-American Activities, 1945–1960.* Ithaca, NY: Cornell University Press, 1952.

Carson, Clayborne. *In Struggle: SNCC and the Black Awakening of the 1960s.* Cambridge: Harvard University Press, 1985.

Carson, Josephine. *Silent Voices: Southern Negro Women Today.* New York: Delacorte Press, 1969.

Chadburn, James. *Lynching and Law.* Chapel Hill: University of North Carolina Press, 1993.

Chafe, William. *The Unfinished Journey: America since World War II.* New York: Oxford University Press, 1999.

Chatfield, Charles. *For Peace and Justice: Pacifism in America, 1914–1941.* Knoxville: University of Tennessee Press, 1971.

Chisholm, Shirley. *Unbought and Unbossed.* Boston: Houghton-Mifflin, 1970.

Church, Annette, and Roberta Church. *The Robert R. Churches of Memphis: A Father and Son Who Achieved in Spite of Race.* Memphis: A. E. Church, 1974.

Clapham, Christopher. *Liberia and Sierra Leone: An Essay in Comparative Politics.* Cambridge: Cambridge University Press, 1976.

Cohen, Jocelyn H., Ellen Dwyer, and Jean Robinson. *Women in Social Protest: The U.S. since 1915 (Photographic Postcard).* Bloomington, IN: Helaine Victoria Press, 1989.

Collins, Patricia Hill. *Black Feminist Thought: Knowledge, Consciousness, and the Politics of Empowerment.* Boston: Unwin Hyman, 1990.

Cott, Nancy. *The Grounding of Modern Feminism.* New Haven: Yale University Press, 1987.

Crawford, Vicki, Jacqueline Rouse, and Barbara Woods, eds. *Women in the Civil Rights Movement: Trailblazers and Torchbearers, 1941–1965.* Brooklyn, NY: Carlson Publishing, 1990.

Curti, Merle. *Peace or War: The American Struggle, 1636–1936.* New York: W. W. Norton and Company, 1936.

Davis, Allen. *American Heroine: The Life and Legend of Jane Addams.* New York: Oxford University Press, 1973.

Davis, Angela. *Angela Davis: An Autobiography.* New York: Random House, 1974.

———. *If They Come in the Morning: Voices of Resistance.* New York: New American Library, 1971.

DeBenedetti, Charles. *An American Ordeal: The Antiwar Movement of the Vietnam Era.* Syracuse, NY: Syracuse University Press, 1990.

———. *The Peace Reform in American History.* Bloomington: Indiana University Press, 1980.

Degen, Marie. *The History of the Woman's Peace Party.* Baltimore: John Hopkins University Press, 1939.

De Lauretis, Theresa. *Feminist Studies/Critical Studies: Issues, Terms and Contexts.* Bloomington: Indiana University Press, 1996.

Detzer, Dorothy. *Appointment on the Hill.* New York: Henry Holt, 1948.

Divine, Robert. *The Illusion of Neutrality: Franklin D. Roosevelt and the Struggle over the Arms Embargo.* Chicago: University of Chicago Press, 1962.

Fahnbulleh, H. Boima, Jr. *The Diplomacy of Prejudice: Liberia in International Politics, 1945–1970.* New York: Vantage Press, 1985.

Foner, Philip S., ed. *The Black Panthers Speak.* New York: Da Capo Press, 1995.

———. *The Voice of Black America: Major Speeches by Negroes in the United States, 1797–1973.* New York: Simon and Schuster, 1972.

Foster, Carrie. *The Women and the Warriors: The U.S. Section of the Women's International League for Peace and Freedom, 1915–1946.* Syracuse, NY: Syracuse University Press, 1995.

Foster, Catherine. *Women for All Seasons: The Story of the Women's International League for Peace and Freedom.* Athens: University of Georgia Press, 1989.

Franklin, John Hope, and Alfred Moss Jr. *From Slavery to Freedom: A History of African Americans.* New York: Alfred A. Knopf, 2000.

Frederickson, George. *The Black Image in the White Mind: The Debate on Afro-American Character and Destiny, 1817–1914*. New York: Harper and Row, 1977.

Gaines, Kevin. *Uplifting the Race: Black Leadership, Politics, and Culture in the Twentieth Century*. Chapel Hill: University of North Carolina Press, 1996.

Gershoni, Yekutiel. *Black Colonialism: The Americo-Liberian Scramble for the Hinterland*. Boulder, CO: Westview Press, 1985.

Giddings, Paula. *In Search of Sisterhood: Delta Sigma Theta and the Challenge of the Black Sorority Movement*. New York: William Morrow and Company, 1988.

———. *When and Where I Enter . . . The Impact of Black Women on Race and Sex in America*. New York: William Morris, 1984.

Goldman, Eric. *The Crucial Decade and After: America, 1945–1965*. New York: Vintage Books, 1950.

Hall, Jacquelyn. *Revolt Against Chivalry: Jessie Daniel Ames and the Women's Campaign Against Lynching*. New York: Columbia University Press, 1979.

Hallowes, Frances. *Women and War: An Appeal to the Women of All Nations*. London: Headley Brothers, 1914.

Halstead, Fred. *Out Now!: A Participant's Account of the American Movement Against the Vietnam War*. New York: Monad Press, 1978.

Haynes, Robert. *A Night of Violence: The Houston Riot of 1917*. Baton Rouge: Louisiana State University Press, 1976.

Hine, Darlene Clark. *Black Women in White: Racial Conflict and Cooperation in the Nursing Profession, 1890–1950*. Bloomington: Indiana University Press, 1989.

———. *Hine Sight: Black Women and the Re-Construction of American History*. New York: Carlson Publishing, 1994.

Hine, Darlene Clark, Elsa Barkley Brown, and Rosalyn Terborg-Penn, eds. *Black Women in America: An Historical Encyclopedia*. 2 vols. Brooklyn, NY: Carlson Publishing, 1993.

Hine, Darlene Clark, and David Gaspar. *More Than Chattel: Black Women and Slavery in the Americas*. Bloomington: Indiana University Press, 1996.

Hine, Darlene Clark, William Hine, and Stanley Harrold. *The African-American Odyssey*. Upper Saddle River, NJ: Prentice-Hall, 2000.

Hine, Darlene Clark, and Kathleen Thompson. *A Shining Thread of Hope: The History of Black Women in America*. New York: Broadway Books, 1998.

Hochschild, Jennifer. *Thirty Years After Brown*. Washington, DC: Joint Center for Political Studies, 1985.

hooks, bell. *Ain't I a Woman?: Black Women and Feminism*. Boston: South End Press, 1981.

Hughes, Langston. *Fight for Freedom: The Story of the NAACP*. New York: Berkeley Publishing, 1962.

Hunt, Michael. *Ideology and U.S. Foreign Policy.* New Haven: Yale University Press, 1983.

Hunter, Tera. *To 'Joy My Freedom: Southern Black Women Lives and Labors after the Civil War.* Cambridge: Harvard University Press, 1997.

Hunton, Addie, and Kathryn Johnson. *Two Colored Women with the American Expeditionary Forces.* Brooklyn, NY: Eagle Press, 1920.

Jones, Beverly Washington. *Quest for Equality: The Life and Writings of Mary Eliza Church Terrell, 1863–1954.* New York: Carlson Publishing, 1990.

Karnga, Abayomi. *History of Liberia.* Liverpool, England: Tyte and Company, 1926.

Kellogg, Charles. *NAACP: A History of the National Association for the Advancement of Colored People, 1909–1920.* Baltimore: John Hopkins University Press, 1967.

King, Coretta Scott. *My Life with Martin Luther King, Jr.* New York: Holt, Rinehart and Winston, 1969.

Kitt, Eartha. *Alone with Me: A New Autobiography.* Chicago: Henry Regnery, 1976.

Kluger, Richard. *Simple Justice: The History of Brown vs. Board of Education and Black America's Struggle for Equality.* New York: Knopf, 1976.

Kolko, Gabriel. *Confronting the Third World: United States Foreign Policy, 1945–1980.* New York: Pantheon Books, 1988.

Kornweibel, Theodore, Jr. *"Seeing Red": Federal Campaigns Against Black Militancy, 1919–1925.* Indianapolis: Indiana University Press, 1998.

Kusmer, Kenneth. *A Ghetto Takes Shape: Black Cleveland, 1870–1930.* Urbana: University of Illinois Press, 1976.

Ladner, Joyce. *Tomorrow's Tomorrow.* Garden City, NY: Doubleday, 1972.

Lemmons, Stanley. *The Woman Citizen: Social Feminism in the 1920s.* Urbana: University of Illinois Press, 1973.

Lerner, Gerda. *Black Women in White America: A Documentary History.* New York: Vintage Books, 1972.

———. *The Creation of a Feminist Consciousness.* New York: Oxford University Press, 1993.

———. *The Majority Finds Its Past: Placing Women in History.* New York: Oxford University Press, 1979.

Liebenow, J. Gus. *Liberia: The Evolution of Privilege.* Ithaca, NY: Cornell University Press, 1969.

Logan, Rayford. *The Diplomatic Relations of the United States with Haiti, 1776–1891.* Chapel Hill: University of North Carolina Press, 1941.

Marchand, C. Roland. *The American Peace Movement and Social Reform, 1898–1918.* Princeton: Princeton University Press, 1972.

Marcus, Robert, and David Burner. *America Firsthand: From Reconstruction to the Present.* New York: St. Martin's Press, 1989.

Millard, Betty. *Women on Guard: How the Women of the World Fight for Peace.* New York: New Century Publishers, 1972.

Miller, Jake. *The Black Presence in American Foreign Affairs.* Washington, DC: University Press of America, 1978.

Mills, Kay. *This Little Light of Mine: The Life of Fannie Lou Hamer.* New York: Penguin Books, 1993.

Moton, Robert. *Finding a Way Out: An Autobiography.* New York: Doubleday, 1920.

Mullen, Robert. *Blacks and Vietnam.* Washington, DC: University Press of America, 1975.

Neverdon-Morton, Cynthia. *Afro-American Women of the South and the Advancement of the Race, 1895–1925.* Knoxville: University of Tennessee Press, 1989.

Murray, Robert. *Red Scare: A Study in National Hysteria, 1919–1920.* Minneapolis: University of Minnesota Press, 1955.

Newman, Shirlee P. *Marian Anderson: Lady from Philadelphia.* Philadelphia: Westminster Press, 1966.

Noer, Thomas. *Cold War and Black Liberation: The United States and White Rule in Africa, 1948–1968.* Columbia: University of Missouri Press, 1985.

O'Neill, William. *Everyone Was Brave: The Rise and Fall of Feminism in America.* Chicago: Quadrangle Books, 1969.

Osofsky, Gilbert. *The Burden of Race.* New York: Harper and Row, 1967.

Padmore, George. *Pan-Africanism or Communism.* New York: Doubleday, 1972.

Patterson, Charles. *Marian Anderson.* New York: Franklin Watts, 1988.

Plummer, Brenda Gayle. *Rising Wind: Black Americans and U.S. Foreign Policy, 1935–1960.* Chapel Hill: University of North Carolina Press, 1996.

Preston, William. *Alien and Dissenters: Federal Suppression of Radicals, 1903–1933.* Urbana: University of Illinois Press, 1994.

Quarles, Benjamin. *The Negro in the Making of America.* New York: Simon and Schuster, 1996.

Randall, Mercedes. *Improper Bostonian: Emily Greene Balch, Nobel Peace Laureate.* New York: Twayne Publishers, 1972.

———, ed. *Beyond Nationalism: The Social Thought of Emily Greene Balch.* New York: Twayne Publishers, 1972.

Raper, Arthur. *The Tragedy of Lynching, 1909–1950.* New York: New American Library, 1969.

Rhodes, Richard. *The Making of the Atomic Bomb.* New York: Touchstone, 1986.

Rudwick, Elliott. *Race Riot at East St. Louis, July 2, 1917.* Cleveland: World Publishing, 1966.

Scharf, Lois, and Joan Jensen, eds. *Decades of Discontent: The Women's Movement, 1920–1940.* Westport, CT: Greenwood Press, 1983.

Schott, Linda. *Reconstructing Women's Thoughts: The Women's International League for Peace and Freedom Before World War II.* Palo Alto: Stanford University Press, 1997.

Scott, James. *Weapons of the Weak: Everyday Forms of Peasant Resistance.* New Haven: Yale University Press, 1985.

Scott, William. *The Sons of Sheba's Race: African-Americans and the Italo-Ethiopian War, 1935–1941.* Indianapolis: Indiana University Press, 1992.

Senechel, Roberta. *The Sociogenesis of a Race Riot: Springfield, Illinois, in 1908.* Urbana: University of Illinois Press, 1990.

Shaw, Stephanie. *What a Woman Ought to Be and Do: Black Professional Workers During the Jim Crow Era.* Chicago: University of Chicago Press, 1996.

Simpson, C. L. *The Symbol of Liberia.* London: Diplomatic Press and Publishing Company, 1961.

Sitkoff, Harvard. *The Struggle for Black Equality, 1954–1992.* New York: Hill and Wang, 1993.

Small, Melvin, and William D. Hoover, eds. *Give Peace a Chance: Exploring the Vietnam Antiwar Movement.* Syracuse, NY: Syracuse University Press, 1992.

Smith, Alice Kimball. *A Peril and a Hope: The Scientists' Movement in America, 1945–1947.* Chicago: University of Chicago Press, 1965.

Smith, John. *An Old Creed for the New South: Proslavery Ideology and Historiography, 1865–1918.* Westport, CT: Greenwood Press, 1985.

Sundiata, Ibrahim K. *Black Scandal: America and the Liberian Labor Class, 1929–1936.* Philadelphia: Institute for the Study of Human Issues, 1980.

Swerdlow, Amy. *Women Strike for Peace: Traditional Motherhood and Radical Politics in the 1960s.* Chicago: University of Chicago Press, 1993.

Terborg-Penn, Rosalyn. *African-American Women in the Struggle for the Vote, 1850–1920.* Bloomington: Indiana University Press, 1998.

Terrell, Mary Church. *A Colored Woman in a White World.* New York: G. K. Hall, 1996.

Theoharis, Athan. *Seeds of Repression: Harry S. Truman and the Origins of McCarthyism.* Chicago: Quadrangle Books, 1971.

Tuttle, William. *Chicago in the Red Summer of 1919.* New York: Atheneum, 1970.

Vivian, Octavia. *Coretta: The Story of Mrs. Martin Luther King, Jr.* Philadelphia: Fortress Press, 1970.

Von Eschen, Penny M. *Race Against Empire: Black Americans and Anti-Colonialism, 1935–1957.* Ithaca, NY: Cornell University Press, 1997.

Watson, Denton. *Lion in the Lobby: Clarence Mitchell, Jr.'s Struggle for Passage of Civil Rights Laws.* New York: Morrow, 1997.

Weinstein, Allen, and Frank Otto Gatell, eds. *The Segregation Era, 1863–1954: A Modern Reader.* New York: Oxford University Press, 1970.

Westheider, James. *Fighting on Two Fronts: African Americans and the Vietnam War.* New York: New York University Press, 1997.

White, Deborah Gray. *Too Heavy a Load: Black Women in Defense of Themselves, 1894–1994.* New York: W. W. Norton and Company, 1999.

Wickstrom, Werner T. *The American Colonization Society and Liberia, 1817–1867*. Monrovia, Liberia: College of West Africa, 1960.

Williams, Juan. *Eyes on the Prize: America's Civil Rights Years, 1954–1965*. New York: Viking–Penguin Press, 1987.

Williams, Lee. *Anatomy of Four Race Riots: Racial Conflict in Knoxville, Elaine (Arkansas), Tulsa, and Chicago, 1919–1921*. Hattiesburg: University and College Press of Mississippi, 1972.

Williamson, Joel. *The Crucible of Race: Black-White Relations in the American South since Emancipation*. New York: Oxford University Press, 1984.

Wittner, Lawrence. *Rebels Against War: The American Peace Movement, 1933–1983*. Philadelphia: Temple University Press, 1984.

Woloch, Nancy. *Women and the American Experience*. New York: McGraw-Hill, 1994.

Wolters, Raymond. *The Burden of Brown: Thirty Years of School Desegregation*. Knoxville: University of Tennessee Press, 1984.

———. *Negroes and the Great Depression: The Problem of Economic Recovery*. Westport, CT: Greenwood Publishing, 1970.

Zaroulis, Nancy, and Gerald Sullivan. *Who Spoke Up? American Protest Against the War in Vietnam, 1963–1975*. Garden City, NY: Doubleday, 1984.

Zinn, Howard. *Vietnam: The Logic of Withdrawal*. Boston: Beacon Press, 1967.

Articles

Anderson, Marian. "My Life in a White World, as Told to Emily Kimbrough." *Ladies' Home Journal*, September 1960, 1–24.

Bevel, Diane Nash. "Journey to North Vietnam." *Freedomways* 7 (Spring 1967): 118–28.

Blackwell-Johnson, Joyce. "African-American Activists in the Women's International League for Peace and Freedom, 1920s–1950s." *Peace and Change: Journal of Peace Research* 23, no. 4 (October 1998): 466–82.

Brown, George W. "Haiti and the United States." *Journal of Negro History* 8 (April 1923): 48–62.

Bussey, Henry. "Peace Worker Finds Small Chink in Russian Public Relations Front." *Portland Reporter*, May 21, 1964, 1–4.

Camp, Kay. "Report of Mission to Vietnam." *Pax et Libertas*, January–June 1971, 1–3.

Chisholm, Shirley. "All We Are Saying Is—." *Freedomways* 12 (Second Quarter 1972): 118–23.

"Chisholm Blasts Hard at Defense Spending." *Pittsburgh Courier*, April 12, 1969, 2.

Cleghorn, Reese. "Who Speaks for Mississippi?" *Reporter*, August 13, 1964, 31–34.

Craig, John. "Redbaiting, Pacifism, and Free Speech: Lucia Ames Meade and Her 1926 Lecture Tour in Atlanta and the Southeast." *Georgia Historical Quarterly* 71 (1987): 587–623.

Cripps, Thomas. "The Reaction of the Negro to the Motion Picture 'The Birth of a Nation.'" *Historian* 25 (May 1963): 350–59.

Davis, Angela. "I Am a Black Revolutionary Woman." In *The Voice of Black America: Major Speeches by Negroes in the United States, 1797–1973*, edited by Philip S. Foner, 1177–82. New York: Simon and Schuster, 1972.

Doughtery, Larry. "Archivist Harris Recalls Her Life Fighting Racism." *Daily Californian*, February 26, 1986.

Dreyfuss, Joel. "Shirley Aids Black GIs' Fight." *Washington Post*, August 11, 1971.

Editorial. *Muhammad Speaks*, February 2, 1968.

"Fighting Race Calumny." *Crisis* 10 (May 1965): 37–45.

Fox, Barbara Coleman. "Philadelphia Woman Meets Mrs. K: Russians Greet Delegates of League for Peace and Freedom." *Women Today*, May 3, 1964, 1–4.

"Free the Camp Allen Brothers." *Winter Soldier* 3 (June 1973): 14.

Garland, Phyl. "Coretta King: In Her Husband's Footsteps." *Ebony*, September 1968, 155–62.

Grimke, R. W. Francis J. "The Logic of Woman Suffrage." *Crisis*, August 1915, 185–198.

Hart, Becky. "Harris Lived an Independent Life." *Wichita State University Alumni News* 3, no. 6 (May–June 1995): 1–7.

Hunton, Addie. "Negro Womanhood Defended." *Voice* 1 (1904): 278–81.

Inscoe, John. "The 'Clansman' on Stage and Screen: North Carolina Reacts." *North Carolina Historical Review* 64 (April 1987): 139–61.

Jensen, Joan. "All Pink Sisters: The War Department and the Feminist Movement in the 1920s." In *Decades of Discontent: The Women's Movement, 1920–1940*, edited by Lois Scharf and Joan Jensen (Westport, CT: Greenwood Press, 1983).

———. "When Women Worked for Peace: Helen Marston and the California Peace Movement, 1915–1945. *California History* 67 (1988): 118–49.

Johnson, Guy. "Negro Racial Movement and Leadership in the United States." *American Journal of Sociology* 63 (1937): 57–71.

King, Coretta Scott. "Statement at WILPF Conference." In *My Country Is the Whole World: An Anthology of Women's Work on Peace and War*, edited by Cambridge Women's Collective, 180–96. London: Pandora Press, 1984.

Lee, Elinor. "She's Off to the Congo to Organize a College." *Washington Post*, July 30, 1962, 1–8.

"Lists Americans as Pacifists." *New York Times*, January 25, 1919, 1:4, 4:4.

Lochard, Metz. "Parley May Skip over Hot Issue of Colonies." *Chicago Defender*, May 5, 1945, 1–9.

Logan, Rayford. "The 'Little Man' Just Isn't Here." *Pittsburgh Courier*, May 5, 1945, 1–10.

McLaurin, Bessie. "Notes on Selma to Montgomery March." *WILPF Journal* (Chapel Hill–Durham branch), June 1965, 1–4.

Miller, Samyne. "First Black Millionaire." *Dawn,* October 3, 1975, 3–18.

Nash, Diane. "Inside the Sit-ins and Freedom Rides: Testimony of a Southern Student." In *The New Negro,* edited by Mathew Ahmann, 43–62. New York: Biblo and Tannen, 1969.

Scammer, Richard. "Report from Black America." *Newsweek,* June 30, 1969, 19–20.

Shepherd, William. "How I Put Over the Klan." *Collier's,* July 14, 1928.

Simcovitch, Maxim. "The Impact of Griffith's 'Birth of a Nation' on the Modern Ku Klux Klan." *Journal of Popular Film* 1 (Winter 1972): 38–49.

Solomon, Barbara Miller. "Dilemmas of Pacifist Women, Quakers and Others in World Wars I and II." In *Witnesses for Change: Quaker Women over Three Centuries,* edited by Elizabeth Potts Brown and Susan Mosher Stuard, 123–48. New Brunswick, NJ: Rutgers University Press, 1989.

Taylor, Arnold. "The Involvement of Black Americans in the Forced Labor Controversy, 1929–1935. In *The Proceedings of the Conference on Afro-Americans and Africans: Historical and Political Linkages, June 13–14, 1974.* Washington, DC: Howard University Press, 1974.

Terborg-Penn, Rosalyn. "African Feminism: A Theoretical Approach to the History of Women in the African Diaspora." In *Women in Africa and the African Diaspora,* edited by Rosalyn Terborg-Penn, Sharon Harley, and Andrea Benton Rushing, 43–64. Washington, DC: Howard University Press, 1987.

———. "Discontented Black Feminists: Prelude and Postscript to the Passage of the Nineteenth Amendment." In *Decades of Discontent: The Women's Movement, 1920–1940,* edited by Lois Scharf and Joan Jensen, 261–78. Boston: Northeastern University Press, 1987.

"Two Black GIs Convicted of Rape Ask Help of Pentagon." *Chicago Tribune,* June 9, 1971, 5.

Van der Kraaij, Fred. "Firestone in Liberia." In *Dependence, Underdevelopment and Persistent Conflicts—On the Political Economy of Liberia,* edited by Eckhard Hinzen and Robert Kappel. Bremen, Germany: Unersee-Museum, 1980.

Weil, Cornelia. "International Peace Delegate Says Irrational Discrimination Must End." *Eugene Register Guard,* May 20, 1964, 1–6.

Dissertations

Forderhase, Nancy. "The Plans That Failed: The United States and Liberia, 1920–1935." Ph.D. diss., University of Missouri, 1971.

Simpson, William. "The Loyalist Democrats of Mississippi: Challenge to a White Majority, 1965–1972." Ph.D. diss., Mississippi State University, 1974.

Index

Joyce Blackwell is the chair of the history department at Saint Augustine's College in Raleigh, North Carolina. Her research and teaching interests include African American women's peace activism, African American international thought, social reform movements, and African American grassroots community activism. She is a member of the Organization of American Historians, the Association of Black Women Historians, the American Historical Association, and the Peace History Society.